Vocabulary Instruction

SOLVING PROBLEMS IN THE TEACHING OF LITERACY
Cathy Collins Block, Series Editor

RECENT VOLUMES

Vocabulary Instruction: Research to Practice
Edited by James F. Baumann and Edward J. Kame'enui

Assessment for Reading Instruction
Michael C. McKenna and Steven A. Stahl

Exemplary Literacy Teachers: Promoting Success for All Children
in Grades K–5
Cathy Collins Block and John N. Mangieri

Rethinking Reading Comprehension
Edited by Anne P. Sweet and Catherine E. Snow

Explaining Reading: A Resource for Teaching Concepts, Skills, and Strategies
Gerald G. Duffy

Struggling Readers: Assessment and Instruction in Grades K–6
Ernest Balajthy and Sally Lipa-Wade

Concept-Oriented Reading Instruction:
Engaging Classrooms, Lifelong Learners
Emily Anderson Swan

Literacy and Young Children: Research-Based Practices
Edited by Diane M. Barone and Lesley Mandel Morrow

Exploring the Literature of Fact: Children's Nonfiction Trade Books
in the Elementary Classroom
Barbara Moss

Teaching Strategic Processes in Reading
Janice F. Almasi

Organizing and Managing the Language Arts Block:
A Professional Development Guide
Lesley Mandel Morrow

A Sound Start: Phonemic Awareness Lessons for Reading Success
Christine E. McCormick, Rebecca N. Throneburg, and Jean M. Smitley

Reading to Learn: Lessons from Exemplary Fourth-Grade Classrooms
Richard L. Allington and Peter H. Johnston

VOCABULARY INSTRUCTION

Research to Practice

Edited by
JAMES F. BAUMANN
EDWARD J. KAME'ENUI

THE GUILFORD PRESS
New York   London

© 2004 The Guilford Press
A Division of Guilford Publications, Inc.
72 Spring Street, New York, NY 10012
www.guilford.com

Printed in the United States of America

This book is printed on acid-free paper.

Last digit is print number: 9 8 7 6 5 4 3

Library of Congress Cataloging-in-Publication Data

Vocabulary instruction : research to practice / edited by James F. Baumann
and Edward J. Kame'enui.
  p. cm. — (Solving problems in the teaching of literacy)
Includes bibliographical references and index.
ISBN 1-57230-933-4 (alk. paper) — ISBN 1-57230-932-6 (pbk. : alk.
  paper)
  1. Vocabulary—Study and teaching. 2. Reading. I. Baumann, James
F. II. Kame'enui, Edward J. III. Series.
LB1574.5.V63 2004
372.44—dc22

                                                              2003019175

About the Editors

James F. Baumann, PhD, is a professor in the Department of Reading Education at the University of Georgia, where he teaches undergraduate and graduate courses in reading and advises graduate students. His research interests include elementary reading instruction, vocabulary teaching and learning, national literacy trends, and teacher inquiry.

Edward J. Kame'enui, PhD, is a professor and Director of the Institute for the Development of Educational Achievement (IDEA) in the College of Education, University of Oregon, where he codirects several research and model-demonstration grants. His research interests include beginning reading, vocabulary development, reading comprehension, and schools as complex organizational systems.

Contributors

James F. Baumann, PhD, Department of Reading Education, University of Georgia, Athens, Georgia

Donald R. Bear, PhD, Educational Specialties, University of Nevada, Reno, Nevada

Isabel L. Beck, PhD, Learning Research and Development Center, School of Education, University of Pittsburgh, Pittsburgh, Pennsylvania

Andrew Biemiller, PhD, Institute of Child Study, Department of Human Development and Applied Psychology, University of Toronto, Toronto, Canada

Camille L. Z. Blachowicz, PhD, National College of Education, National-Louis University, Evanston, Illinois

Eileen Boland, MEd, Department of Reading Education, University of Georgia, Athens, Georgia

Michael D. Coyne, PhD, Department of Educational Psychology, Neag School of Education, University of Connecticut, Storrs, Connecticut

Elizabeth Carr Edwards, MEd, Department of Reading Education, University of Georgia, Athens, Georgia

Peter Fisher, PhD, National College of Education, National-Louis University, Evanston, Illinois

George Font, PhD, Department of Curriculum and Instruction, Purdue University, West Lafayette, Indiana

Michael F. Graves, PhD, Department of Literacy Education, University of Minnesota, Bloomington, Minnesota

Lori Helman, MA, Educational Specialties, University of Nevada, Reno, Nevada

Bonnie von Hoff Johnson, PhD, Human Development and Learning, Dowling College, Oakdale, New York

Dale D. Johnson, PhD, Literacy Education, Dowling College, Oakdale, New York

Edward J. Kame'enui, PhD, Department of Special Education, College of Education, University of Oregon, Eugene, Oregon

Robert J. Marzano, PhD, Mid-continent Research for Education and Learning, Aurora, Colorado, and Cardinal Stritch University, Milwaukee, Wisconsin

Margaret G. McKeown, PhD, Learning Research and Development Center, University of Pittsburgh, Pittsburgh, Pennsylvania

William E. Nagy, PhD, School of Education, Seattle Pacific University, Seattle, Washington

Kathleen Schlichting, PhD, Literacy Education, Dowling College, Oakdale, New York

Judith A. Scott, PhD, Language, Literacy and Culture, Department of Education, University of California, Santa Cruz, California

Deborah C. Simmons, PhD, Department of Special Education, College of Education, University of Oregon, Eugene, Oregon

Katherine A. Dougherty Stahl, EdD, Curriculum and Instruction, College of Education, University of Illinois, Urbana–Champaign, Illinois

Steven A. Stahl, EdD, Curriculum and Instruction, College of Education, University of Illinois, Urbana–Champaign, Illinois

Shane Templeton, PhD, Center for Learning and Literacy, University of Nevada, Reno, Nevada

Acknowledgments

This project was supported in part by a Field-Initiated Study (PR/Award Number R305T990271) administered by the National Institute for Student Achievement, Curriculum and Assessment, of the Office of Educational Research and Improvement within the U.S. Department of Education. The research and practice suggestions expressed herein do not necessarily reflect the position or policies of the National Institute for Student Achievement, Curriculum and Assessment, the Office of Educational Research and Improvement, or the U.S. Department of Education.

Contents

Introduction

1 Vocabulary: The Plot of the Reading Story   3
   Edward J. Kame'enui and James F. Baumann

**Part I
TEACHING SPECIFIC VOCABULARY**

2 Direct and Rich Vocabulary Instruction   13
   Margaret G. McKeown and Isabel L. Beck

3 Teaching Vocabulary in the Primary Grades: 28
   Vocabulary Instruction Needed
   Andrew Biemiller

4 Vocabulary Instruction for Young Children at Risk   41
   of Experiencing Reading Difficulties: Teaching Word
   Meanings during Shared Storybook Readings
   *Michael D. Coyne, Deborah C. Simmons,
   and Edward J. Kame'enui*

5 Word Wizards All!: Teaching Word Meanings   59
   in Preschool and Primary Education
   Steven A. Stahl and Katherine A. Dougherty Stahl

Part II
TEACHING VOCABULARY-LEARNING STRATEGIES

6 Teaching Prefixes: As Good as It Gets?   81
   Michael F. Graves

7 The Developing Vision of Vocabulary Instruction   100
   Robert J. Marzano

8 The Vocabulary–Spelling Connection: 118
   Orthographic Development and Morphological
   Knowledge at the Intermediate Grades and Beyond
   Shane Templeton

9 Word Study for Vocabulary Development   139
   in the Early Stages of Literacy Learning:
   Ecological Perspectives and Learning English
   Donald R. Bear and Lori Helman

10 Unlocking Word Meanings: Strategies and Guidelines   159
   for Teaching Morphemic and Contextual Analysis
   *Elizabeth Carr Edwards, George Font, James F. Baumann,
   and Eileen Boland*

Part III
TEACHING VOCABULARY THROUGH WORD
CONSCIOUSNESS AND LANGUAGE PLAY

11 Logology: Word and Language Play   179
   *Dale D. Johnson, Bonnie von Hoff Johnson,
   and Kathleen Schlichting*

12 Developing Word Consciousness   201
   Judith A. Scott and William E. Nagy

13 Keep the "Fun" in Fundamental: Encouraging Word   218
   Awareness and Incidental Word Learning
   in the Classroom through Word Play
   Camille L. Z. Blachowicz and Peter Fisher

   Index   239

INTRODUCTION

1

Vocabulary

The Plot of the Reading Story

EDWARD J. KAME'ENUI
JAMES F. BAUMANN

In his book *How to Read and Why*, Harold Bloom (2001), well-known literary critic of Shakespeare and the written word, observes, "Ultimately we read . . . in order to strengthen the self, and to learn its authentic interests" (p. 22). He further observes that self-trust "cannot come without years of deep reading" (p. 25). The idea that years of deep reading is shrewd service to self-trust is provocative and compelling. However, for educational researchers charged with understanding the nature of reading, and for classroom practitioners charged with teaching reading to all children, Bloom's insight unwittingly betrays the elusive nature of reading in a complicated writing system and the teaching of reading in complex school environments (Berliner, 2002; Simmons et al., 2002; Taylor & Pearson, 2002).

To engage in years of deep reading that ostensibly builds self-trust requires acquiring skills and experiences that include (1) negotiating an alphabetic writing system and phonological code (National Reading Panel, 2000; Snow, Burns, & Griffin, 1998); (2) reading words effortlessly and fluently (Dowhower, 1994; Rasinski, 1990; Samuels, 1979); (3) reading for understanding, learning, and appreciation (Block, Gambrell, & Pressley, 2002; Block & Pressley, 2002; RAND Reading Study Group, 2002); and (4) understanding what Pinker (1999) characterizes as the "first trick" to appreciating the "boundless expressive power" of our language (pp. 1–2),

3

that is, understanding associations between word pronunciation and meaning—reading vocabulary. As Bloom notes, "There is no single way to read well. . . . [but] Reading well is one of the great pleasures that solitude can afford you, because it is . . . the most healing of pleasures" (p. 19).

Vocabulary Instruction: Research to Practice addresses what it takes to teach the meanings of words if all children are to "read well" and enjoy the "most healing of pleasures." Naturally, the ultimate purpose of reading is to read for meaning. However, in order to read for meaning, a reader must first read the words (Adams, 1990). Word pronunciation alone, of course, is incomplete and reveals only part of the reading story. The purpose of this edited volume is to provide readers another essential part of the story: gaining access to the meanings of words we read.

This compendium presents contemporary theoretically and empirically based information about reading vocabulary instructional techniques that are useful and usable in the classroom. Contributors draw from their own research and theoretical work to underpin the instructional approaches they present. The authors provide detailed descriptions of diverse vocabulary instructional strategies or components, including concrete examples of their use with students. Thus, each chapter is developed within a research-to-practice framework that recognizes that research in reading becomes implemented in the complex environment of classrooms and schools (Taylor & Pearson, 2002).

The remaining chapters of *Vocabulary Instruction: Research to Practice* are organized into three parts. Part I, "Teaching Specific Vocabulary," consists of Chapters 2–5 and addresses research and strategies for promoting students' vocabulary and comprehension through explicit instruction of individual words. Chapters 6–10 make up Part II, "Teaching Vocabulary-Learning Strategies," in which authors present strategies for students to increase vocabulary independently through application of generalizable vocabulary-acquisition strategies. Finally, Part III, "Teaching Vocabulary through Word Consciousness and Language Play," consists of Chapters 11–13 and addresses vocabulary development by promoting students' metacognitive awareness of, interest in, and curiosity about words.

The consummate vocabulary enthusiast who is thoroughly marinated in the semantic sauce of vocabulary research and practice will quickly recognize that the three parts of this text align with three of Michael Graves's (2000) four components of a comprehensive vocabulary program: teaching individual words (Part I), teaching strategies for learning words independently (Part II), and fostering word consciousness (Part III). As editors, we are indebted to Graves for this organizational grammar, which we think offers a clear and compelling structure for negotiating the research-to-practice linkages in vocabulary learning. Graves's fourth component—

providing children frequent, extensive, and varied opportunities to engage in independent reading—is implicitly at the heart of vocabulary teaching and learning and serves as the proverbial catalyst for appreciating the "boundless expressive power" (Pinker, 1999, p. 1) of our language. In the following sections, we preview each of the three parts in more detail to provide readers a more complete appreciation of the promise of vocabulary research and instruction, that is, the plot of the reading story.

PART I: TEACHING SPECIFIC VOCABULARY

We open Part I with a chapter by two authors who have become synonymous with cutting-edge research on vocabulary instruction, Margaret McKeown and Isabel Beck. When McKeown and Beck speak about vocabulary learning and development, teachers and researchers listen. Not surprisingly, these researchers have titled their chapter "Direct and Rich Vocabulary Instruction," which asserts that "direct instruction is an effective way for students to acquire vocabulary knowledge." However, the goal for McKeown and Beck is not "simply having students become familiar with definitions of words" but "to enhance students' ability to use—both comprehend and produce—their language." Toward this end, McKeown and Beck deliver on their promise by providing practitioners details on "How to choose which words to teach," "How to teach vocabulary effectively," "When to teach," "What to expect from context clues," and "How to keep it going."

The second chapter in Part I is titled "Teaching Vocabulary in the Primary Grades: Vocabulary Instruction Needed," and its author, Andrew Biemiller, clearly knows what is needed for beginning readers who have a limited grasp of words as they enter kindergarten. Biemiller observes that after second grade "children in all vocabulary quartile groups acquire new words at about the same rate (Biemiller & Slonim, 2001). Therefore, it seems likely that the most important vocabulary differences before grade 3 reflect differences in experiences rather than simply constitutional factors." Like McKeown and Beck, Biemiller believes that instruction and what teachers do matter, especially for children with limited vocabularies. Biemiller outlines a program of storybook instruction that can result in children's acquiring 3 words a day, or up to 400 words a year.

In Chapter 4 Coyne, Simmons, and Kame'enui offer an empirically tested storybook reading strategy to develop the vocabulary knowledge of children who enter kindergarten knowing fewer word meanings than their peers. These researchers rely on the following critical features to accelerate vocabulary growth within the context of storybook reading activities: (1)

repeated reading of stories, (2) targeted vocabulary selection and instruction, (3) multiple exposures to target vocabulary, and (4) systematic review and integration of vocabulary words within and between lessons.

It seems only fitting to conclude Part I on teaching specific vocabulary with a chapter by Steven Stahl and Katherine A. Dougherty Stahl, who offer readers a range of strategies for engaging and expanding children's knowledge and experiences with words. As the authors observe, "To expand a child's vocabulary is to teach that child to think about the world." Like other authors of Part I, Stahl and Stahl lament the "large gaps in vocabulary knowledge, beginning in the preschool years and persisting through the elementary school years and probably beyond." They, like other Part I authors, call for teaching word meanings directly. They also promote teaching " 'Goldilocks' words, words that are not too difficult but just right," engaging in "cognitively challenging talk" about words, and focusing on words that comprise the "language of school." For readers, Stahl and Stahl offer advice that is not too abstract, not too naïve, but just right!

PART II: TEACHING VOCABULARY-LEARNING STRATEGIES

Part II is composed of Chapters 6–10 on word-learning strategies designed to promote the magic of generalization in learning unfamiliar words. What we gain from these chapters is a keen respect for the intricate requirements of teaching selected instances of particular words or word parts (e.g., roots, prefixes, suffixes) that permit readers to know or infer more about novel or unknown instances of similar words or classes of words.

It is our good fortune to open Part II with Michael F. Graves's masterful example of a word-learning strategy designed to teach prefixes. But this offering is not without a tease, as Graves ponders whether our knowledge of teaching prefixes is "as good as it gets." In Graves's hands, the getting is pretty good for teaching prefixes! After all, 15 of the most frequently occurring prefixes occur in over 4,000 words; using a newer word list, 20 of the most frequently occurring prefixes are found in some 3,000 words, with the most common three prefixes—*un-*, *re-*, and *in-* (meaning "not")—accounting for 51% of the total. Thus, teaching selected prefixes will permit readers to infer the correct meaning of many newly encountered words.

In contrast to teaching the elements of words, Robert J. Marzano reaches for nothing less than developing a "vision of vocabulary instruction" that recognizes the "slippery nature of words." This vision is anchored to several provocative ideas, such as expanding the "representations" (e.g., such referents as key images, specific examples, objects or classes of objects, prototypes) we use to teach children the meanings of words. Marzano calls for expanding the "mode" of these representations when teaching vocabulary words from linguistic or language forms to nonlinguistic or nonverbal forms involving auditory or visual images. This proposed vision of vocabulary instruction will require practitioners to think about words seriously, imaginatively, and thoughtfully.

Shane Templeton's call in Chapter 8 for unifying spelling and vocabulary instruction through morphology offers a different kind of vision. In this vision, "Spelling knowledge provides the basis for explicit awareness and understanding of morphology, which, in turn, may guide the systematic growth of vocabulary knowledge." Invoked at least two decades ago, Templeton's vision of the *spelling–meaning connection* is clear and succinct: "Words that are related in meaning are often related in spelling as well." This perceptive observation is then supplemented by specific recommendations regarding the general scope and sequence for an integrated spelling and vocabulary curriculum, a set of four teacher-based factors, and concrete examples of activities and strategies for learning words that involve teacher modeling and scaffolding and rule-based instruction.

In Chapter 9, Donald R. Bear and Lori Helman insist on a new image of vocabulary development during the early stages of literacy that requires matching students' "social and perceptual ecologies" with literacy instruction. Bear and Helman pose six questions that serve to frame their analysis:

1. What are students' oral and written vocabularies?
2. What oral language resources do students bring to literacy?
3. What written language resources do students bring to oral language development?
4. What are students' exposure to and experiences with reading and writing?
5. What do students read accurately and automatically?
6. How does literacy support vocabulary development?

The answers to these questions are anchored to a "synchrony in literacy learning" that includes the reciprocal development of orthographic knowledge, spelling, writing, phonics, reading, and vocabulary learning.

In Chapter 10, the final chapter of Part II, Elizabeth Carr Edwards, George Font, James F. Baumann, and Eileen Boland offer readers another empirically tested set of generalized strategies and guidelines for "unlocking word meanings" through teaching morphemic and contextual analysis. After acknowledging the elements of Graves's (2000) comprehensive vocabulary development program and providing a concise review of research on teaching morphemic and contextual analysis, these researchers provide readers an instructive analysis for why morphemic and contextual analysis deserve attention. In addition, they offer a set of guidelines for teaching morphemic and contextual analysis, including teaching these strategies in tandem.

PART III: TEACHING VOCABULARY THROUGH WORD CONSCIOUSNESS AND LANGUAGE PLAY

Part III is the final section of our text and consists of three chapters. This section is designed to address vocabulary development by enhancing students' awareness of, interest in, and curiosity about the mischievous nature and vagaries of words. It seems only appropriate that Dale D. Johnson, Bonnie von Hoff Johnson, and Kathleen Schlichting lead off this section with their chapter on logology, word and language play. These authors offer a delightful description of eight categories of word play, including an instructive review of the research and a compelling argument for the study of word play: "Every genre of written and oral language requires an understanding of word play devices." In the end, the major focus of this chapter is on "the category most overlooked in schools—onomastics, the study of names," including, for example, eponyms, aptronyms, toponyms, anemonyms, and nicknames. After all, names are everywhere, and these authors are especially clever in communicating the playful wit underlying so many words, names, and expressions in the English language.

In Chapter 12, "Developing Word Consciousness," Judith A. Scott and William E. Nagy argue for the "generative" nature of vocabulary learning, that is, "knowledge and dispositions that will transfer to and enhance students' learning of other words." They provide readers ideas and guidelines for increasing students' "word consciousness" that include morphological awareness, syntactic awareness, and metasemantic awareness, as well as the "knowledge and beliefs about word learning, and the various instructional practices and tools used to achieve it." To promote word consciousness in classrooms, Scott and Nagy describe a "7–year teacher research project called The Gift of Words," which advances the "need to learn to value words in order to spend the time and energy trying to learn them."

In the final chapter of Part III and the book, Camille L. Z. Blachowicz and Peter Fisher insist on keeping the "fun" in fundamental, because "Vocabulary instruction can be pretty grim sometimes." These researchers provide readers "four research-grounded statements about word play" that emphasize the importance of word play as motivating, engaging, and noteworthy to the development of metalinguistic awareness of words, word parts, and context and the social construction of meaning. Blachowicz and Fisher have been around words and classrooms enough to appreciate that research-based statements are not enough; attention to instructional details, the development of materials and games, and access to Internet resources are essential to "creating a word-rich environment."

CONCLUSION

Hart and Risley (1995) document that children come to school with considerable variation in their vocabulary knowledge. *Vocabulary Instruction: Research to Practice* bears witness to the importance of ensuring that all children, regardless of their place in the vocabulary development continuum, are taught, encouraged, and inspired to gain access to the meanings of words. As editors, we are privileged to receive the contributions of these authors and researchers who represent many of the field's most knowledgeable scholars of vocabulary teaching and learning. Finally, the message of this text is somewhat unremarkable: Learning the meanings of unfamiliar words is essential to fully understanding the story—the plot, if you will. Central to understanding the plot, therefore, is the manner in which teachers create instructional environments, craft lessons, and engage students in activities that promote students' vocabulary learning. As Bloom (2001) reminds us, reading is the most "healing of pleasures" (p. 19).

REFERENCES

Adams, M. J. (1990). *Beginning to read: Thinking and learning about print.* Cambridge, MA: MIT Press.

Berliner, D. C. (2002). Educational research: The hardest science of all. *Educational Researcher, 31*(8), 18–20.

Biemiller, A., & Slonim, N. (2001) Estimating root word vocabulary growth in normative and advantaged populations: Evidence for a common sequence of vocabulary acquisition. *Journal of Educational Psychology, 93,* 498–520.

Block, C. C., Gambrell, L. B., & Pressley, M. (Eds.). (2002). *Improving comprehension instruction: Rethinking research, theory, and classroom practice.* San Francisco: Jossey-Bass.

Block, C. C., & Pressley, M. (Eds.). (2002). *Comprehension instruction: Research-based best practices.* New York: Guilford Press.

Bloom, H. (2001). *How to read and why.* New York: Simon and Schuster.

Dowhower, S. L. (1994). Effects of repeated reading on second-grade transitional readers' fluency and comprehension. *Reading and Writing Quarterly, 10,* 343–358.

Graves, M. F. (2000). A vocabulary program to complement and bolster a middle-grade comprehension program. In B. M. Taylor, M. F. Graves, & P. van den Broek (Eds.), *Reading for meaning: Fostering comprehension in the middle grades* (pp. 116–135). Newark, DE: International Reading Association.

Hart, B., & Risley, T. R. (1995). *Meaningful differences in the everyday experiences of young American children.* Baltimore: Brookes.

National Reading Panel. (2000). *Teaching children to read: An evidence-based assessment of the scientific research literature on reading and its implications for reading instruction: Reports of the subgroups* (NIH Publication No. 00–4754). Washington, DC: National Institutes of Health and National Institute of Child Health and Human Development.

Pinker, S. (1999). *Words and rules: Ingredients of language.* New York: Harper-Collins.

RAND Reading Study Group. (2002). *Toward an R & D program in reading comprehension.* Santa Monica, CA: RAND Corporation.

Rasinksi, T. V. (1990). Effects of repeated reading and listening-while-reading on reading fluency. *Journal of Educational Research, 83,* 147–150.

Samuels, S. J. (1979). The method of repeated reading. *The Reading Teacher, 32,* 403–408.

Simmons, D. C., Kame'enui, E. J., Good, R. H., Harn, B. A., Cole, C., & Braun, D. (2002). Building, implementing, and sustaining a beginning reading improvement model: Lessons learned school by school. In M. R. Shinn, H. M. Walker, & G. Stoner (Eds.), *Interventions for academic and behavior problems II: Preventive and remedial approaches* (pp. 537–569). Bethesda, MD: National Association of School Psychologists.

Snow, C. E., Burns, M. S., & Griffin, P. (Eds.). (1998). *Preventing reading difficulties in young children.* Washington, DC: National Academy Press.

Taylor, B. M., & Pearson, P. D. (Eds.). (2002). *Teaching reading: Effective schools, accomplished teachers.* Mahway, NJ: Erlbaum.

PART I

TEACHING SPECIFIC VOCABULARY

2

Direct and Rich Vocabulary Instruction

MARGARET G. McKEOWN
ISABEL L. BECK

Research indicates that direct instruction in vocabulary can increase vocabulary learning and comprehension. If instruction is to influence comprehension, it needs to involve a breadth of information about the instructed words and engage active processing by getting students to think about and use the words. This chapter considers how a teacher might set up a vocabulary program whose goal, beyond having students become familiar with definitions of words, is to enhance students' ability to both comprehend and produce language. The discussion will include how to select which words to teach, how to teach, when to teach, how to deal with context, and how to keep the learning process going.

The basis for this chapter is the assumption that direct instruction is an important component in students' vocabulary development. This assumption derives from numerous studies, findings that direct instruction in vocabulary can increase vocabulary learning and comprehension. The contrasting viewpoint offers two counterarguments to the need for vocabulary instruction (Nagy & Herman, 1987), the first being that there are too many words to teach for direct instruction to be feasible and the second that words can be learned easily from context during reading.

ARE THERE TOO MANY WORDS TO TEACH?

If one thinks of teaching all the words in the language, then, yes, of course, there are too many to teach through direct instruction. But consider a mature, literate individual's vocabulary as comprising three tiers. The first tier consists of the most basic words—*brother, bed, sky, run*, and so on. Words in this tier rarely require instructional attention to their meanings in school. The third tier is made up of words whose frequency of use is quite low and often limited to specific domains. Some examples might be *apogee, precinct, peninsula*, and *ecclesiastical*. In general, a rich understanding of these words would not be of high utility for most learners. These words are probably best learned when a specific need arises, such as introducing *coagulate* during a biology lesson.

The second tier contains words that are of high frequency for mature language users and are found across a variety of domains. Examples include *compromise, scrutinize, diligent*, and *typical*. Because of the large role they play in a language user's repertoire, rich knowledge of words in the second tier can have a powerful impact on verbal functioning. Thus, instruction directed toward tier 2 words can be most productive (Beck & McKeown, 1985).

LEARNING FROM CONTEXT: HOW EASILY?

Words *are* learned from context, but just how readily that learning takes place is still a question. Contexts are tricky; they are not always laden with appropriate information for deriving a word's meaning. A good illustration of this comes from a bright little 4-year-old named Rebecca, who was protesting being put to bed one night. She told her mother that she felt "soggy." Puzzled, her mother asked her what soggy meant, and Rebecca replied, "sad and lonely." This puzzled Rebecca's mother even more—until she realized that the context in which Rebecca had often heard the word was "Rebecca, come back and eat your cheerios; they're getting soggy." Using the context, Rebecca drew some inferences and came up with a meaning for the word.

The effectiveness of context for learning new words has been explored by several studies that have given readers natural text containing unknown words and then tested whether learning of those words has occurred. One such study concluded that context clues do not reveal the meanings of low-frequency words in naturally occurring prose and that the clues appear to be as likely to result in confusion as in the correct identification of word meaning (Schatz & Baldwin, 1986).

Other studies that presented similar tasks to students concluded that readers *do* use context to learn new words but that learning takes place in small increments (Nagy, Anderson, & Herman, 1987; Swanborn & de Glopper, 1999). So, learning from written contexts does happen, of course, but at a rather low rate; the best estimate is that, of 100 unfamiliar words met in reading, a reader may learn 3–15 of them.

Considering all the words that people read, learning from context at this rate can mean learning hundreds of new words a year in this fashion. However, some people read a great deal and some do not, and those students who most need boosts in vocabulary are usually the same students who have trouble reading, so they do not read as much (Cunningham & Stanovich, 1998).

Students who encounter difficulty in their reading are also likely to be less successful in deriving meanings from context. One study that gave evidence of difficulties in using context clues presented a series of contexts that provided increasingly stronger clues to a word's meaning (McKeown, 1985). Contexts as strong as the following were presented, after a series of other clues: "It was hot inside and I knew I would be more comfortable if I could *bafe* my sweater." Choices were then presented as to whether *bafe* meant *remove, lose, punch, wear, repair,* or *turn off*. Even after such strong contexts, 25% of the students could not derive correct meanings of words. Yet, consider how information-rich this situation was; students were presented with a series of contexts, choices for the word's meaning—one of which was always correct—and had the material read to them. The evidence suggests that naturally occurring written contexts are not highly effective learning environments.

Despite counterarguments to the need for vocabulary instruction, the perspective of this chapter is that direct instruction is an effective way for students to acquire vocabulary knowledge. Research over the past two decades offers direction on the kind of vocabulary instruction that is most productive. In early vocabulary research, virtually all studies that presented vocabulary instruction resulted in the students learning words. However, the instruction in these studies focused on associating words with definitions, and the evidence of learning was most often the ability to choose a correct definition or synonym from a number of choices. Higher-order goals that one might associate with vocabulary learning, such as text comprehension, were rarely attained (e.g., Gipe, 1978–1979; Jackson & Dizney, 1963; Pany, Jenkins, & Schreck, 1982; Tuinman & Brady, 1973). Subsequent research has tried to discover the characteristics of instruction that make a difference between remembering word meanings and being able to use the words in comprehension. Toward this end, two research study reviews (Mezynski, 1983; Stahl & Fairbanks, 1986) examined vocabulary instructional experiments that had both succeeded and failed to improve comprehension. In general, both reviews indicate that if instruction is to influence comprehension it needs to (1) present multiple exposures of the words being taught; (2) involve a breadth of information—not just repeat definitions but present contexts, examples, and the like; and (3) engage active or deep processing by getting students to think about the words and interact with them. Breadth and depth of information enable students to establish networks of connections from the new words being learned to words, experiences, and ideas they already have. These connections then facilitate students' ability to use a new word in appropriate circumstances and to understand it when they read it or hear it used in new contexts; the word comes to mind very readily.

The rest of this chapter is devoted to consideration of how a teacher might set up a vocabulary program whose goal, beyond simply having students become familiar with definitions of words, is to enhance students' ability to use—both comprehend and produce—their language. The discussion will include how to select which words to teach, how to teach, when to teach, how to teach use of context, and how to keep the learning going (for a detailed discussion of these topics, see Beck, McKeown, & Kucan, 2002).

HOW TO CHOOSE WHICH WORDS TO TEACH

No formula exists for selecting age-appropriate vocabulary words despite lists that identify "fifth-grade words" or "seventh-grade words"; there are no principles that determine which words students should be learning at different grade levels. For example, that *coincidence* is an "eighth-grade word" according to a frequency index means only that most students do not know the word until eighth grade. It does not mean that students in the seventh grade or even the fifth grade cannot learn the word or should not be taught it. There are only two things that make a word inappropriate for a certain level. One is not being able to define it in terms known to the students at that grade level. If the words used to define a target word are likely unknown to the students, then the word is too hard. The other consideration is that the words be useful and interesting—ones that students will be able to find uses for in their everyday lives. Of course this is a judgment call, best made by those who know the individual students best.

With the choice so wide open, how might a teacher go about selecting words to teach? The most likely place to start choosing words for instruction is school materials—readers, social studies and science books, language arts texts. A good start is to look for words that will be important for comprehension. For example, for a selection about the night the lights went out in New York City and thousands of people were stuck in subways, good candidates would be *blackout* and *commuters*.

In addition, though, the candidates for instruction should include good general words, even if their role in the text is not crucial. An illustration of this is found in a selection appearing in a basal reader (Holt, Rinehart & Winston, 1989) from *Fog Magic*, a Newbery Award-winning book in which a girl who loves to walk in the fog finds herself transported to a long-ago era (Sauer, 1986). This selection's conceptual structure, setting, and types of characters are likely familiar to children, and thus, in one sense, there is not any critical vocabulary to teach. However, this story represents a situation found frequently in literature: the rich and effective use of language by a good writer. Words such as the following are used: *convenient, hastily, miserable, amazement, treacherous, prosperous, protective, dignity,* and *graceful*. Unfamiliarity with these words might not interfere with comprehension of the story, but it could diminish an appreciation for good writing by lessening the impact of effective language use.

Besides school materials, there are many other sources of words to teach. Classroom and community events, news stories, television programs, and even commercials offer good candidates for instruction. For example, you may have seen the American Egg Board's commercials about the "incredible edible egg." Here are two splendid words to introduce to students, *incredible* and *edible*. A teacher might start a lesson by asking if students had seen the commercial and then ask if they think eggs are incredible—or edible. The discussion could include explanations of what the words mean and then could consider what students find edible and the kinds of things they think of as incredible.

The use of a television commercial that students have probably seen brings up another point about choosing words. Words do not have to be completely unknown to be good candidates for instruction. For example, students might know the egg commercial by heart and understand the message about eggs being tasty and good for you, but that does not mean that they have a full understanding of the words and the various ways they can be used.

HOW TO TEACH VOCABULARY EFFECTIVELY

In earlier research we created a vocabulary program based on the notion of "rich instruction" (Beck, McCaslin, & McKeown, 1980). Our aim was to produce the kind of deep and thorough word knowledge that we hypothesized was needed to affect comprehension. Earlier studies that we examined had focused on the learning of definitions and produced no improvement in comprehension. We hypothesized that, because comprehension is a complex process, a reader may well need knowledge of a different character than mere accuracy of definitions of words in the text to facilitate the process.

The aim of rich instruction was to have students engage in active thinking about word meanings, about how they might use the words in different situations, and about the relationships among words. For example, we would present the verb *console* accompanied by its definition and then ask students to think of a time they had consoled someone. Or in discussing the word *hermit*, we asked students to think of what a hermit might have a nightmare about. Students were asked to compare and contrast words by answering questions such as "Would you *berate* someone who *inspired* you?" "Could a *miser* be a *tyrant*?" Students spent a week on groups of 8–10 words, so they had many interactions with each word. In our research we found that rich instruction led not only to knowledge of word meanings but also to improved comprehension of stories containing those words (Beck, Perfetti, & McKeown, 1982; McKeown, Beck, Omanson, & Perfetti, 1983; McKeown, Beck, Omanson, & Pople, 1985).

But teaching every word that you want to introduce to students in a rich way is not necessary or practical. Some words in many situations do not require rich knowledge. For example, consider a selection from *Call It Courage*, in which a young Polynesian boy conquers his fear of the sea (Sperry, 1983). Many terms that relate to the sea setting appear in the story, such as *barrier reef, sea urchins, outrigger, coral,* and *bonitos.* These words do not play a crucial role in the story; the level of information that is needed about them is available from context, such as that an outrigger is a type of boat and sea urchins are creatures that live in the sea.

The answer to the how-to-teach question is to do whatever seems appropriate depending on the goals of instruction. Rich instruction is particularly important for words that seem necessary for comprehension, or for words that turn up in a wide variety of contexts, or for words that are hard to get across with just a brief explanation. More narrow instruction, such as a simple definition, can be efficacious for words that are easy to explain or words that do not need to be well known, such as the sea-related ones cited above. Giving limited attention to meanings of individual words has the advantage that it enables a teacher to increase the number of words introduced to students.

We now offer some specific examples of activities that exemplify rich instruction. These activities are taken from the vocabulary program created for our research. They are examples of activities that were presented to students after the words and their meanings had been introduced.

An activity called *Overheard Conversations* asked students to apply the words they were learning to situations. The idea was that students were to imagine themselves walking along a street, overhearing bits of conversation, and were asked to think of a vocabulary word that would fit the things they were hearing. Part of the student's worksheet appears as Figure 2.1. The words to be applied were, respectively, *monotonous, unique, peculiar,* and *extraordinary.*

1. "This is a drag!"

2. "There's nothing else like this in the world!"

3. "That was a weird one."

4. "It's fantastic! Better than I could have imagined!"

FIGURE 2.1. Overheard conversations.

For many of the activities designed for the program, students had to make decisions by comparing and contrasting words or contexts. One such activity asked students to compare descriptions of very similar situations that differed only on the definitional features of the target word. For pairs of situations, the teacher asked students to decide which was the example of the word and which was the nonexample and then explain why. For instance, a student might say that "The whole class says the Pledge of Allegiance to the flag" is an example of *chorus*, because *chorus* means to say something all together. Figure 2.2 shows the scenarios that were presented to students for the words *urge, chorus, wail,* and *mention.*

The next example illustrates a very flexible activity called *word lines*. The activity asks students to place situations that contain vocabulary words along a continuum. For the word line represented in Figure 2.3, students considered the amount of energy that different activities would require. But word lines can be created with a wide variety of end points, such as slow–fast, hard–easy, fun–not fun, and so forth. In this seemingly simple activity, students are asked to do some sophisticated thinking; they have to interpret how much energy each situation would take and compare it to the energy needed for others. In introducing the activity, the teacher would explain to urge

A mother tells her children that they should remember to take their vitamins every morning.	Children tell their mother that they already took their vitamins.

chorus

The whole class says the Pledge of Allegiance to the flag.	The class makes plans for a Flag Day assembly.

wail

A child screams after falling down.	A child asks politely for a band-aid after falling down.

mention

Our neighbors once told us that they had lived in Florida.	Our neighbors are always talking about when they lived in Florida.

FIGURE 2.2. Example–nonexample.

students that they were to decide how much energy each situation would take in comparison to the others and place each on the line from "least energy" to "most energy." The teacher emphasizes that there are no right or wrong answers but that the students should be able to give reasons for their choices.

Another important feature of the word line activity is that it does not have preestablished correct answers. Students rank each activity according to their view of the energy it would take; then students take turns discussing and comparing their rankings. An important factor in rich instruction is the discussion that follows individually completed activities. This gives students a chance to make their thinking explicit, and to defend or revise their ideas—all of which helps students to reinforce and deepen their understanding of the words they are learning.

The sample activities just presented exemplify but do not define rich instruction. Rich instruction is very open-ended; it is not some particular set of activities but rather any activity that gets students to use, think

How much energy does it take to . . .

1. flex your little finger?
2. thrust a heavy door shut?
3. embrace a teddy bear?
4. beckon to someone for five straight hours?
5. seize a feather floating through the air?

Least energy _____ Most energy

FIGURE 2.3. Word line.

about, and become involved with words. The major concept is to provoke thought. Give students a lot of information about the words, and a variety of information—examples, contexts, pictures, relationships. Then have them engage in interactions—create contexts, compare features of words, explain their reasoning, and discuss meanings and uses.

WHEN TO TEACH

The key to a successful vocabulary program is to use both formal and informal encounters so that attention to vocabulary is happening any time and all the time. First, there are the vocabulary words taught in conjunction with formal lessons. Second, opportunities arise within the classroom routine that can be used for vocabulary learning. Teachers and students interact verbally all day long, beyond formal lessons, as assignments are discussed, classroom management is attended to, and spontaneous conversations arise about some situation at hand. Within this *verbal environment* abundant opportunities exist for drawing attention to vocabulary. A teacher might use sophisticated words—sometimes stopping to define them—comment on a student's use of particular words, create or point out new uses for vocabulary learned in class, play with words, or use new words to label familiar situations.

For example, one teacher we observed discussed with her fourth and fifth graders the selection of classroom jobs. She asked students to spend a *portion* of their morning thinking about the jobs and to *indicate* which job they wanted, and she asked for *alternatives* in assigning students to jobs. Sophisticated, likely unfamiliar words were used within the context of a very familiar situation, so understanding their meanings was not crucial to comprehending the teacher's discourse. Thus there was no need for the teacher to define the words, but they served to enrich the verbal environment, perhaps piqued some interest from students, and even laid a preliminary trail of understanding.

Later in the discussion about classroom jobs, one boy said that the teacher could pick names from a hat if several students wanted the same job. The teacher concurred, saying, "Yes, *random selection*," thus supplying a new, sophisticated label for a familiar idea. This is yet another way to bring new words on the scene in a way that is not going to cause comprehension problems and may result in some learning. And it costs virtually nothing in terms of materials or time.

Using opportunities to sprinkle a classroom with vocabulary helps to create a rich verbal environment. The notion of a rich verbal environment in school is especially important for students who do not have a language-rich environment at home. Consider that by first grade there is already a wide gap in the number of words known orally between students from homes of higher socioeconomic status and those from homes of lower socioeconomic status (Graves, Brunetti, & Slater, 1982).

WHAT TO EXPECT FROM CONTEXT CLUES

Teaching students that they should use context to derive word meanings is a traditional part of reading and vocabulary instruction. But, as indicated earlier, using context is not always a reliable way to get information about word meaning. A reader can, in many instances, learn a word's meaning from context, but many contexts are not transparent, that is, fully informative. In some cases no amount of effort will assure getting the correct meaning of a word. Take, for example, this context: "Dan heard voices in the hall downstairs and wondered who had arrived. Then he recognized the lumbering footsteps of Aunt Grace on the stairs." If you did not know the word *lumbering*, a wide range of meanings would be possible: *familiar, lively, heavy, high-heeled*. The context just does not have enough clues.

The message here is not that teaching about context clues should not be done. Rather, it is to point out that it should be handled carefully in instruction. Students should not be given the impression that meaning can be readily derived from all contexts. To emphasize the varying reliability of contexts, we have demonstrated that not all contexts are created equal (Beck, McKeown, & McCaslin, 1983). We examined stories in basal readers for their contexts surrounding new words and classified the contexts as to the degree of assistance they seemed to offer to readers who did not know the words. We developed four classifications to indicate the range of helpfulness of contexts: directive, general, nondirective, and misdirective.

Directive contexts were those that seemed likely to lead to a correct inference about a word's meaning. For example, consider the context "Madelaine watched as Nora grew smaller and smaller and finally *vanished*. Now she was really alone." These sentences make it quite clear that *vanish* means disappear; the clues direct a reader to the meaning.

General contexts were those that provided enough clues to meaning to place the word in a general category. For example, "Brian said *morosely*, 'This miserable town will be the death of us.' " This context makes it easy to infer that *morosely* describes a negative feeling, but its specific features remain undefined; the emotion expressed might be anger, fear, or unhappiness, for example.

Nondirective contexts provide little assistance in directing a reader toward any particular meaning for a word. Consider, for example, "Freddie looked over the members of the team she'd been assigned. Each looked more *hapless* than the next." From this context the team members could be almost anything—*happy, eager, untrained*, and so forth. But the context does give some information about the word—it describes something a person can be, but, as to the particular meaning of the word, the context gives little guidance.

Misdirective contexts seem to direct a reader to an incorrect meaning for a word. For example, consider the following context: "The climb up the mountain took longer than John and Patrick expected. The cliffs were steeper than Patrick remembered, and they had to walk an extra mile because the path was blocked at one point. It was John's first experience mountain climbing, and he was *exhilarated* at the end of the day." Here the word *exhilarated* is somewhat unexpected—one would more likely think, from the description of the day's activities, that John would be exhausted or even discouraged, not enlivened.

We tested the effectiveness of the four types of contexts in helping readers derive word meanings (Beck et al., 1983). The contexts consisted of stories from fourth- and sixth-grade basal readers in which we had blacked out the words recommended for attention, and our subjects were all adults. The results were that readers could identify word meanings for each of the categories as follows: directive, 86%; general, 49%; nondirective, 27%; misdirective, 3%. What these results mean is that adults, reading stories for fourth and sixth graders, were able to identify meanings of words already in their vocabularies slightly less than half the time.

One of the texts used in our study was an Encyclopedia Brown story, "The Case of the Blueberry Pies" (Sobol, 1976). The story is about a pie-eating contest in which each contestant is to eat two blueberry pies and then run half a mile. The competition seems to be shaping up between Chester, a friend of Encyclopedia Brown's who had won the year before, and the Thompson twins, who are the local bad guys. As Encyclopedia and his friend Sally arrive at the contest, they notice that only one twin has entered. Following the pie-eating section, the race boils down, as expected, to Chester and the one twin. Chester approaches the finish line, but is passed by the twin, who wins the race. As the twin takes his victory lap, the exchange below occurs between Sally and Encyclopedia. The blanks indicate the words we asked subjects to determine from context and thus illustrate the variability of contexts for deriving word meanings.

"He sure has beautiful teeth," said Sally _____ingly.

"Look at him _____. You'd think he was on television doing a toothpaste _____."

Encyclopedia stared bitterly at the twin's white-toothed smile.

"He'll be smiling on the other side of his face soon," said the boy detective. "Chester is the _____ful winner."

The words to be determined are, in order, *grudgingly, strut, commercial*, and *rightful*. (And Encyclopedia figures out that Chester was the rightful winner because the twin's smile revealed that he had not eaten any blueberry pies—the cheating twins pulled a switch during the race!) The demonstration provided by our study suggests that the ability to derive word meaning from context is greatly influenced by the nature of particular contexts.

The implication for instruction is that it makes sense to tell students that context will not always give strong clues to the meaning of a word. Students need to know that some contexts will give sufficient information to understand a word's meaning and some will not give much information at all. It is helpful to demonstrate those differences to students by giving them examples of contexts that offer a range of support for deriving word meaning.

Having sufficient information available from which to derive meaning is not the only factor in successful use of context, however. For many students, the most difficult part of deriving word meaning from context is the process of reasoning about how to put together information from the context and what kind of conclusions are valid to draw. In a study of fifth graders' ability to use context clues, it was found that even when students identified the information in the context that gave clues to word meaning, they were often not able to use the information to infer a correct meaning for the word (McKeown, 1985). For example, in the context presented earlier about Aunt Grace's footsteps on the stairs, a student might recognize that *lumbering* had to do with footsteps but then reason as follows to derive a meaning for the word: "Dan was probably glad it was Aunt Grace because he really liked her, so lumbering probably means being happy to see someone." The information about footsteps does not get used at all.

Because students do not always understand what kinds of associations are valid in determining what a word means in relation to a context, it can be useful for a teacher to occasionally work through some contexts by reading and thinking aloud to model for students how to use information to infer a word's meaning. For example, suppose the following sentences appeared in a story the class was reading: "Leah was usually glad to be called on in class and felt confident about her answers. But last night's homework had been really confusing and she was apprehensive as the teacher looked her way." The teacher might say, "Leah felt apprehensive. Let's think about what that could mean. She usually feels confident and happy about answering in class, but this day she doesn't want to be called on, and the teacher is looking her way. So it seems like apprehensive means she is worried or afraid of what might happen."

Eventually a teacher can modify this sort of activity so that students do the reading and thinking aloud on contexts. Practice in modeling context use can guide students to develop strategies for approaching context. A study that provided instructional practice in such activities showed growth in students' abilities to derive meaning from context (Goerss, Beck, & McKeown, 1999).

HOW TO KEEP IT GOING

In a successful vocabulary program, words do not appear as part of a classroom exercise and then drop from sight. Many of the words that have been introduced return again and again, both to refresh students' memories about words encountered earlier and to enrich knowledge of those words by relating them to new contexts or to more recently taught words. For example, if students have learned *gregarious*, a teacher might introduce *hermit* by asking, "Would a hermit be gregarious?"

One way to assure that vocabulary learning is ongoing is to have students keep a record of words they have learned. This record can be in the form of personal word journals in which students record new words and what they have learned about them. Or there can be a more public record in a classroom, such as a bulletin board that is designated as a word wall, exhibiting words and their definitions that have been worked with in class.

Another important aspect of keeping it going is to motivate students to take their learning beyond the classroom. The more that students discover how words are used and where they crop up outside of class, the greater the chance that they will really use the words in their own speaking and writing, and come to own them.

In our vocabulary research, we used a device called the Word Wizard Chart to encourage students to take their learning with them. We challenged students to find the words they had been taught outside of class—in books, newspapers, on the radio or television, on billboards, by hearing their parents use them, or they could simply use the words in their own conversation or writing. When students brought in an explanation of how the word was used, they earned points that were recorded on a large chart in the classroom. Every few weeks, the teacher tallied the points earned, and students were given certificates for achieving certain categories such as Word Wizard, Word Whirlwind, Word Wildcat, Word Worker, or Word Watcher.

The use of the Word Wizard Chart turned out to be a very powerful technique in the vocabulary program. The students responded to its challenge with great enthusiasm; it was not an unusual day if every child in the class came in with a Word Wizard entry!

Even beyond reinforcing words that have been learned, "keeping it going" means promoting word awareness, getting students to notice new words in the environment and to be aware of their uses. This kind of noticing and interest in learning more words opens the pores for independent vocabulary learning. Of course, the ultimate goal of any effective instruction is to put the learners in a position to take on responsibility for their own learning.

One more ingredient in a successful vocabulary program is the teacher as an active, enthusiastic vocabulary learner. The teacher should be a partner in word awareness and discovering new words and new uses for words. The teacher can tempt students with words by giving them a new word to find out about or dropping clues to a word's meaning in creative ways. For example, if a student is dawdling in getting out her work, a teacher might say, "I think you're procrastinating." The student may respond with a puzzled look; the teacher might then pursue by asking her if she is procrastinating, or ask other students if they think she is procrastinating or if they ever procrastinate. Students quickly catch on to the game and are likely to start hypothesizing a meaning for the word or situations in which it seems to apply. Frequent impromptu attention to vocabulary can help instill in students a feeling of the power of words and the value of knowing words.

IN CONCLUSION

Direct instruction in vocabulary can be an effective way to enrich students' language abilities. To make instruction most effective, it should focus on words that students are likely to meet often and that are useful to them. Both formal and informal opportunities should be used to create vocabulary learning that engages students' thinking and offers a variety of ways to apply the words learned. Words introduced to students should remain part of the vocabulary program so that students continue to reinforce and enrich their understanding of them. Attention given to context clues can be most beneficial if variations in contexts are discussed and students are exposed to models of how to integrate information from context to derive word meanings. Focusing attention on vocabulary in the ways described can establish a way of thinking about words that leads to a lively and productive verbal environment in the classroom.

REFERENCES

Beck, I. L., McCaslin, E. S., & McKeown, M. G. (1980). *The rationale and design of a program to teach vocabulary to fourth-grade students* (LRDC Publication 1980/25). Pittsburgh: University of Pittsburgh, Learning Research and Development Center.
Beck, I. L., & McKeown, M. G. (1985). Teaching vocabulary: Making the instruction fit the goal. *Educational Perspectives, 23*(1), 11–15.
Beck, I. L., McKeown, M. G., & McCaslin, E. S. (1983). Vocabulary development: All contexts are not created equal. *The Elementary School Journal, 83*(3), 177–181.
Beck I. L., McKeown, M. G., & Kucan, L. (2002). *Bringing words to life: Robust vocabulary instruction.* New York: Guilford Press.
Beck, I. L., Perfetti, C. A., & McKeown, M. G. (1982). Effects of long-term vocabulary instruction on lexical access and reading comprehension. *Journal of Educational Psychology, 74*(4), 506–521.

Cunningham, A. E., & Stanovich, K. E. (1998). What reading does for the mind. *American Educator, 22*(1–2), 8–15.

Gipe, J. P. (1978–1979). Investigating techniques for teaching word meaning. *Reading Research Quarterly, 14,* 624–644.

Goerss, B. L., Beck, I. L., & McKeown, M. G. (1999). Increasing remedial students' ability to derive word meaning from context. *Reading Psychology, 20*(2), 151–175.

Graves, M. F., Brunetti, G. J., & Slater, W. H. (1982). The reading vocabularies of primary-grade children of varying geographic and social backgrounds. In J. A. Harris & L. A. Harris (Eds.), *New inquiries in reading research and instruction* (pp. 99–104). Rochester, NY: National Reading Conference.

Holt, Rinehart & Winston, Inc. (1989). *Reading today and tomorrow.* Austin, TX: Author.

Jackson, J. R., & Dizney, H. (1963). Intensive vocabulary training. *Journal of Developmental Reading, 6,* 221–229.

McKeown, M. G. (1985). The acquisition of word meaning from context by children of high and low ability. *Reading Research Quarterly, 20*(4), 482–496.

McKeown, M. G., Beck, I. L., Omanson, R. C., & Perfetti, C. A. (1983). The effects of long-term vocabulary instruction on reading comprehension: A replication. *Journal of Reading Behavior, 15*(1), 3–18.

McKeown, M. G., Beck, I. L., Omanson, R. C., & Pople, M. T. (1985). Some effects of the nature and frequency of vocabulary instruction on the knowledge and use of words. *Reading Research Quarterly, 20*(5), 522–535.

Mezynski, K. (1983). Issues concerning the acquisition of knowledge: Effects of vocabulary training on reading comprehension. *Review of Educational Research, 53,* 253–279.

Nagy, W. E., Anderson, R. C., & Herman, P. A. (1987). Learning word meanings from context during normal reading. *American Educational Research Journal, 24,* 237–270.

Nagy, W. E., & Herman, P. A. (1987). Breadth and depth of vocabulary knowledge: Implications for acquisition and instruction. In M. G. McKeown & M. E. Curtis (Eds.), *The nature of vocabulary acquisition* (pp. 19–35). Hillsdale, NJ: Erlbaum.

Pany, D., Jenkins, J. R., & Schreck, J. (1982). Vocabulary instruction: Effects on word knowledge and reading comprehension. *Learning Disability Quarterly, 5,* 202–215.

Sauer, J. L. (1986). *Fog magic.* New York: Puffin.

Schatz, E. K., & Baldwin, R. S. (1986). Context clues are unreliable predictors of word meaning. *Reading Research Quarterly, 21,* 439–453.

Sobol, D. (1976). The case of the blueberry pies. In Ginn and Company, *Reading 720.* Lexington, MA: Ginn.

Sperry, A. (1983). *Call It Courage.* New York: Simon & Schuster.

Stahl, S. A., & Fairbanks, M. M. (1986). The effects of vocabulary instruction: A model-based meta-analysis. *Review of Educational Research, 56,* 72–110.

Swanborn, M. S. L., & de Glopper, K. (1999). Incidental word learning while reading: A meta-analysis. *Review of Educational Research, 69*(3), 261–285.

Tuinman, J. J., & Brady, M. (1973, December). *How does vocabulary account for variance on reading comprehension tests?* Paper presented at the National Reading Conference, Houston.

3

Teaching Vocabulary in the Primary Grades
Vocabulary Instruction Needed

ANDREW BIEMILLER

By the end of grade 2, there is a 4,000-word difference in root vocabulary knowledge between children in the highest vocabulary quartile and those in the lowest quartile. Until primary grade children with low vocabularies have a chance to build vocabulary in school, they will continue to lag seriously behind more advantaged children. There is evidence that words are acquired in roughly the same order by most children. A number of studies suggest a gain of 3 words per day when teachers read books aloud several times in a week and provide explanations of 8 to 10 words a day. Further details on several published tests and two new studies are reported. Suggestions for classroom practice are provided.

There is much evidence that vocabulary levels are strongly correlated with reading comprehension (Chall, Jacobs, & Baldwin, 1990; Scarborough, 1998). Even in the primary grades the range in vocabulary between children with smaller and bigger vocabularies is large (Biemiller & Slonim, 2001). By the end of grade 2, children in the lowest vocabulary quartile had acquired about 1.5 root words a day over 7 years, for a total of about 4,000 root word meanings. Children in the highest quartile had acquired more than 3 root words a day, for a total of about 8,000 root word meanings. Average vocabulary increases from an estimated 3,500 root word

28

meanings at the beginning of kindergarten to 6,000 at the end of second grade (Biemiller, 2001; Biemiller & Slonim, 2001). These estimates, which have been increased slightly since the 2001 publication, are consistent with findings by Anglin (1993) and my own work (Biemiller & Slonim, 2001) as well as studies of root word knowledge by beginning college students (Hazenberg & Hulstijn, 1996; D'Anna, Zechmeister, & Hall, 1991; Goulden, Nation, and Read, 1990).

These large differences reflect many things: (1) levels of parental language support and encouragement, (2) other language sources (e.g., caregivers, day care, preschool, school, etc.), and (3) child constitutional differences in the ease of acquiring new words. However, after second grade, children in all vocabulary quartile groups acquire new words at about the same rate (Biemiller & Slonim, 2001). Therefore, it seems likely that the most important vocabulary differences before grade 3 reflect differences in experiences rather than simply constitutional factors.

Unfortunately, several studies suggest that, at present, primary school attendance is not a major source of vocabulary acquisition. Age, not school experience, apparently affects vocabulary. Both Cantalini (1987) and Morrison, Williams, and Massetti (1998) report that, unlike early academic skills, vocabulary is affected by age but not by school experience in the primary years. Thus the vocabulary of old kindergarten children and young first-grade children is similar. So too is the vocabulary of old first-grade children and young second-grade children.

Becker (1977) suggested that the school emphasis on reading (word identification) skills in the early grades without emphasis on books with challenging vocabulary results in problems for many middle elementary children's reading comprehension. Those with restricted oral vocabularies comprehend at lower levels. Other studies have shown that (1) developed vocabulary size in kindergarten is an effective predictor of reading comprehension in the middle elementary years (Scarborough, 1998); (2) orally tested vocabulary at the end of first grade is a significant predictor of reading comprehension 10 years later (Cunningham & Stanovich, 1997); and (3) children with restricted vocabulary by third grade have declining comprehension scores in the later elementary years (Chall, Jacobs, & Baldwin, 1990). In each of these studies, observed differences in vocabulary were related to later comprehension. None of these studies had any evidence that schooling was responsible for vocabulary size.

In short, vocabulary levels diverge greatly during the primary years, and virtually nothing effective is done about this in schools. It is true that some children arrive in kindergarten with less vocabulary than others. Schools cannot change what happens before children start school. However, when children fall further behind while in primary school, it becomes less likely that they can later catch up. Our chances of successfully addressing vocabulary differences in school are greatest in the preschool and early primary years. In this chapter, I will mention the problem of assessing vocabulary in primary classes and briefly describe some methods that have been used with primary and preprimary children to teach and assess vocabulary. In addition, I will describe two recent studies of vocabulary support with kindergarten to grade 2 children, discuss some of the problems teachers will encounter in teaching vocabulary, and present some guidelines for using children's books to support vocabulary.

ASSESSING VOCABULARY IN THE PRIMARY YEARS: A MAJOR PROBLEM

A major barrier for including vocabulary in the primary curriculum is the difficulty of assessing vocabulary, especially under classroom conditions. Testing children's vocabulary orally on a one-to-one basis is not difficult. The Peabody Picture Vocabulary Test (PPVT; Dunn & Dunn, 1997) and the Expressive Vocabulary Test (Williams, 1997) are well established. These tests are predictive of later school achievement (Scarborough, 1998). My own Root Word Inventory can also be used with young children, especially if prompts are used (Biemiller & Slonim, 2001; Biemiller, 2001). This test is also highly correlated with reading comprehension. However, none of these methods is feasible for classroom teachers, for such assessments typically take 10–15 minutes per student.

I believe that the inability to readily assess vocabulary and vocabulary growth has been a major reason why vocabulary receives little attention in the primary grades. It may be that feasible methods for assessing vocabulary in the primary grades will be developed. For now, I think the best teachers can do is to try to get a general idea of how well words are reported to be known by children. Children could be asked to raise hands if they know a word. This should be followed by asking one child what the word means.

WHAT SEQUENCE OF WORD ACQUISITION EXISTS, AND HOW CAN YOU FIND A LISTING OF WORD SEQUENCE?

The data in any standardized test of vocabulary (e.g., PPVT) identifies words learned early and words learned later. A child with a relatively large vocabulary will know more of the "later" words than a child with a small vocabulary, even if they are the same age. Biemiller and Slonim (2001) showed that words known best by children from grades 1–5 are likely to be known by even children with relatively small vocabularies, while those with larger vocabularies know those words plus words known less well. Our data suggest that, at any given point in time, children are adding words from an estimated 2,000–3,000 of the 15,000 root words known by the majority of grade 12 students. Words selected for classroom instruction or explanation should be from the 2,000–3,000 words being learned.

However, there are two problems. One problem is that children within a particular grade enter with different vocabulary sizes, and hence they are learning somewhat different words. Addressing the vocabulary needs of the lower half of the class (in vocabulary) may not meet the needs of more advanced children and vice versa. The other problem is that we lack an accurate, comprehensive listing of most word meanings known by children at different ages or, better, children with different sizes of vocabulary. Our relatively accurate data on word knowledge is based on 120 word meanings sampled from Dale and Rourke's (1981) *Living Word Vocabulary* (LWV; Biemiller & Slonim, 2001).

The LWV is the best available source on when word meanings are likely to be learned, and very much more accurate than word frequency measures. The LWV contains some 44,000 word meanings and the grade level at which a word is first known by 67% or more of children or adults. Grade levels at which two-thirds or more of children know a word range from grade 4 to grade 16+. There are about 30,000 word meanings known by students in high school or younger. Of these, about 17,500 entries are root word meanings. Note that the same root word will often have several word meanings, which may be known at different ages. For example, *lean* as in *Lean the rake against the wall* is known by children younger than grade 4. In contrast, *lean* as in *Lean on me when you're having troubles* is first known by a majority of students in grade 8. These are just two of the eight root word meaning entries listed for *lean* in the LWV.

The LWV levels were ascertained using written tests, and hence weren't used with children younger than grade 4. We determined that a grade level 2 can be formed using words known by 81% or more of children in grade 4 (Biemiller & Slonim, 2001). In fact, we have found that grade level 2 words are usually learned before the other words. This level really refers to words learned by grade 2 or earlier. Grade level 2 words include the more common meanings used in Chall and Dale's (1995) readability test. These words are also listed at the end of my book *Language and Reading Success* (Biemiller, 1999). Neither list specifies meanings. For practical purposes, one can assume the most common meanings of these words.

Unfortunately, we have found that the middle LWV levels (4–6, and 8–10) are not very good indicators of the sequence of word learning. At present, the best I can suggest is using LWV words from levels 4 and 6 for vocabulary work with children in grades 1 and 2. Kindergartners need some of these and some words from level 2 (level 4 words known at 80% or better). I now have usable lists of root word meanings from grade levels 2, 4, 6, 8, 10, and 12. I hope these will soon be made available through the publisher of LWV, World Book/Childcraft International. These LWV grade levels should probably be best thought of as roughly indicating the sequence of word learning rather than specific grades by which the words should be taught or acquired.

RESEARCH ON PROMOTING VOCABULARY IN THE PRIMARY YEARS

I have found few classroom studies of teaching or promoting vocabulary in the primary grades, whereas there are many more vocabulary studies with children from grade 3 and up. Methods with older children can be carried out using print material and printed tests. These are not feasible in the primary years, when children's reading skills are nonexistent or too low to help with advanced vocabulary. The few studies I found on vocabulary in the primary grades all make use of story contexts within which some vocabulary instruction occurs. Overall, these studies show that it is possible to have most children acquire as many as three words a day.

One study shows that reading a book several times leads to more word learning than reading several different books once each (Senechal, 1997). Several studies show that when some words are explained while reading a book, more of these words are retained than when books are read without word explanation (Brabham & Lynch-Brown, 2002; Brett, Rothlein, & Hurley, 1996; Elley, 1989; Senechal, 1997). These studies all used three readings of books. Two or three different books were repeatedly read over a period of two to three weeks. Overall, individual children learned the meanings of about a quarter of the words explained, across a range of 3–10 words taught per day. Thus, if 10 words were taught, an average of 2.5 words were learned. Results were similar for children from age 3 to age 10 (grade 4). Note that when we speak of learning a quarter of the words explained, different children are learning different words. Some will have known more of the words to begin with. Overall, there may be an upper limit of about three words learned per day. All of these studies used multiple-choice vocabulary pretests and posttests, usually administered orally. Those studies that compared immediate posttests with posttests 6 weeks to 3 months after reading found word knowledge to be about the same at both times. In short, when learned in context, words appear to be retained well.

In another study by Feitelson, Goldstein, Iraqi, and Share (1991) data on specific words explained were not tested before or after readings. In this study with kindergarten children, 12 books were each read nine or more times over the course of the year. Dramatic and significant gains in language competence (vocabulary and grammatical competence) were reported in comparison to children in control classes without extensive oral reading. This study was conducted with Arabic children. Especially noteworthy is the fact that the children were acquiring not only the vocabulary and knowledge of story structure needed to comprehend this material but also the more formal dialect of Arabic used in most written communications. In disadvantaged English-speaking communities, there is also a need to acquire standard forms of the language used in educated contexts.

Current Classroom Research

I have replicated the findings of Brabham and Lynch-Brown (2002), Brett, Rothlein, and Hurley (1996), Elley (1989), and Senechal (1997) in my ongoing classroom research (Biemiller, 2003). I have been particularly concerned with promoting vocabulary in the primary grades—before children are reading independently. In the first study of the report, whole-class instruction provided by regular teachers in kindergarten to grade 2 classes resulted in learning 20–30% of the words explained. Most of these children spoke more than one language at home. My method of assessing vocabulary is more demanding than most studies—requiring children to explain meanings of words presented in context sentences. My conclusions about word learning are based on posttests given 6 weeks after reading. Children not exposed to the books learned 5% of the words explained. Results were similar in kindergarten, grade 1, and grade 2.

In the second study of the report, when compared to comparable story words that were not explained, I found an average gain of 19% for explained words and 12% for unexplained words. Furthermore, I found a substantial classroom effect. The average of the larger gains in classrooms across the grades was 27% while the average of smaller gains was 9%. Again there was no clear grade difference. These classroom results strongly suggest that classroom implementation influenced the outcomes. Part of the differences between the classrooms was caused by my procedure. I had instructed teachers to ask children if they knew a word to be explained. Children's explanations were used when correct. However, I now suspect that other children did not attend as well to children's explanations as they did to teacher explanations. In the third study of the report, I found that having the same teachers explain words, and adding daily and weekly reviews of words taught, raised the percentage of words learned to 35%. This resulted in learning 6 to 12 words per week, depending on the number of words taught (Biemiller, 2003). In the next section, I will outline my conclusions about promoting vocabulary.

Summary of Studies of Reading to Children

All of these kindergarten, first-, or second-grade studies are remarkable for the magnitude of language gains produced from relatively short, daily whole-class or half-class interventions. In the long run, effective intervention will involve extended vocabulary work as a normal part of a primary curriculum. At two to three words a day, the impact of work over 2 or 3 weeks is limited. However, over 140 days of instruction (allowing that instruction will not occur every day), up to 400 words could be learned across a school year. If this gain proves to be largely *in addition* to words learned at home, many low-vocabulary children would have a serious chance of moving close to grade-level vocabulary.

PRACTICAL PROBLEMS
IN PROMOTING VOCABULARY

Adding an oral teacher read-aloud component with some direct vocabulary and comprehension instruction should provide a significant opportunity to improve vocabulary. While reading aloud to children is a common component of primary classroom programs, it is often used as a transition activity for changes of instruction or as a relaxation just after lunch (Lickteig & Russell, 1993). In my observation, books are rarely reread and rarely used in conjunction with any direct instruction (e.g., word or comprehension explanations). If teachers are to include a read-aloud component with some deliberate instruction, there will be a number of practical issues to address.

Choosing Books

The first problem is choosing books to read to children. In my opinion, teachers should select books that are somewhat challenging for children in the less advanced half of the class when read orally. (You'll be able to tell how challenging the book is when you check children's knowledge of some vocabulary you have targeted.) There should be a number of words not known by at least half of the class.

It is not desirable to concentrate on words known by only a few of the children in a class nor to select books which contain many such words. Allowing children with below-average vocabulary to acquire vocabulary known by children with above-average vocabulary will probably be most important. This will move them up in the sequence of words learned. The studies outlined previously showed either that low-vocabulary children acquired as many words as higher-vocabulary children when words are explained, or in some cases even more words (Biemiller, 2003; Elley, 1989).

Selecting Words for Explanation

Which words in the book you've chosen should be selected for attention? We have found that our intuition is good but not perfect. We start by simply selecting words that we think will be challenging. We then check to see whether these words we selected are on Chall and Dale's (1995) list of familiar words. These are largely what Beck, McKeown, and Kucan (2002) refer to as "Tier One" words—common words known by most children. If we are selecting words for preschool or kindergarten children or English-language learners, a focus in part on these familiar words may be necessary. For most first-grade and second-grade children, exclude words that are on Chall and Dale's list of familiar words, which are reproduced in Appendix A in *Language and Reading Success* (Biemiller, 1999). The LWV does not provide clear evidence beyond that. Words from LWV grade levels 4, 6, 8, and 10 all appear to be learned across the elementary years. (Clearly, there are also words in each of those grade levels that are not usually learned in the elementary years.) Thus the only advice I can give at this point is to exclude grade level 2 words and use your judgment regarding the appropriateness of other words. I recommend not explaining really rare words for primary children (e.g., *settee, woofer*). You can only address a limited number of words, and even though children may be able to learn rare words, they will rarely encounter them in the primary grades. (Of course, if a rare word is to be used in part of the curriculum, for example in science, the meaning should be taught.)

As I indicated above, I have completed a list of all root words in the LWV between grades 2 and 12. In general, the words to focus on are those which do *not* appear as the first 3,000 words from the Dale and Chall (1995) readability assessment list. Again, refer to the root word list in Biemiller (1999, Appendix).

Assessing Word Knowledge in the Primary Years

It would be desirable to have some basis for knowing how well a word is known prior to explaining it. As discussed previously, it is not feasible for elementary teachers to assess all children's knowledge of each word prior to (or after) word explanation. After reading a book aloud with word explanations, one possibility is to invite children to consider each word presented in a sentence from the story, and then ask one child who "knows" the word to explain it. Some rough estimate of word knowledge can thus be obtained, while children are on notice to report honestly.

Reading with Word Explanations

Having established that target words are not well known, at least by those in the lower half of the class, we undertake reading with explanations. In our experience, it is important to read the book once with minimal interruptions. After this initial reading, we find that we can interrupt up to 8 or 10 times to explain words while rereading a book, depending on the length of the book. However, we try not to interrupt more than once every 75–100 running words while reading. With very young children, we try not to interrupt more than once a page in a specific reading. Books for very young children are typically short. Two such books may have to be read to be able to explain 10 words a day.

We try to keep word explanations simple. These are being given in a specific context. We explain only what is needed to understand the content being read. For example, in a kindergarten, the teacher reading *Clifford at the Circus* (Bridwell, 1977) comes to "A sign said the circus needed help. " The teacher rereads this sentence and then explains, "*Help* in this story has a different meaning. *The circus needed help* means the circus show wants to hire some people to work at the show—to help put on the show." (Somewhat to our surprise, children have not had difficulty with the use of the word *means*.)

KEEPING TRACK OF WORDS TAUGHT

As a teacher proceeds with reading and word explanations, it would be very useful to keep a list of words introduced to the children and preferably some idea of whether the words were learned. I recommend keeping an alphabetical list of words introduced, and brief notes on the books in which the words appeared and the teacher's estimate of children's mastery of the words. It is rare for words to go from unknown by all to known by all. Rather, we can expect a significant increase in the percentage of children knowing a word. Unfortunately, as noted above, teachers will typically not have the resources to make such assessments before and after every book used. Some highly abbreviated version of word assessment is the best we can hope for.

I urge teaching 8–10 words a day. In the studies described and in our own experience, we can expect children to acquire 2–3 out of 10 words. Most target words may already be known by some children. Some words will not be learned. We hope that with further work the proportion of words learned can be increased to 40%.

TEACHING VOCABULARY
USING CHILDREN'S LITERATURE

The research literature and our studies reported here suggest that acquiring an average of 3 words a day is possible, assuming explanation of around 10 words a day. While this may not seem like a lot of words, vocabulary work on 140 instruction days could add 400 root words to individual children's vocabularies. Adding three root words a day is the average daily number of words learned by primary age children with the largest vocabularies (Biemiller & Slonim, 2001). That may be as many words as we can expect to see on an ongoing basis. Senechal's (1997), Elley's (1989), and our data all suggest that children with initially smaller vocabularies (specific to the books instructed) have at least the same gains and sometimes larger gains. Those with relatively smaller vocabularies are most in need of added words.

Increasing vocabulary gains by 400 words a year would have a measurable effect on vocabulary size. If sustained over 3 years, this would add about two-thirds of the number of words needed to bring children from the lowest vocabulary quartile to average vocabulary levels, assuming that these children would continue to learn some words outside of school. However, I suggest that there is no magic bullet in vocabulary acquisition. Unlike early work with reading mechanics (e.g., Becker, 1977) or numbers (e.g., Griffin, Case, & Siegler, 1994), promoting vocabulary in the primary grades is not likely to increase self-learning of word meanings through inference. This is true of children who are not reading fluently or widely. (Among older children, especially in middle and high school, there is some evidence that active inference may help with vocabulary learning.) During the primary years, new root words are learned mainly from explanations by others.

Other vocabulary methods could be used in addition. A "word of the day" could be added (preferably a word that will be used in the room). If children can be encouraged to ask about unfamiliar words—and parents can be persuaded to encourage such questions—more gains could be achieved. However, total gains greater than three words a day have yet to be seen (or attempted!).

A classroom intervention along the lines described in this chapter would take about 30 minutes. I realize that asking for 30 minutes a day is a lot, as state and provincial curricula become ever more demanding. For example, some of the teachers I have worked with have complained that "they were not able to complete the curriculum" (content relating to science, social studies, and art) if they had to focus on stories and vocabulary 30 minutes a day. Their principal suggested that becoming literate was probably more important than some of the details in the prescribed curriculum. Curricula that result in children reaching Grade 3 without the best possible vocabulary instruction and opportunities are curricula that hold disadvantaged children back. Some of this reading aloud and word explanation can be conducted with specified curriculum materials related to social studies or science. However, in the primary grades, we should be more concerned with children acquiring an adequate normal vocabulary than mastering specific social studies or science facts. It is now widely accepted that children need basic academic skills—word identification, handwriting and spelling, and number skills. We will not begin to close gaps between advantaged and disadvantaged children until we also succeed in ensuring adequate vocabulary development and use.

SUMMARY

Most differences in vocabulary occur prior to third grade. After second grade, most children acquire new words at about the same rate. However, by fifth grade, lower-quartile children have not yet attained the same size vocabulary as high-quartile children have in the second grade. Furthermore, there is evidence that the low-vocabulary children are largely acquiring the same words in roughly the same order as other children.

In this chapter, I have described several studies that have demonstrated that primary-level children can acquire new vocabulary at a rate of two or three words a day. The programs demonstrating this success have all used books read aloud to children several times, combined with word explanations of specific words. Typically, 8–10 words a day are explained. Individual children acquire two or three words a day when this is done. In most of these studies, knowledge of words learned was demonstrated some weeks after instruction.

Some suggestions are provided in this chapter for reading stories, selection of words for explanations, examples of reading with explanations, and assessment of vocabulary levels and gains. As noted, individual oral assessment of children is not possible under classroom conditions with one teacher. Some alternatives were briefly discussed.

Overall, I suggest planning on about 30 minutes a day for reading aloud, word explanations, maintaining some focus on comprehension, and on assessment. I realize that 30 minutes is a large part of the day that primary grade teachers have with their children. I also know that failure to de-

velop an adequate vocabulary is as limiting for a child as failing to learn to
identify words or understand numbers.

REFERENCES

Anglin, J. M. (1993). Vocabulary development: A morphological analysis. *Mono-graphs of the Society for Research in Child Development, 58*(10, Serial No. 238).

Beck, I. L., McKeown, M G., & Kucan, L. (2002). *Bringing words to life: Robust vocabulary instruction.* New York: Guilford Press.

Becker, W. C. (1977). Teaching reading and language to the disadvantaged—What we have learned from field research. *Harvard Educational Review, 47,* 518–543.

Biemiller, A. (1999). *Language and reading success.* Cambridge, MA: Brookline Books.

Biemiller, A. (2001, June). *The relationship between vocabulary assessed with picture vocabulary methodology, same words with sentence context method, root word inventory, and reading comprehension.* Paper presented at the Annual Conference of the Society for Scientific Study of Reading, Boulder, CO.

Biemiller, A. (2003, April). *Teaching vocabulary to kindergarten to grade two children.* Paper presented at the annual meeting of the American Educational Research Association, Chicago, IL.

Biemiller, A., & Slonim, N. (2001) Estimating root word vocabulary growth in normative and advantaged populations: Evidence for a common sequence of vocabulary acquisition. *Journal of Educational Psychology, 93,* 498–520.

Brabham, E. G., & Lynch-Brown, C. (2002). Effects of teachers' reading-aloud styles on vocabulary acquisition and comprehension of students in the early elementary grades. *Journal of Educational Psychology, 94,* 465–473.

Brett, A., Rothlein, L., & Hurley, M. (1996). Vocabulary acquisition from listening to stories and explanations of target words. *Elementary School Journal, 96,* 415–422.

Bridwell, N. (1977). *Clifford at the circus.* New York: Scholastic.

Cantalini, M. (1987). *The effects of age and gender on school readiness and school success.* Unpublished doctoral dissertation, Ontario Institute for Studies in Education. Toronto, Canada.

Chall, J. S., & Dale, E. (1995). *Readability revisited: The new Dale–Chall readability formula.* Cambridge, MA: Brookline Books.

Chall, J. S., Jacobs, V. A., & Baldwin, L. E. (1990). *The reading crisis: Why poor children fall behind.* Cambridge, MA: Harvard University Press.

Cunningham, A. E., & Stanovich, K. E. (1997). Early reading acquisition and its relation to reading experience and ability 10 years later. *Developmental Psychology, 33,* 934–945.

Dale, E., & O'Rourke, J. (1981). *The living word vocabulary.* Chicago: World Book/Childcraft International.

D'Anna, C. L., Zechmeister, E. B., & Hall, J. W. (1991). Toward a meaningful definition of vocabulary size. *Journal of Reading Behavior, 23,* 109–122.

Dunn, L. M., & Dunn, L. M. (1997). *Peabody picture vocabulary test* (3rd ed.). Circle Pines, MN: American Guidance Service.

Elley, W. B. (1989). Vocabulary acquisition from listening to stories. *Reading Research Quarterly, 24,* 174–186.

Feitelson, D., Goldstein, Z., Iraqi, J., & Share, D. I. (1991). Effects of listening to story reading on aspects of literacy acquisition in a diglossic situation. *Reading Research Quarterly, 28,* 70–79.

Goulden, R., Nation, P., & Read, J. (1990). How large can a receptive vocabulary be? *Applied Linguistics, 11,* 341–363.

Griffin, S., Case, R., & Siegler, R. (1994). Rightstart: Providing the central conceptual prerequisites for first formal learning of arithmetic to students at risk for failure. In K. McGilly (Ed.), *Classroom lessons: Integrating cognitive theory and classroom practice* (pp. 25–50). Cambridge, MA: MIT Press.

Hazenberg, S., & Hulstijn, J. H. (1996). Defining a minimal receptive second-language vocabulary for non-native university students: An empirical investigation. *Applied Linguistics, 17,* 145–163.

Lickteig, M., & Russell, J. (1993). Elementary teachers read-aloud practices. *Reading Improvement, 30,* 202–208.

Morrison, F. J., Williams, M. A., & Massetti, G. M. (1998). *The contributions of IQ and schooling to academic achievement.* Paper presented at the annual meeting of the Society for the Scientific Study of Reading, San Diego, CA.

Scarborough, H. S. (1998). Early identification of children at risk for reading disabilities: Phonological awareness and some other promising predictors. In B. K. Shapiro, P. J. Accardo, & A. J. Capute (Eds.), *Specific reading disability: A view of the spectrum* (pp. 75–119). Timonium, MD: York Press.

Senechal, M. (1997). The differential effect of storybook reading on preschoolers' acquisition of expressive and receptive vocabulary. *Child Language, 24,* 123–138.

Williams, K. T. (1997). *Expressive vocabulary test.* Circle Pines, MN: American Guidance Service.

4

Vocabulary Instruction
for Young Children
at Risk of Experiencing
Reading Difficulties

Teaching Word Meanings
during Shared Storybook Readings

MICHAEL D. COYNE
DEBORAH C. SIMMONS
EDWARD J. KAME'ENUI

This chapter describes an experimental storybook intervention designed
to help children at risk of experiencing reading difficulties to develop critical vocabulary knowledge in the primary grades. This instructional intervention incorporates principles of explicit vocabulary instruction within
shared storybook reading activities. In this chapter, we first summarize
the research literature on storybook or shared book reading activities followed by the literature base on explicit vocabulary instruction. We then
describe and give examples of the storybook intervention informed by
these two distinct literatures.

Beginning reading research has converged on a profound and irrefutable
finding over the past decade: children enter kindergarten with "meaningful
differences" in early literacy experiences (Hart & Risley, 1995). Even at
this early age, children are characterized by differences in skills, exposure,

and opportunities with the form, functions, and conventions of language and print (National Research Council, 1998).

For example, young children differ considerably in their understanding of and familiarity with the phonologic features of language and the alphabetic nature of our writing system (Torgesen et al., 1999). While some children come to school having already grasped the insight that language can be broken down into individual phonemes that map onto letters, many other children have only the most rudimentary awareness of sounds and print. A large body of research evidence suggests that these differences in phonological awareness and letter knowledge have important implications for learning to read and predicting success in acquiring beginning reading skills (National Reading Panel, 2000).

Similarly, young children possess vastly divergent vocabularies (Biemiller, 2001; Hart & Risley, 1995; National Research Council, 1998). While some children enter school with thousands of hours of exposure to books and a wealth of rich oral language experiences, other children begin school with very limited knowledge of language and word meanings. Just as the research base on phonological awareness and alphabetic understanding attests, teachers and researchers have long recognized the important and prominent role that vocabulary knowledge plays in becoming a successful reader (Becker, 1977; Cunningham & Stanovich, 1998; National Reading Panel, 2000).

The research evidence is unequivocal: children enter kindergarten with significant differences in critical early literacy skills, and these differences place many children at serious risk for failing to learn how to read and understand text. As a result, early intervention matters, and it matters more for children who enter with less. These children not only begin school with limited skills and knowledge, but also these initial differences grow larger and more discrepant over time (Stanovich, 1986). The goal of early intervention, therefore, is to target differences in early literacy skills and experiences at the outset of formal schooling before reading difficulties become entrenched and intractable (Coyne, Kame'enui, & Simmons, 2001). To this end, educators, policy makers, and researchers have actively and increasingly promoted prevention and early intervention efforts in beginning reading (e.g., Reading First, 2002).

The results of early intervention have been largely encouraging. Over the past 10 years, researchers have engaged in a concerted and ever more successful effort to develop effective instructional strategies and interventions to increase the phonological awareness and word identification skills of young children at risk for reading difficulties and disability (e.g., Foorman, Francis, Fletcher, Schatschneider, & Mehta, 1998; Simmons et al., 2002; Torgesen et al., 1999). Yet, while the research community has concentrated its collective attention on helping children *read* words, there has been very little corresponding research conducted on helping children *understand* words or develop equally critical vocabulary knowledge (National Reading Panel, 2000). As Biemiller and Slonim (2001) recently asserted, "Although vocabulary development is crucial for school success, it has not received the attention and interest that work on identifying printed words and spelling have received" (p. 511).

There is a need for research-based, intensive vocabulary interventions for young children at risk of experiencing reading difficulties. To address this need, we conceptualized and implemented an intervention that integrated knowledge from two distinct literatures: the storybook literature and the vocabulary literature. In developing the intervention, we incorporated validated principles of explicit and systematic vocabulary instruction from research conducted with students in grades 3 and above into storybook reading activities typically used with children in preschool through grade 2.

In this chapter, we first summarize the research literature on storybook or shared book reading activities followed by the literature base on explicit vocabulary instruction. We then describe and give examples of an experimental storybook intervention designed for kindergarten children who are at risk for experiencing reading difficulties. This instructional intervention integrates principles of explicit vocabulary instruction within storybook reading experiences.

SHARED STORYBOOK READING ACTIVITIES
IN PRESCHOOL TO GRADE 2

Older students acquire a great deal of new vocabulary through wide independent reading (Anderson & Nagy, 1992). Younger students who have yet to become skilled readers, however, must learn word meanings through a different medium (Becker, 1977). The primary way for young nonreaders to be exposed to new vocabulary is within the context of oral language experiences such as shared storybook reading. Storybook reading activities are an excellent means for language and vocabulary development because of the opportunities for using decontextualized language during interactive discussion (Snow, 1991) and the relative rarity of the vocabulary encountered in storybooks compared with speech (Cunningham & Stanovich, 1998). For example, the complexity of vocabulary found in children's books is greater than in all of adult conversation, except for courtroom testimony (Hayes & Ahrens, 1988).

There is a growing literature documenting the effects of listening to storybooks on language and vocabulary development (Bus, van IJzendoorn, & Pellegrini, 1995; National Reading Panel, 2000). For example, studies have found that children can learn the meanings of unknown words through incidental exposure during shared storybook reading activities (Elley, 1989; Nicholson & Whyte, 1992; Senechal & Cornell, 1993; Robbins & Ehri, 1994).

Much of this research has been informed by an influential series of studies by Whitehurst and his colleagues (Whitehurst, Arnold, et al., 1994; Whitehurst, Epstein, et al., 1994; Whitehurst et al., 1999). These studies investigated the effects of a storybook reading intervention called "dialogic reading." In contrast to traditional storybook reading activities which typically consist of an adult reading and a child listening passively, dialogic reading actively involves the child in the overall literacy experience. According to Whitehurst et al. (1999), the "adult assumes the role of an active listener, asking questions, adding information, and prompting the child to increase the sophistication of descriptions of the material in the picture book. The child's active engagement is encouraged through praise and repetition, and more sophisticated responses are encouraged by expansions of the child's utterances and by scaffolding by means of more challenging questions from the adult reading partner" (p. 262).

Results from studies evaluating dialogic reading with preschool children reported significant effects on young children's emergent literacy and language skills (Whitehurst, Epstein, et al., 1994; Whitehurst et al., 1999). In a converging program of related research, Senechal and her colleagues similarly found that preschool children's active participation and engagement during shared storybook reading increased the likelihood that they would learn new vocabulary (Hargrave & Senechal, 2000; Senechal, Thomas, & Monker, 1995).

Researchers have begun to isolate factors that increase the likelihood that children will learn new vocabulary from listening to storybooks. In addition to engaging in rich dialogic discussion about the storybook, these factors include reading storybooks multiple times (Robbins & Ehri, 1994; Senechal, Thomas, & Monker, 1995), providing performance-oriented readings (Dickinson & Smith, 1994), and reading storybooks with small groups of students (Whitehurst, Arnold, et al., 1994). Finally, it is important to choose engaging storybooks with beautiful pictures and appealing stories that will capture and hold children's interest and attention.

The results of these studies suggest that shared storybook reading activities are a valuable way to support vocabulary development in young children. However, evidence also reveals that these activities are not equally effective for all students. Children who are at risk for reading difficulties with smaller initial vocabularies are less likely to learn unknown words from incidental exposure during storybook reading activities than their peers with larger vocabularies (Nicholson & Whyte, 1992; Robbins & Ehri, 1994; Senechal, Thomas, & Monker, 1995). In other words, with traditional storybook reading activities, the initial vocabulary differences among students grow larger over time (Stanovich, 1986; Penno, Wilkinson, & Moore, 2002).

In response to this finding, researchers have called recently for more conspicuous teacher-directed vocabulary instruction to complement traditional storybook reading activities for young children who are at risk for experiencing reading difficulties (Biemiller & Slonim, 2001; Simmons et al., 2002; Stahl & Shiel, 1999). For example, Robbins and Ehri (1994) concluded that "because children with weaker vocabularies are less likely to learn new words from listening to stories than children with larger vocabularies, teachers need to provide more explicit vocabulary instruction for children with smaller vocabularies" (p. 61).

Two recent studies (Penno, Wilkinson, & Moore, 2002; Wasik & Bond, 2001) reported promising results of interventions that included more focused attention on teaching target vocabulary words within the context of shared storybook readings. Penno and her colleagues (2002) conducted a study in which 47 young children (mean age, 6 years and 6 months) were randomly assigned to two storybook reading conditions. In the control condition, children listened to three readings of a storybook distributed over 3 weeks. In the treatment condition, children listened to three readings of the same storybook but also received explanations of target vocabulary words within the context of the story. The researchers found that at posttest children in the treatment condition identified more target words in a multiple-choice test and included more target words in a retelling of the story. The results of this study support the findings of earlier studies documenting the benefits of providing simple explanations of target words in storybook reading activities (Brett, Rothlein, & Hurley, 1996; Elley, 1989).

Wasik and Bond (2001) conducted a more intensive 15-week intervention study with 121 preschool children from a Title 1 early learning center. Four classroom teachers were randomly assigned to either a treatment or control condition. In the treatment condition, teachers read storybooks with groups of 12–15 children and engaged them in extended and interactive discussion about the book, using target vocabulary before, during, and after the readings.

Children in the interactive book reading condition outperformed children in the control condition on experimenter-developed measures assessing receptive and expressive knowledge of target vocabulary. Additionally, and more impressively, children in the treatment group scored significantly higher on the Peabody Picture Vocabulary Test (PPVT-III), a general measure of receptive vocabulary knowledge. Wasik and Bond (2001) concluded that providing multiple opportunities to interact with target vocabulary in meaningful contexts both within and "beyond the pages of the book" can result in increased vocabulary learning for low-income children.

Findings from studies such as these hold promise for improving early intervention efforts for young children at risk of reading difficulties with less developed vocabularies. By intensifying shared book reading activities with direct teaching of target vocabulary, these interventions increased the amount of vocabulary that children learned. Interventions that maximize learning are a critical component of prevention efforts because children who begin school with less require the most effective and efficient instruction to catch up to their peers who are not at risk (Coyne et al., 2001).

The goal of our intervention was also to optimize the vocabulary development of young children by increasing the effectiveness of teaching the meanings of target words within the context of shared storybook reading activities. To accomplish this, we looked to a separate but related knowledge base, the research on explicit vocabulary instruction (Baumann, Kame'enui, & Ash, 2003). In the next section, we summarize the vocabulary instructional literature.

EXPLICIT VOCABULARY INSTRUCTION IN GRADES 3 AND ABOVE

Although there is little research on explicit vocabulary instruction in grades K–2, there is a more extensive literature on direct vocabulary instruction in grades 3 and above (Baker, Kame'enui, & Simmons, 1998; Baumann et al., 2003). There is especially strong evidence regarding the effectiveness of explicit vocabulary instruction that focuses on teaching students the meanings of specific words and instructional principles that maximize vocabulary learning (National Reading Panel, 2000).

Explicit vocabulary instruction should teach directly the meanings of words that are important for understanding the text and words that children will encounter often (Stahl, 1986). Effective strategies for directly teaching vocabulary include using both contextual and definitional information, giving multiple exposures of target words, and encouraging deep processing (National Reading Panel, 2000; Stahl, 1986; Stahl & Fairbanks, 1986). Activities that encourage deep processing challenge students to move beyond memorizing simple dictionary definitions to understanding words at a richer, more complex level by, for example, describing how they relate to other words and to their own experiences (Beck, McKeown, & Omanson, 1987; Chapter 2, this volume).

Direct instruction of target words is also more effective when it adheres to validated principles of instructional and curricular design (Kame'enui, Carnine, Dixon, Simmons, & Coyne, 2002). For example, vocabulary instruction should be conspicuous (Baker et al., 1998). Conspicuous instruction is explicit and unambiguous and consists of carefully designed and delivered teacher actions. During vocabulary instruction, this would include direct presentations of word meanings using clear and consistent wording and extensive teacher modeling of new vocabulary in multiple contexts. Vocabulary instruction should also provide students with carefully scheduled review and practice to help them more firmly incorporate new vocabulary into their lexicon (Baker et al., 1998).

A program of research that evaluated the effectiveness of explicit vocabulary instruction was conducted by Beck, McKeown, and their colleagues with students in upper elementary grades (Beck, Perfetti, & McKeown, 1982; McKeown, Beck, Omanson, & Perfetti, 1983; McKeown, Beck, Omanson, & Pople, 1985). Their program of rich vocabulary instruction provided students with definitions of words but also extended instruction by providing experiences that promoted and reinforced deep processing of word meanings. Students were exposed to target words frequently within and across lessons and given opportunities to manipulate words in varied and rich ways. Results of these studies demonstrated that a carefully designed program of direct vocabulary instruction can have positive effects on both students' word learning and comprehension.

The vocabulary instruction literature has important implications for younger students at risk of reading difficulties. Previously, many researchers have argued that the number of words that children need to learn is so great that the role of direct instruction in helping children develop vocabulary knowledge is insignificant and inconsequential (Anderson & Nagy, 1992). Recently, however, other researchers have begun to question this assertion. Lower estimates of the number of root-word meanings that typical students acquire in a year suggest that direct instruction can, in fact, provide students with a significant proportion of words they will learn, especially students with less developed vocabularies (Biemiller, 2001; Stahl & Shiel, 1999; Chapter 3, this volume).

To date, most research on explicit vocabulary instruction has been carried out with older children in grade 3 and above (e.g., Beck et al., 1982; Kame'enui, Carnine, & Freschi, 1982). Unfortunately, waiting until third grade to systematically address vocabulary development for students with low vocabularies may be too late for children who enter school at risk for experiencing reading difficulties. The urgency of targeting vocabulary development in the early grades was made acutely apparent in recent research conducted by Biemiller and Slonim (2001). Their findings revealed that most of the vocabulary differences between children occur before grade 3, at which point children with high vocabularies know *thousands* of more word meanings than children who are experiencing delays in vocabulary development.

In summary, research highlights the need for early interventions that offer effective classroom-based vocabulary instruction for young children at risk of experiencing reading difficulties. The two distinct research literatures outlined previously provide a conceptual and empirical basis for developing such an intervention by incorporating validated principles of explicit and systematic vocabulary instruction from research conducted with students in grades 3 and above into storybook reading activities for young children in kindergarten through grade 2. In the following section, we describe and give examples of a storybook intervention informed by this conceptual framework.

LINKING RESEARCH TO PRACTICE

We are currently engaged in a longitudinal program of research to investigate ways to optimize early literacy instruction and intervention for children at risk of experiencing reading difficulties (Simmons et al., 2002). As part of this larger program of research, we developed a storybook intervention to increase children's vocabulary knowledge and enhance their comprehension, two critical components of early literacy instruction.

When designing the elements of the intervention targeting vocabulary development, we explicitly incorporated and integrated the instructional principles distilled from our review of the storybook and vocabulary research. To make the linkage between the research principles and their application more transparent, we outline these connections in the following two tables. Table 4.1 summarizes the research principles gleaned from the

TABLE 4.1. Shared Storybook Reading Literature

Research principle	Application
Interesting and engaging storybooks	Storybooks chosen were either classics (e.g., *Bread and Jam for Francis, Harry the Dirty Dog*) or recent award winners (e.g., *Hush! A Thai Lullaby, McDuff Moves In*)
Rich dialogic discussion about storybooks	Teachers engaged children in scaffolded discussion of the story by activating prior knowledge, eliciting responses about story elements, linking story themes to children's own experiences, and facilitating story recalls.
Performance-oriented readings	Discussion took place primarily before and after story readings. Teachers read stories with expression and enthusiasm.
Multiple readings of storybooks	Each storybook was read two times over four lessons. Students also retold each story one additional time with prompted connections to the storybook's illustrations.
Small groups of students	Storybooks were read with groups of two to five children.

shared storybook reading literature and how we incorporated them into our intervention. Table 4.2 summarizes our application of the research principles synthesized from the vocabulary instruction literature.

We evaluated the effects of our storybook intervention within the context of a large-scale experimental study with kindergarten children identified as at risk of experiencing reading difficulties (Simmons et al., 2002). Children who received the storybook intervention scored significantly higher than a control group on an experimenter-developed expressive measure of taught vocabulary at posttest ($d = .85$). These results suggest that explicitly teaching word meanings within the context of shared storybook

TABLE 4.2. Vocabulary Instruction Literature

Research principle	Application
Carefully selected target words	Three target words were chosen to teach directly from each storybook. Words were selected because they were important for understanding the story and likely to be unfamiliar to kindergarten students.
Simple definitions within the context of the story	When introducing a new vocabulary word, teachers provided students with a simple definition or synonym (e.g., *rumpus* means *wild play*). Teachers then used the definition within the context of the story. In the story *Where the Wild Things Are*, for example, the teacher says, "I'll say the sentence with the words that mean the same as *rumpus*. 'Let the wild play start.' "
Conspicuous instruction	Definitions of target words were presented through instruction that was direct and unambiguous. Definitions were explicitly modeled by teachers using clear and consistent wording.
Rich instruction	Teachers provided children opportunities to discuss target words in extended discourse before and after stories. Additionally, teachers provided children with structured discrimination and generalization tasks that challenged them to process word meanings at a deeper and more complex level (e.g., Is *rumpus* more like sitting quietly or wild play? Have you ever been in a rumpus?).
Multiple exposures to target words and carefully scheduled review and practice	Target vocabulary words were introduced and reviewed a minimum of 6 days in a carefully scaffolded sequence. Each target word was first used by the teacher in context, practiced in sentences by students, incorporated into story recalls, and discussed in multiple novel contexts.

reading is an effective method for increasing the vocabulary of young children at risk of experiencing reading difficulties.

STORYBOOK INTERVENTION

In this section we describe in more detail the storybook intervention evaluated in the kindergarten study (Simmons et al., 2002). The intervention consisted of 108 half-hour lessons developed to accompany 40 children's picture books. The picture books were either classics or recent award winners. Three target vocabulary words were identified from each storybook to be taught explicitly. Target words were selected because they are important for understanding the story and likely to be unfamiliar to young children. Selected examples of picture books, target vocabulary, and definitions are included in Appendix 4.1.

Lessons were sequenced in 20 6-day cycles. Each cycle was designed to complement two storybooks. One storybook was read on days 1 and 3 of the cycle, while the other storybook was read on Days 2 and 4. Days 5 and 6 focused on integrating and applying target vocabulary to generalized contexts. During days 5 and 6, children were also given opportunities to retell the stories using selected illustrations as prompts. Teachers encouraged children to use target vocabulary during retells.

To illustrate the intervention, we provide examples of lessons that accompanied the storybook *The Snowy Day* written and illustrated by Ezra Jack Keats (1963). The three target words selected from this picture book were *tracks*, *firm*, and *adventure*. Because children at risk of experiencing reading difficulties benefit from instruction that is highly explicit, we designed lessons with a considerable degree of instructional specificity (Simmons et al., 2002). For example, lessons were broken down into a series of specific instructional tasks, opportunities for corrective feedback were provided, and teachers were supplied with precise and consistent wording (Kame'enui et al., 2002).

The day 1 lesson was divided into four sections, (1) teacher preparation, (2) story introduction, (3) the reading, and (4) postdiscussion. The teacher preparation section offered suggestions for gathering and organizing materials and reviewing the storybook. During the story introduction, the teacher introduced the children to the target vocabulary words and their definitions. Children were also given opportunities to predict what will happen in the story and preview important story elements. The teacher then read the storybook to the children, pausing briefly to discuss target words within the context of the story. Finally, in the postdiscussion, children engaged in an extended discourse about the storybook. Children were encouraged to explore story elements and target vocabulary and were challenged to draw on their own experiences to increase the richness and complexity of the discussion. (Note that suggested teacher wording in this and following lessons is shown in *italics*.)

DAY 1: *THE SNOWY DAY*, READING 1

Teacher Preparation

1. Find the vocabulary tagboard for today's words.
2. Rehearse the story prior to reading it with the children—practice reading with expression (Your reading should take approximately 3 minutes).
3. Pencil in the pauses that you will make in the story.
4. Remember to reinforce good listening behaviors.

Story Introduction

1. Point to the title on the cover. *The title of this story is **The Snowy Day**. The story was written by Ezra Jack Keats, who also drew the pictures.*
2. ***The Snowy Day** is a story about things to do on a snowy day. Listen to discover all of the things that Peter does on a snowy day.*
3. Showing the cover, ask, *What do you think this story is about?*
   a. Build on students' responses by emphasizing the characters and problem: *Yes, the main character will be a boy who goes out in the snow, or Yes, the boy is going to look for things to do on a snowy day.*
4. *Stories that we read have characters, problems, and settings. Thinking about these will help you remember what happens in the story.*
5. *When I read this story, I am going to read and say a lot of words. I want you to listen for three magic words in the story. Here they are.* (Point to each word on the tagboard as you repeat it.) ***Tracks**. Say it with me . . . tracks. **Firm**. Say it with me . . . firm. **Adventures**. Say it with me . . . adventures. When you hear these words in the story, raise your hand.*

The Reading

1. Pay attention to volume, suitable speed, enunciation, and intonation.
2. Pause at the following breaks and ask these questions:
   a. The page with the long tracks. *Oh, good. Some of you raised*

your hands! What word did you hear? Yes, "tracks." OR Did anyone hear one of the magic words? The words are "tracks," "firm," and "adventures." Listen and raise your hands. "He dragged his feet s-l-o-w-l-y to make tracks."
        THEN ADD:
    *Tracks are **marks left on the ground**. Peter dragged his feet to make tracks.*

b. The page with Peter, making a snowball. *Terrific, some of you raised your hands! What word did you hear? Yes, "firm." OR Did anyone hear one of the magic words? The words are "tracks," "firm," and "adventures." Listen and raise your hand. "He packed it round and firm and put the snowball in his pocket for tomorrow."*
        THEN ADD:
c. *Firm is **hard**. Peter packed the snow round and firm to make a snowball.*

d. The next page with Mom taking off Peter's socks. *Oh, good, some of you raised your hands! What word did you hear? Yes, "adventures." OR Did anyone hear one of the magic words? The words are "tracks," "firm," and "adventures." Listen and raise your hand. "He told his mother all about his adventures."*
        THEN ADD:
    *Adventures are **exciting times**. Peter told his mother about his adventures.*

Post Discussion

1. *How does Peter make tracks? What else could he use to make tracks?* (Provide answers if necessary.) *Have you ever left tracks in the snow? What did they look like? Have you ever left tracks in the house? Have you ever seen animal tracks?* (Call on several students.)

2. *Why did Peter pack his snowball round and firm? Did he have the snowball when he went to bed? Why not?* (Provide answers if necessary.) *Have you ever made a snowball? Did you pack the snow firm? Are the muscles in your arms firm? Is the table firm? Are your socks firm?* (Call on several students.)

3. *What adventures did Peter have in the snow? What adventures do you think Peter and his friend will have the next day in the snow?* (Provide answers if necessary.) *Have you had adventures in the snow? Have you had adventures at the beach? Have you had adventures with your friends?* (Call on several students.)

The second reading of *The Snowy Day* took place on day 3 of the cycle. (On days 2 and 4, the students listened to and discussed the other storybook included in the cycle.) The day 3 lesson followed the same organization and procedures as day 1. However, during this lesson more emphasis was placed on discussing the target vocabulary within the context of the story. For example, during the story introduction, teachers reviewed target words by showing children the illustration from the story depicting the word's use. For *The Snowy Day*, the teacher displayed the illustration with the long tracks and said, "Peter made tracks in the snow with his boots and a stick." Additionally, some teacher scaffolding was removed and children took over more responsibility when discussing target words as well as story elements. For example, whereas in day 1 children only listened to the teacher define the target word, in day 3 they produced the definitions as well.

The day 5 and 6 lessons were divided into two sections: (1) vocabulary activity and (2) story retell. Teachers did not reread the storybooks during these lessons but rather engaged children in structured vocabulary and comprehension activities. The vocabulary activity reviewed and integrated target words introduced in the two storybooks read during days 1 through 4 of the cycle. These activities were also designed to extend children's understanding of target words by providing them with opportunities to process word meanings at a deeper and richer level. During the story retell, children retold each storybook using illustrations from the story and interactive discourse as scaffolded prompts. Teachers also encouraged children to use target vocabulary and incorporate story elements in their retells. Below are examples of vocabulary activities from days 5 and 6. Although target words from both storybooks in the cycle are discussed, for clarity only examples of vocabulary from *The Snowy Day* are presented.

DAY 5: VOCABULARY ACTIVITY

Here is the story, **The Snowy Day**. *Let's talk about the new words we learned in this book.*

1. Show picture of long tracks. *Peter left marks on the ground in the snow with his feet and a stick. What is our magic word for left marks on the ground? Yes, tracks.*
2. Show page with Peter making the snowball. *Peter made the snowball hard. What's our magic word for hard? Yes, firm.*
3. Show page with Mom taking off Peter's socks. *Peter told his mom about all of his exciting times in the snow. What's our magic word*

for exciting times? Yes, adventures. We are going to play a game using the magic words. This is the "Guess the Word Game." You are going to tell me which word goes with another word.

   a. *Which words go with adventures? Bathtub or exciting times?* (exciting times)
   b. *Which word goes with firm? Sloppy or hard?* (hard)
   c. *Which words go with tracks? Snowballs or marks left on the ground?* (marks left on the ground)

DAY 6: VOCABULARY ACTIVITY

*Here is the story **The Snowy Day**. Let's remember the words that we talked about in this book. I'm going to say some sentences, and then I want you to use our magic words to finish them.*

   1. *The girl's shoes left marks on the ground. Her shoes left . . .* (tracks)
   2. *In the story, Peter had many exciting times in the snow. Peter had many . . .* (adventures)
   3. *The dirt was packed down very hard. The dirt was . . .* (firm)

We are going to play a game using the words. This is the "What Am I Talking about Game." See if you can tell me what I am talking about.

   1. *We went to the beach. We dug up clams. We played in the waves. We had an exciting time at the beach. What is our magic word for exciting times? If incorrect or no response, ask, tracks or adventures? We had adventures at the beach. Say that.*
   2. *The girl stomped her feet in the snow leaving marks on the ground. What is our magic word for leaving marks on the ground? Yes, tracks. If incorrect or no response, ask, tracks or adventures? The girl left tracks in the snow. Say that.*
   3. *Mother packed the cookie dough into a pan. She made the dough hard. What is our magic word for hard? Yes, firm. If incorrect or no response, ask, cozy or firm? Mother made the cookie dough firm. Say that.*

SUMMARY

In this chapter we outlined a conceptual and empirical framework for incorporating direct instruction of specific word meanings into storybook reading activities. To support this conceptual framework, we summarized research findings from two different literature bases: the research on shared storybook reading activities carried out with young children in preschool through grade 2 and the research on explicit vocabulary instruction conducted primarily with students in grades 3 and above.

We then illustrated how these research principles could be translated into instructional practice by providing examples of a storybook intervention designed to help kindergarten children at risk of experiencing reading difficulties increase their vocabulary knowledge. Results from an experimental study evaluating this intervention demonstrated that these students can be taught the meanings of specific words within the context of storybook reading activities. These and similar findings (e.g., Penno et al., 2002; Wasik & Bond, 2001) are important because previous research suggests that traditional storybook reading activities benefit children with higher initial vocabularies to a greater extent than their peers with less developed vocabularies. Interventions that increase the effectiveness of storybook reading activities through explicit teaching of word meanings hold promise for decreasing the vocabulary differences among students in the primary grades.

REFERENCES

Anderson, R. C., & Nagy, W. E. (1992). The vocabulary conundrum. *American Educator, 16*(4), 14–18, 44–47.

Baker, S. K., Simmons, D. C., & Kame'enui, E. J. (1998). Vocabulary acquisition: Research bases. In D. C. Simmons & E. J. Kame'enui (Eds.), *What reading research tells us about children with diverse learning needs* (pp. 183–218). Mahwah, NJ: Erlbaum.

Baumann, J. F., Kame'enui, E. J., & Ash, G. E. (2003). Research on vocabulary instruction: Voltaire redux. In J. Flood, J. Jensen, D. Lapp, & J. R. Squire (Eds.), *Handbook of research on teaching the English language arts* (pp. 752–785). New York: Macmillan.

Beck, I. L., McKeown, M. G., & Omanson, R. C. (1987). The effects and uses of diverse vocabulary instructional techniques. In M. G. McKeown & M. E. Curtis (Eds.), *The nature of vocabulary acquisition* (pp. 147–163). Hillsdale, NJ: Erlbaum.

Beck, I. L., Perfetti, C. A., & McKeown, M. G. (1982). Effects of long-term vocabulary instruction on lexical access and reading comprehension. *Journal of Educational Psychology, 74*(4), 506–521.

Becker, W. C. (1977). Teaching reading and language to the disadvantaged: What we have learned from field research. *Harvard Educational Review, 47,* 518–543.

Biemiller, A. (Spring, 2001). Teaching vocabulary: Early, direct, and sequential. *American Educator, 25*(1), 24–28, 47.

Biemiller, A., & Slonim, N. (2001). Estimating root word vocabulary growth in normative and advantaged populations: Evidence for a common sequence of vocabulary acquisition. *Journal of Educational Psychology, 93*(3), 498–520.

Brett, A., Rothlein, L., & Hurley, M. (1996). Vocabulary acquisition from listening to stories and explanations of target words. *The Elementary School Journal*, 96, 415–422.

Bus, A. G., van IJzendoorn, M. H., & Pellegrini, A. D. (1995). Joint book reading makes for success in learning to read: A meta-analysis on intergenerational transmission of literacy. *Review of Educational Research*, 65, 1–21.

Coyne, M. D., Kame'enui, E. J., & Simmons, D. C. (2001). Prevention and intervention in beginning reading: Two complex systems. *Learning Disabilities Research & Practice*, 16, 62–72.

Cunningham, A. E., & Stanovich, K. E. (1998). What reading does for the mind. *American Educator*, 22(1–2), 8–15.

Dickinson, D. K., & Smith, M. W. (1994). Long-term effects of preschool teachers' book readings on low-income children's vocabulary and story comprehension. *Reading Research Quarterly*, 29, 104–122.

Elley, W. B. (1989). Vocabulary acquisition from listening to stories. *Reading Research Quarterly*, 24, 174–187.

Foorman, B. R., Francis, D. J., Fletcher, J. M., Schatschneider, C., & Mehta, P. (1998). The role of instruction in learning to read: Preventing reading failure in at-risk children. *Journal of Educational Psychology*, 90, 37–55.

Hargrave, A. C., & Senechal, M. (2000). A book reading intervention with preschool children who have limited vocabularies: The benefits of regular reading and dialogic reading. *Early Childhood Research Quarterly*, 15, 75–95.

Hart, B., & Risley, R. T. (1995). *Meaningful differences in the everyday experience of young American children*. Baltimore: Brookes.

Hayes, D. P., & Ahrens, M. (1988). Vocabulary simplification for children: A special case of "motherese." *Journal of Child Language*, 15, 395–410.

Kame'enui, E. J., Carnine, D. W., Dixon, R. C., Simmons, D. C., & Coyne, M. D. (2002). *Effective teaching strategies that accommodate diverse learners* (2nd ed.). Columbus, OH: Merrill.

Kame'enui, E., Carnine, D., & Freschi, R. (1982). Effects of text construction and instructional procedures for teaching word meanings on comprehension and recall. *Reading Research Quarterly*, 17(3), 367–388.

Keats, E. J. (1963). *The snowy day*. New York: Viking.

McKeown, M. G., Beck, I. L., Omanson, R. C., & Perfetti, C. A. (1983). The effects of long-term vocabulary instruction on reading comprehension: A replication. *Journal of Reading Behavior*, 15, 3–18

McKeown, M. G., Beck, I. L., Omanson, R. C., & Pople, M. T. (1985). Some effects of the nature and frequency of vocabulary instruction on the knowledge and use of words. *Reading Research Quarterly*, 20, 482–496.

National Reading Panel. (2000). *Teaching children to read: An evidence-based assessment of the scientific research literature on reading and its implications for reading instruction: Reports of the subgroups*. Bethesda, MD: National Institute of Child Health and Human Development.

National Research Council. (1998). *Preventing reading difficulties in young children*. Washington, DC: National Academy Press.

Nicholson, T., & Whyte, B. (1992). Matthew Effects in learning new words while listening to stories. In C. K. Kinzer & D. J. Leu (Eds.) *Literacy research, theory, and practice: Views from many perspectives: Forty-first Yearbook of the National Reading Conference* (pp. 499–503). Chicago, IL: The National Reading Conference.

Penno, J. F., Wilkinson, I. A. G., & Moore, D. W. (2002). Vocabulary acquisition from teacher explanation and repeated listening to stories: Do they overcome the Matthew Effect? *Journal of Educational Psychology, 94,* 23–33.

Reading First. (2002). United States Department of Education. Retrieved September 6, 2002 from http://www.ed.gov/offices/OESE/readingfirst/index.html

Robbins, C., & Ehri, L. C., (1994). Reading storybooks to kindergartners helps them learn new vocabulary words. *Journal of Educational Psychology, 86,* 54–64.

Senechal, M., & Cornell, E. H. (1993). Vocabulary acquisition through shared reading experiences. *Reading Research Quarterly, 28,* 360–374.

Senechal, M., Thomas, E., & Monker, J. (1995). Individual differences in 4–year-old children's acquisition of vocabulary during storybook reading. *Journal of Educational Psychology, 87,* 218–229.

Simmons, D. C., Kame'enui, E. J., Harn, B. A., Edwards, L. A., Coyne, M. D., Thomas-Beck, C., Kaufman, N, Peterson, K., & Smith, S. B. (2002). *The effects of instructional emphasis and specificity on early reading and vocabulary development of kindergarten children.* Manuscript submitted for publication.

Snow, C. E. (1991). The theoretical basis for relationships between language and literacy in development. *Journal of Research in Childhood Education, 6,* 5–10.

Stahl, S. A. (1986). Three principles of effective vocabulary instruction. *Journal of Reading, 29*(7), 662–668.

Stahl, S. A., & Fairbanks, M. M. (1986). The effects of vocabulary instruction: A model-based meta-analysis. *Review of Educational Research, 56,* 72–110.

Stahl, S. A., & Shiel, T. G. (1999). Teaching meaning vocabulary: Productive approaches for poor readers. In *Read all about it! Readings to inform the profession* (pp. 291–321). Sacramento: California State Board of Education.

Stanovich, K. E. (1986). Matthew effects in reading: Some consequences of individual differences in the acquisition of literacy. *Reading Research Quarterly, 21,* 360–406.

Torgesen, J. K., Wagner, R. K., & Rashotte, C. A., Rose, E., Lindamood, P., Conway, T., & Garvan, C. (1999). Preventing reading failure in young children with phonological processing disabilities: Group and individual responses to instruction. *Journal of Educational Psychology, 91,* 1–15.

Wasik, B. A., & Bond, M. A. (2001). Beyond the pages of a book: Interactive book reading and language development in preschool classrooms. *Journal of Educational Psychology, 93,* 243–250.

Whitehurst, G. J., Arnold, D. H., Epstein, J. N., Angell, A. L., Smith, M., & Fischel, J. E. (1994). A picture book reading intervention in day care and home for children from low-income families. *Developmental Psychology, 30,* 679–689.

Whitehurst, G. J., Epstein, J. N., Angell, A. L., Payne, A. C. Crone, D. A., & Fischel, J. E. (1994). Outcomes of an emergent literacy intervention in Head Start. *Journal of Educational Psychology, 86,* 542–555.

Whitehurst, G. J., Zevenbergen, A. A., Crone, D. A., Schultz, M. D., Velting, O. N., & Fischel, J. E. (1999). Outcomes of an emergent literacy intervention from Head Start through second grade. *Journal of Educational Psychology, 91,* 261–272.

APPENDIX 4.1. Selected Storybooks, Target Vocabulary, and Definitions

Book	Vocabulary taught	Definition
Harry the Dirty Dog	buried	put in the ground and covered with dirt
	strange	someone (or something) that you don't know
	furiously	fast and wildly
Pete's a Pizza	mood	how you act or feel
	kneading	pushing and squeezing
	giggling	silly laughing
Hush! A Thai Lullaby	nearby	close
	ceiling	top of a room
	dozes	sleeps lightly
A Chair for My Mother	tips	extra money for good work
	spoiled	messed up
	delivered	brought
Caps for Sale	peddler	someone who travels and sells things
	stamped	to put your foot down hard
	disturb	to move out of place
McDuff Moves In	tumbled	fell and rolled
	pairs	sets of two
	celebrated	had a party
I Lost My Bear	care	be interested
	remember	bring to mind again
	favorite	best-liked
Yoko	treasure	something special
	sushi	rice roll
	foreign	from another country
Hot Hippo	strolled	walked slowly
	promised	said would truly do
	bottom	the lowest part
Curious George Feeds the Animals	exhibit	place that shows something
	zookeeper	a person who takes care of animals at the zoo
	idea	a plan
Anansi and the Moss-Covered Rock	forest	woods
	spinning	turning
	satisfied	happy
Monkey and Crocodile	banks	sides of a river
	cunning	tricky smart
	searched	looked for

5

Word Wizards All!
Teaching Word Meanings in Preschool and Primary Education

STEVEN A. STAHL
KATHERINE A. DOUGHERTY STAHL

The research of Hart and Risley (1995) found significant gaps in vocabulary knowledge among children, demonstrating a need to address vocabulary knowledge in preschool and primary aged children. Most vocabulary development in those years will come through adults reading storybooks to children. We suggest a few approaches that might improve vocabulary learning from listening to storybooks. We also suggest that some approaches validated on older children, such as semantic mapping and Venn diagrams, can be adapted for younger children.

Consider the power that a name gives a child. Now this is a *table* and that is a *chair*. No longer are they merely things that one must crawl around. Having a name for something means that one has some degree of control. The child can say *milk* and get some to drink, or *eat* and get a cracker or some baby food. As children get more words, they get more control over their environment. To move from *eat* to *cracker* or *bottle* or *cookie* or *fruit*, from *milk* to *juice*, allows the child to better communicate wants and needs, and to have a better chance of having them fulfilled.

As the child learns new words, the child can further classify the environment. The child can go from gross categories—things that sit on the

59

floor, things that one can get nourishment from—to more precise labels. A child's ability to name establishes the ability to form categories (Nelson, 1996). As knowledge about the named item increases, that word may be transferred to related situations. This pattern is true for first vocabulary and extends to each new or expanding knowledge domain. Language and reading both act as the tools of thought to bring representations to a new level and to allow the formation of new relationships and organizations.

This process does not end in early childhood, but goes on and on as long as the person continues to learn. To follow the *juice* example to *orange juice* to the various kinds of juice available (*fresh squeezed, no pulp, from concentrate*) in your local supermarket may be absurd, but a good deal of the process of knowing about your world is learning the categories and subcategories of objects and actions within that world. For example, Berlin and Kay (1969) examined color naming in peoples all over the world. They found that most advanced or industrialized civilizations had more words for colors. Very primitive societies may have terms for only *dark* and *light*, slightly more advanced societies may add one for *red* until we get to very advanced societies with a panoply of color names.

Even if one cannot argue that having as many color names as we do allows for the development of a Renoir or a Monet, having more words enables one to think more precisely about one's environment and to manipulate that environment. Classification, the basic mental process underlying naming, is important not only in naming but also in summarizing (Kintsch & van Dijk, 1978), inferencing (Anderson & Pearson, 1984; Trabasso, 1981), among other things. To expand a child's vocabulary is to teach that child to think about the world.

This chapter will discuss the teaching of word meanings to children from pre-kindergarten to grade 2. This is an area that is not widely researched, but vitally important.

GAPS IN VOCABULARY KNOWLEDGE

Given the importance of the words we know, it is distressing that there are large gaps in vocabulary knowledge, beginning in the preschool years and persisting through the elementary school years, and probably beyond. Hart and Risley (1995), in a troubling study, found that children from advantaged homes (i.e., children of college professors) had receptive vocabularies as much as five times larger than children from homes receiving Aid to Families with Dependent Children (AFDC). They found that children in AFDC homes had concomitantly fewer words spoken to them, with more words spoken in imperative sentences and fewer in descriptive or elaborative sentences. Their picture is that of a widening gap between well-off and poor, one which threatens to grow with time.

These differences in vocabulary knowledge, even in the young years, can influence children's reading throughout the elementary years. Dickinson and Tabors (2001) found that children's word knowledge in preschool still had significant correlations with their comprehension in upper elementary school.

Another study, of elementary school students, found a gap in word knowledge persisting through the elementary years. White, Graves, and Slater (1990) examined the reading and meaning vocabularies of children in first through fifth grades in three schools—a largely white suburban school, an inner-city school with mainly African American students, and a semirural school enrolling largely Pacific Island children. They found that both reading vocabulary and meaning vocabularies grew rapidly over the school years, with meaning vocabularies growing at an estimated average of 3,000 words per year. This average, though, concealed large variations, with estimated vocabulary growth ranging from 1,000 to 5,000 words per year. The reading and meaning vocabularies of children in the suburban school grew more rapidly than those in the two schools serving low-income children.

In contrast, Biemiller and Slonim (2001), who examined children's growth in word meanings between grades 2 and 5, found that children in the bottom quartile learned more words per day (averaging 3 root words) than did children in the upper quartile (averaging 2.3 root words per day). They suggested that children in the lower quartile had more words to learn, so, given the same exposure to words in school, were able to learn more. However, children in the lowest quartile still knew only as many word meanings by grade 5 as a typical fourth grader, because they started so far behind in second grade. Biemiller and Slonim suggested that vocabulary instruction should begin earlier to close the gap.

The vocabulary gap between children of different socioeconomic status can be conceived of as a Matthew Effect (Stanovich, 1986). The term *Matthew Effect* comes from the Book of Matthew, in which it is foretold that the "rich get richer and the poor get poorer." Stanovich suggested that children who are more proficient readers tend to read more and read more challenging materials than children who struggle in reading. Because most words that children acquire are learned from reading them in context (Kuhn & Stahl, 1998) and because proficient readers read more challenging materials, those which contain rarer or more difficult words, they tend to learn more of those words, enabling them to read yet more challenging materials. Thus, the gap between proficient and struggling readers grows each year.

GAPS IN EXPERIENCES

Hart and Risley (1995) also found that parents of lower SES children spoke significantly fewer words to their children than did the professional parents. Part of this was attributable to discourse patterns. Parents of children receiving AFDC tended to use more imperatives, or commands, and fewer elaborated explanations than did the professional parents. The fewer words also may have reflected the more limited resources available to the parents of AFDC children (Nunberg, 2002).

To expand children's vocabularies, then, one must not only provide more words for children to learn, through expanding the number of words used when speaking to children, but also expand children's experiences. After all, the words have to label something. These experiences do not have to be firsthand experiences. There are many things that we know about without having seen them directly. For example, we have a clear idea of what dinosaurs look like (or at least what scientists have posited that they look like) and had such an idea even before seeing the movie *Jurassic Park*. Children learn from television, the movies, and descriptions in books. What is important is that they have experiences with a wide variety of concepts.

HOW WORD KNOWLEDGE DEVELOPS

The philosopher W. V. Quine (1960, cited in Woodward, 2000) presents the basic problem in word learning. In his example, a linguist sees an aboriginal point to a rabbit and hears the native say *gavagai* just as the rabbit runs by. What does *gavagai* mean? Does it refer to the rabbit, to the act of running, to some characteristic of the rabbit such as its color, or to something else, such as dinner? The essential problem of attaching words to concepts is that, because each concept has multiple dimensions, the learner must choose which aspect of the word is referred to. Because young children are presented with many examples in the context of words they do not know, often with a single exposure, they cannot know which aspect of the context to attend to. We are most interested in how words are learned in storybooks, but the process should be similar in other settings.

In one model (Stahl, 1991), when a word such as *gavagai* is first encountered, the hearer creates a phonological representation of the word. Because the hearer has not encountered this word before, this phonological representation is not connected to any stored semantic or syntactic information. The hearer might assume that the term refers to the whole object, *rabbit*, but this is not necessarily so. Smith (2000) suggests that children initially learning words have a predisposition to assume that words refer to objects as a whole. They use overall shape as an initial definition. However, the linguist would realize that this is just a guess and that *gavagai* might refer to any aspect of what was seen. Thus, the linguist would store all aspects of the experience. Piaget (1990) describes a young child who pointed to a dog through a window. His mother labeled it *chien* (dog). The child for a short time used that word to describe any object seen from the window, only gradually learning to accurately label *dog*.

Children also often overgeneralize words during this initial learning. Thus, *daddy* refers to any male, *dog* to any animal, and *cookie* to anything cookie-shaped or the cookie jar (Woodward, 2000). The process of word learning is not only learning what the word refers to but also constraining the use of the word to actual examples.

As the word is encountered repeatedly in different contexts, the linguist will be able to constrain the possible meanings. Thus, if *gavagai* is next used to refer to a sitting rabbit, the possible aspect of running is removed. If it is used to refer to another animal of the same color, the linguist may conclude that it refers to that color. In this view, a word is learned by repetitive exposure in context. For each exposure, the child learns a little about the word, until the child develops a full and flexible knowledge of the word's meaning. This will include definitional aspects, such as the category to which it belongs and how it differs from other members of the category, but this knowledge will be implicit and not conventionalized, as in a dictionary definition. It will also contain information about the various contexts in which the word was found, and how the meaning differed in the different contexts. Schwanenflugel, Stahl, and McFalls (1997), working with older children, found that children's learning from context seemed to fit this model. They were able to document the gradual growth of knowledge about a word after a single exposure in context. Other studies have found that children gradually learn words from both reading (e.g., Nagy, Anderson, & Herman, 1987) and from listening (e.g., Elley, 1989).

This model of word learning is a fairly passive one. As children are exposed to words, they gradually pick up information about words they encounter. This model ignores the importance of children's agency in word learning (Bloom, 2000). However, children will learn words from context only if they attend to them. Bloom argues that words must be relevant to children, that is, they must describe something that children are interested in for word learning to occur. In addition, the words need to describe states that children have experienced and need to communicate. According to Bloom, without engagement in a world of ideas and concepts, children will not develop a rich knowledge and use of language. This engagement occurs in a supportive and motivating atmosphere.

These needs will not be met, however, if the words required for expression are not available. Hart and Risley (1995) found that children in AFDC homes were not exposed to the same quantity of language as children from advantaged homes. Regardless of the child's cognitive capacity and need to express those cognitive states, the child's vocabulary will not grow unless the words are available in social and interactive settings. Further, they were given more imperatives and fewer opportunities for elaboration. Parents in the advantaged homes gave children more *motherese*, or repetitions with expansions. For example, Hart and Risley (1999) cite the following example:

> A parent asked a 23-month-old, "What happened to Marlon?" When the child did not answer, the parent gave a hint, "What does he have on his arm?" The child said, "Cast." The parent confirmed, "A cast," and returned to "What happened to his arm?" The child said, "Cast." The parent then supplied the answer she would expect (and the child would be able to give) at 36 months old, "Yes, the cast is on because he broke his arm. He fell and broke his arm." (p. 103)

In this and other examples, parents elaborate on children's knowledge and expand it. This expansion moves from the child's knowledge and expands it.

TALKING TO CHILDREN

One aspect of expanding the vocabulary of children should be to talk to them. It is striking not only from Hart and Risley's (1995, 1999) work that there are wide variations in how much adults talk to children. For children to develop rich vocabularies, they need to have many interactions with adults. It is from these interactions that they will develop the words they need to negotiate their world. Huttenlocher, Haight, Bryk, Seltzer, and Lyons (1991) found both the total volume of words and the number of different words mothers spoke to children significantly influenced the child's vocabulary learning

"Goldilocks" Words

It is not enough to just throw big words into conversations with children. This does not seem to be effective in improving children's vocabularies. Juel (2002) observed children in various kindergartens. She found that the one teacher who used the most rare words in her lessons was among the least effective in aiding children's vocabulary growth. Her interpretation is that the children could not understand the rare words because they did not have enough conceptual knowledge to understand the new words. Instead, they disregarded them.

Beck and McKeown (2003) suggest teaching what they call Tier 2 words. These are words that are in general use, but are not common. Tier 1 words would be common words, such as common sight words and simple nouns and verbs. Tier 3 words are words that are rare, limited to a single context, or represent concepts that young children might not have such as *cogitate, amble,* or *photosynthesis.* Tier 2 words include words such as *dome, beret, wade, nocturnal, accountant, chef, amble,* and *emerge.* We call them "Goldilocks" words, words that are not too difficult, not too easy, but just right.

There is evidence that children learn words in a similar order. Biemiller and Slonim (2001) found that the order of vocabulary acquisition was similar between children, with high correlations in word knowledge between children. That is, children will learn a word like *stride* before they learn *amble.* Their findings suggest that words grow in complexity and that children cannot learn a more complex word without learning the simpler words. Thus, we should make sure that the words we are teaching are of appropriate complexity. This sounds harder than it is. In natural conversation, mothers and teachers seem quite able to get the right level, if they keep their ears open to how the children are responding to them.

Talk around Words

The type of talk around words is important. That example of motherese cited above is a good example of what effective teachers and parents do to expand their children's vocabulary. In that case, the parent started with what the child knew and expanded it through a series of questions. This type of expansion through questioning seems effective in helping older children learn new words encountered in context.

deTemple and Snow (2003) suggest that nonimmediate and cognitively challenging talk is effective in helping children develop new word meanings. Nonimmediate talk is talk that goes beyond what is in front of the child that enables the child to make connections to past experiences, to analyze information or draw inferences, or to discuss the meaning of words. Mother's use of this type of talk was found to relate to their children's later performance on vocabulary measures (deTemple, 1994). deTemple and Snow (2003) use storybook reading for examples of this type of talk, but it can be done when talking about things that one encounters on a walk or on a trip. It can be of a "What's that?" kind of discussion, as in the following. In this segment, a mother and her 3-year-old son were reading *The Very Hungry Caterpillar.*

MOTHER: What's that (*pointing to the sun*)?
CHILD: (*Shrugs.*)

MOTHER: What's that? What make you hot?

CHILD: I don't know. Huh?

MOTHER: What make you hot?

CHILD: (*Shrugs.*)

MOTHER: The sun don't make you hot?

CHILD: Mmhm. (*Nods.*)

MOTHER: It make you real hot (*nodding*)?

CHILD: Mmhm. (*Nods.*)

(deTemple & Snow, 2003, pp. 21–22)

In this segment, the mother tries (unsuccessfully) to get her son to use the word *sun*. When he was unable to say it, she gave a defining characteristic (very hot) and then provided the word for him.

In cognitively challenging talk, the adult tries to get the child to extend her or his thinking about the topic. Such talk not only expands vocabulary knowledge, in terms of the numbers of words known, but also the depth of that knowledge.

MOTHER: That's a tusk see? It's white. Know what Domingo?

CHILD (*Domingo, age 5.11 years*): Hmm?

MOTHER: Hunters kill these elephants for that.

CHILD: Why?

MOTHER: Because they want it for, um, well, they use it for different things. I think um some museums buy them and I don't know about museums but I know that they kill the for this white um.

CHILD: There's no tusk on these elephants though.

MOTHER: See? That one's bigger so some of them die because of that. That is sad.

CHILD: I wish there was not such things as hunters and guns.

MOTHER: I know it me too. Oh there's a herd. That's a lot of them. See how they walk?

CHILD: Ma here's ones that's dead.

MOTHER: I don't think he's dead! Well we'll find out. "They use their tusks to dig" Oh see he's digging a hole! "They use their tusks to dig for salt. . . . "

CHILD: Hmm.

MOTHER: Let's look and see if there's another page you might like. It's ivory! The tusks are made of ivory. And they can make things with these tusks and that's why some animals, they die, hunters kill them.

CHILD: No wonder why they have hunters.

MOTHER: Yeah that's sad.

CHILD: I'm never gonna be a hunter when I grow up.

(deTemple & Snow, 2003, pp. 23–24)

The talk in this excerpt shows how a mother can take an experience as a springboard to new concepts. In this case, the mother begins by pointing out the *tusk*, then expands it to the uses of the tusk by the elephant and by the hunters, finally ending on an emotional reaction to hunting. The richness of the language expands the child's knowledge of the word *tusk*, by connecting it to *hunting*, *digging*, etc.

Just talking is important. However, it is equally important to have something to talk about. This means that adults (teachers and parents) need to consciously provide experiences that expand children's horizons. These experiences might include trips around one's neighborhood, to the grocery store (to talk about all those varieties of orange juice), to the park, the zoo, or any other place that gives the child new experiences or a chance to expand on older experiences.

WHERE THE WORDS ARE

Most vocabulary learning, however, comes from books. Storybook reading is the most powerful source of new vocabulary, including those academic words that are valued in school discourse. Books are literally "where the words are." Hayes and Ahrens (1988) examined the vocabulary used in a variety of sources. The average difficulty of a typical children's book ranks above that of either a children's or an adult television program and above that of a typical conversation between two college-educated adults. The number of rare words per 1,000 in children's books also ranks above that of television programs, adult conversation, and cartoon shows. Even a book like *Curious George Gets a Job* (Rey, 1947), intended for first graders to read and younger children to listen to, contains relatively rare words, not only *curious* but also *cozy*, *dizzy*, *wound*, *scold*, *attention*—just from the first 20 pages.

Stanovich (2000) and Cunningham and Stanovich (1991) have found that exposure to books, as measured by author recognition or title recognition measures, can account for a great deal of the variation in vocabulary knowledge among children and adults. In their studies, they looked at exposure specifically to books, but we believe that the same effect would hold true for exposure to all verbal language, written or spoken. As Hart and Risley (1995) found, increased exposure to a breadth of words will lead to increased words in a child's vocabulary.

Neuman and Celano (2001) examined the availability of print resources in low-income and middle-income communities. They found striking differences in the availability of print resources between these communities. For example, in one middle-class community, there were 13 venues selling children's books with 358 titles available. In a contrasting low-income community, there were 4 venues with only 55 titles available. Thus, the gap that begins with differences in the richness of language continues through differences in print resources available.

If we are to decrease the gap between children, we should start where the gap begins, in the preschool or at least the primary grades. By addressing the gap early, we might be able to diminish some of the differences between children later on in school, allowing more children to succeed in school.

THE LANGUAGE OF SCHOOL

All words are not valued equally. Instead, what we want children to learn is the language of school. For many children, this is a foreign language (Nagy & Stahl, in press). This language of school includes words that are used in school, but not necessarily in one's homes or neighborhoods.

Olson (1977) makes a useful distinction between utterance and text. *Utterance* refers to the conversational language that often contains sentence fragments, reliance on deixis (e.g., "over there") and other contextualized referents, a reduced vocabulary, and a shared knowledge base between speaker and hearer. Utterance tends to be a relatively restricted form of language, capable of communicating in the here and now, but dependent on a shared context for communication. *Text*, on the other hand, is relatively autonomous, contains more complex sentence forms, uses a more complex and exact vocabulary, and makes fewer assumptions about a shared knowledge base. It is text that is the language of school.

Although we use the term *text* usually to refer to written text, in Olson's (1977) notion, Text[1] could be written or oral, as long as it contains the autonomous and elaborated language typical of written text. One could argue that the college professor parents in Hart and Risley's (1995) study were speaking in Text, with more full sentences and rarer, more academic

---

[1]*Text*, when capitalized, refers to Olson's usage of that term. When used in lowercase letters, *text* refers to the conventional meaning.

words, even to their preschoolers. Children's books also are Text, containing more formal language, especially rarer vocabulary words. We will call this *academic vocabulary*, because this is the vocabulary of school. Children need to be exposed to Text, both spoken Text as in the rich utterances of Hart and Risley's professor parents and reading written children's books, in order to learn the language of schooling.

Children without the exposure to Text can be predicted to have difficulties in learning academic vocabulary. And, again, there are wide disparities in the amount of Text that children are exposed to. Adams (1990) estimated that she spent at least 1,000 hours reading storybooks to her son prior to his entrance into first grade. In contrast, Teale (1984) observed children from low-income homes and saw an average of 2 minutes per day with a projected average of 60 hours prior to first grade. Teale did not observe any storybook reading in the majority of homes in which he observed. The differences between the exposures given to the children studied by Teale and Adams's own child can be assumed to have profound effects on children's learning, including the learning of word meanings.

One solution to the problem posed by Hart and Risley (1995) would seem to involve increased reading of storybooks to children. This is not the only solution. Storybook reading might occur 45 minutes to an hour per day. Children need to be in an environment rich in vocabulary in order to learn words. This involves having children involved in elaborated interactions that involve academic vocabulary. In addition to reading storybooks, some direct teaching of word meanings will help.

Of special note should be alphabet books. Although we do not think about alphabet books when we think about vocabulary teaching, many alphabet books are well suited for that purpose. There are animal alphabet books, machine alphabet books, bird alphabet books, and so on, which can be a wonderful source for new words. Even ordinary alphabet books have surprise words that will help children's knowledge of word meanings to grow.

DIRECT TEACHING
IN EARLY CHILDHOOD CLASSES

For older children, Stahl and Fairbanks (1986) found that teaching word meanings significantly improved children's vocabulary knowledge as well as improving the comprehension of texts containing the taught words. For older children, such vocabulary teaching is done before reading a story, as in the directed reading activity. For younger children, the teaching might be done before a book, in a picture walk (Fountas and Pinnell, 1996), but it also might be done after reading or apart from reading entirely. We will discuss several activities that might be used to teach word meanings in K–2 classes.

Text Talk

Beck and McKeown (2001, 2003) suggest an interchange with young children called Text Talk. Text Talk is an approach to read-alouds designed to promote comprehension and language development. It involves the selection of texts that exhibit an event structure and enough complexity to prompt discussion and higher-level thinking. The strategic use of open-ended questioning encourages children to explain, elaborate, and formulate their own questions surrounding the text. Salient features of Text Talk have to do with the way background knowledge and vocabulary are addressed as part of the read-aloud. Background knowledge discussion should be limited to that which is directly related to the text. "Birdwalking," or encouraging elaborations that are only tangentially related to the text, has been found to disrupt the comprehension process and distract students from the text itself. Extensive vocabulary work follows each story. The meaning of three or four words is given, with examples of how each word is used. Children are encouraged to generate their own sentences for each word immediately after the reading, and an incentive chart records each child's use of the words over time. An example of a dialogue in Text Talk about the word *absurd* follows.

> **absurd:** In the story, when the fly told Arthur he could have three wishes if he didn't kill him, Arthur said he thought that was absurd. That means Arthur thought it was silly to believe a fly could grant wishes. When something is absurd—it is ridiculous and hard to believe.
>
> If I told you that your teacher was going to stand on his/her head to teach you—that would be absurd. If someone told you that dogs could fly—that would be absurd.
>
> I'll say some things, and if you think they are absurd, say: "That's absurd!" If you think they are not absurd, say: "That makes sense."
>
> I have a singing cow for a pet. (absurd)
>
> I saw a tall building that was made of green cheese. (absurd)
>
> Last night I watched a movie on TV. (makes sense)
>
> This morning I saw some birds flying around the sky. (makes sense)
>
> If I said let's fly to the moon this afternoon, that would be absurd. Who can think of an absurd idea? (When a child answers, ask another if they think that was absurd, and if so, to tell the first child: "That's absurd!") (Beck & McKeown, 2003, p. 165)

This discussion extends the meaning of the word as encountered in the story. From a single encounter, it is unlikely that children would gain much information about the word. This "text talk" both gives the child a rough definition for the word and extends its use into other contexts. Including both types of information was found to be characteristic of vocabulary instruction that improved children's comprehension (Stahl & Fairbanks, 1986). In addition, the discussion requires children to not only listen but also generate new knowledge about the word ("Who can think of an absurd idea?"). Generating new understandings is also important in word learning. Through generation words become more memorable. And all this interaction, as with the interactions around storybooks described earlier, leads to more vocabulary learning (Beck & McKeown, 2003).

Picture Walk

A picture walk is a guided reading book introduction in which the teacher goes through the pictures methodically, carefully supporting children's predictions about the text. Although we stress the use of picture walks for vocabulary development, they are used more broadly than just for vocabulary. Picture walks are based on the work of Marie Clay and her descriptions of an effective book introduction for novice readers (Clay, 1991, 1993; see Fountas & Pinnell, 1996, for more explicit descriptions). These conversations typically occur as the teacher and students preview each page or few pages of the new book before reading. The pictures are used as a catalyst for discussion of what the book is likely to be about. The picture walk does not have a specific set of procedures. It is used flexibly and in response to the students' needs and the challenges of a particular text. Teachers follow a few guidelines to ensure that students have a successful, independent first reading of the text.

- The introduction is conducted as a conversational social interaction around the text.
- The conversation prompts student engagement in activating background knowledge and experiences that relate to the text.
- The teacher provides an overview of the plot, theme, or important ideas.
- Children's attention is directed to text structure and language structure.
- Teachers use the book's language structure and vocabulary in the conversation about the book.
- Teachers may direct attention to using letter–sound relationships in one or two places in the text.

The extensiveness of the introduction depends on the expected challenges caused by content or text readability. A few vocabulary words may be introduced during the story introduction and conversation. The teacher selects vocabulary that the particular group of students may need introduced or developed. Unlike a vocabulary workbook page taught prior to reading, the discussion and the illustrations help situate the vocabulary in the story context. After reading the students and teacher might include the new vocabulary in their discussion or writing activity.

Word Wizard

The Word Wizard activity was designed by Beck, Perfetti, and McKeown (1982) to sensitize children to a wide range of words and to provide encouragement and incentive for the repeated use of new vocabulary. Individual classroom teachers apply the Word Wizard ideas in a variety of ways. In some classrooms, interesting words from class read-alouds, including Text Talk, are posted on a vocabulary word wall. A class poster contains the children's names along the side and the words along the top. When the children use the vocabulary in their conversations or written products, they receive a check on the poster. They may also receive a check for noticing the word in a new book, conversation, or elsewhere. The student with the most checks at the end of a designated time period becomes the Word Wizard.

In one second-grade class, Wednesday was word day, and each child brought in an unfamiliar or interesting word that he or she had heard or read during the preceding week. The Word-of-the-Week (WOW) sheet included the interesting word, where it had been heard or seen, the meaning, and the word in a sentence. The words were posted on a vocabulary word wall. Again, a poster was used to reflect the students' names and the weekly words. Checks were given, as in the original example. Each Wednesday both the children who had received the most checks and the children who had contributed the words with the most checks since the previous Wednesday ate lunch with the teacher in a special section of the cafeteria. Rewarding the contributors resulted in a wider range of student participants receiving the special lunch. It also resulted in the selection of sophisticated words that were likely to be used in conversation rather than obscure words that were difficult to apply in classroom conversations.

Teaching Children to Classify

As discussed at the beginning of the chapter, classification is a basic mental process, one that underlies vocabulary knowledge as well as other cognitive processes. Teaching children to classify can be done as early as preschool. An activity such as "Which one does not belong?" forces children to think about concepts in terms of their attributes. For example, you can give children as young as preschool age pictures of a bird, an airplane, a cat, and a kite and ask them which one does not belong. Then ask them why they chose what they chose. In this case, you want children to verbalize that a bird, an airplane, and a kite fly or are in the air, while cats do not fly.

A little more advanced activity is a type of sorting game. A teacher can take a flannel board divided into two sections, and a group of children sorts pictures into two groups. Sample categories might be farm animals versus zoo animals, things found in a kitchen versus things found in a living room, or the like. This can be an opportunity to introduce words that refine existing knowledge, such as *sofa*, *couch*, *stool*, or *spatula*. To take this one step further, children can sort by more than two categories.

Venn diagrams can be used to show children that some items can be part of more than one class. A Venn diagrams consists of two intersecting circles. For example, one circle might be labeled "Things with fur" and the other "Things that fly." On the "fur" side, a *cat*, *dog*, *lion*, *ocelot*, *leopard*, and so on might be included, taking care to include animals that might not be known to children (i.e., Tier 2 words). The other side might include a *bird*, *butterfly*, *bee*, *owl*, *hornet*, and so on. A *bat* might be in the middle because it fits in both categories.

Although we have used a fairly simple set of categories in this example, Venn diagrams can be used with many sets of concepts. We have used them with the terms *rebellion* and *protest* to discuss concepts surrounding the American Revolution. (In the years preceding the American Revolution, the colonists protested various taxes and laws. King George viewed these protests as rebellion, and acted to suppress them. This difference in perception may be one of the causes of the revolution.) We used the Venn diagram to compare and contrast the features of these words. Venn diagrams can be a fast and easy way to talk about many different concepts.

Semantic Maps

Another activity that extends the child's ability to classify are semantic maps. These have been used in vocabulary instruction for a long time (Heimlich & Pittelman, 1986; Johnson, Toms-Bronowski, & Pittelman, 1982; Stahl & Vancil, 1986), especially in content area instruction. However, they adapt very easily to young children, even prereaders. A semantic mapping lesson has four parts.

1. *Brainstorming.* The teacher and the class brainstorm ideas that relate to a topic. For example, for the topic *weather*, a class might come up with *rain*, *snow*, *wind*, *hot*, *thermometer*, *hurricane*, *blizzard*, and so on. The teacher might stop and explain some of the terms that the students come up with. The teacher might also add some other terms, again explain-

ing what they mean. These terms can be written on the board or pictured for young children.

2. *Mapping.* These terms can be drawn into a map. To draw the map, children (with the aid of the teacher) would come up with three or four categories that describe the terms on the board. These are arranged into a map. A possible map for *weather* is shown in Figure 5.1. A map made of pictures for prereaders on the topic *animals* is shown in Figure 5.2. The *animals* map might be used to introduce terms such as *insects* or *mammals* or particular types of each.

3. *Reading.* After the map is complete, the students and teacher read a book or selection about that topic. For younger children, the teacher can read the text aloud; for children who can read, they might read in partners or by themselves. An alternative might be an observation. For a lesson on weather, this might involve going outside to see the current weather. For a lesson on plants, this might involve growing a plant.

4. *Completing the map.* After the reading, teachers and children as a group discuss what they have learned from the book. At this time, they might change categories or add another category to reflect what they have learned

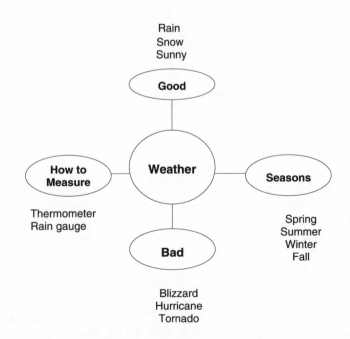

FIGURE 5.1. Semantic map for *weather.*

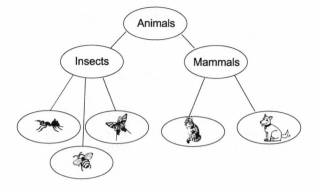

FIGURE 5.2. Semantic map made of pictures for prereaders.

It is important that semantic maps not be used as an end in themselves. Instead, they should be connected to a book, an observation, or an ongoing part of the curriculum.

TEACHING WORD MEANINGS IN PRESCHOOL AND EARLY ELEMENTARY CLASSROOMS

Although we have given some techniques that can be useful for teaching word meanings in early education, what is more important is maintaining a dialogue about words. This dialogue should be cognitively challenging, pushing students to expand their knowledge about the world by expanding the words they use to describe that knowledge. There should be an interplay between what the student knows and this ongoing dialogue. Words should not be too difficult—or they will be beyond the child's ability to learn—nor should they be too easy. Instead, they should be Goldilocks words—just right. Finding the right level is not hard. It comes from the kinds of interactions we have illustrated in this chapter.

Further, effective vocabulary teaching in the early years should make children curious about words. To be a good word learner, one must be hungry for words. Learning (and using) new words can be exciting because a new word not only is a sign of growing up, but it also is a sign of greater control and understanding about one's world. Effective instruction should make children seek out words, be sensitive about hearing and learning more about new words. It is not enough to fill children up with words as if they were an empty vessel. Instead, teachers and parents should create an environment where children go out and seek new words as well. Good vocabulary teaching in the primary grades is talking about words, when found in books, on trips, in the classroom, bringing them in and sending children out to find more.

REFERENCES

Adams, M. J. (1990). *Beginning to read: Thinking and learning about print.* Cambridge, MA: MIT Press.

Anderson, R. C., & Pearson, P. D. (1984). A schema-theoretic view of basic processes in reading. In P. D. Pearson (Ed.), *Handbook of reading research* (pp. 255–292). White Plains, NY: Longman.

Beck, I. L., & McKeown, M. G. (2001). Text talk: Capturing the benefits of read aloud experiences for young children. *The Reading Teacher, 55*, 10–35.

Beck, I. L., & McKeown, M. G. (2003). Text Talk: An approach to storybook reading in kindergarten. In A. v. Kleeck, S. A. Stahl, & E. B. Bauer (Eds.), *On reading books to children: Parents and teachers* (pp. 10–35). Mahwah, NJ: Erlbaum.

Beck, I. L., Perfetti, C. A., & McKeown, M. G. (1982). Effects of long-term vocabulary instruction on lexical access and reading comprehension. *Journal of Educational Psychology, 74*, 506–521.

Berlin, B., & Kay, P. (1969). *Basic color terms: Their universality and evolution.* Berkeley, CA: University of California Press.

Biemiller, A., & Slonim, N. (2001). Estimating root word vocabulary growth in normative and advantaged populations. *Journal of Educational Psychology, 93*, 498–510.

Bloom, L. (2000). The intentionality model of word learning: How to learn a word, any word, *Becoming a word learner: A debate on lexical acquisition* (pp. 19–50). Oxford, UK: Oxford University Press.

Clay, M. M. (1991). Introducing a new storybook to young readers. *The Reading Teacher, 45*, 264–273.

Clay, M. M. (1993). *Reading recovery: A guidebook for teachers in training.* Portsmouth, NH: Heinemann.

Cunningham, A. E., & Stanovich, K. E. (1991). Tracking the unique effects of print exposure in children: Associations with vocabulary, general knowledge, and spelling. *Journal of Educational Psychology, 83*, 264–274.

deTemple, J. (1994). *Book reading styles of low-income mothers with preschoolers and children's later literacy skills.* Unpublished doctoral dissertation, Harvard Graduate School of Education, Cambridge, MA.

deTemple, J., & Snow, C. (2003). Learning Words from Books. In A. v. Kleeck, S. A. Stahl, & E. B. Bauer (Eds.), *On reading storybooks to children: Parents and teachers* (pp. 16–36). Mahwah, NJ: Erlbaum.

Dickinson, D. K., & Tabors, P. O. (2001). *Beginning literacy with language: Young children learning at home and school.* Baltimore: Brookes.

Elley, W. B. (1989). Vocabulary acquisition from listening to stories. *Reading Research Quarterly, 24*, 174–187.

Fountas, I. C., & Pinnell, G. S. (1996). *Guided reading: Good first teaching for all children.* Portsmouth, NH: Heinemann.

Hart, B., & Risley, T. R. (1995). *Meaningful differences in the everyday experiences of young American children: The everyday experience of one and two year old American children.* Baltimore: Brookes.

Hart, B., & Risley, T. (1999). *The social world of the child learning to talk*. Baltimore: Brookes.

Hayes, D. P., & Ahrens, M. G. (1988). Vocabulary simplification for children: A special case of "motherese." *Journal of Child Language, 15*, 395–410.

Heimlich, J. E., & Pittelman, S. D. (1986). *Semantic mapping: Classroom applications*. Newark, DE: International Reading Association.

Huttenlocher, J., Haight, W., Bryk, A., Seltzer, M., & Lyons, T. (1991). Early vocabulary growth: Relation to language input and gender. *Developmental Psychology, 27*, 236–248.

Johnson, D. D., Toms-Bronowski, S., & Pittelman, S. D. (1982). *An investigation of the effectiveness of semantic mapping and semantic feature analysis with intermediate grade children* (Program Report 83–3). Madison, WI: Wisconsin Center for Educational Research, University of Wisconsin.

Juel, C. (2002, May). *Presentation at the Reading Hall of Fame meeting*. Annual convention of the International Reading Association, San Francisco, CA.

Kintsch, W., & van Dijk, T. A. (1978). Toward a model of text comprehension and production. *Psychological Review, 85*, 363–394.

Kuhn, M. R., & Stahl, S. A. (1998). Teaching children to learn word meanings from context: A synthesis and some questions. *Journal of Literacy Research, 30*, 119–138.

Nagy, W. E., Anderson, R. C., & Herman, P. A. (1987). Learning word meanings from context during normal reading. *American Educational Research Journal, 24*, 237–270.

Nagy, W. E., & Stahl, S. A. (in press). *Teaching word meanings*. Mahwah, NJ: Erlbaum.

Nelson, K. (1996). *Language in cognitive development: Emergence of the mediated mind*. Cambridge, UK: Cambridge University Press.

Neuman, S. B., & Celano, D. (2001). Access to print in low-income and middle-income communities: An ecological study of four neighborhoods. *Reading Research Quarterly, 36*, 8–27.

Nunberg, G. (2002, Sept. 3). A loss for words. *Fresh Air Commentary, National Public Radio*.

Olson, D. R. (1977). From utterance to text: The bias of language in speech and writing. *Harvard Educational Review, 47*, 257–281.

Piaget, J. (1990). *The child's conception of the world*. New York: Littlefield Adams.

Rey, H. (1947). *Curious George gets a job*. New York: Houghton Mifflin.

Schwanenflugel, P. J., Stahl, S. A., & McFalls, E. L. (1997). *Partial word knowledge and vocabulary growth during reading comprehension* (Research Report No. 76): University of Georgia, National Reading Research Center.

Smith, L. B. (2000). Learning how to learn words: An associative crane, *Becoming a word learner: A debate on lexical acquisition* (pp. 51–80). Oxford, UK: Oxford University Press.

Stahl, S. A. (1991). Beyond the instrumentalist hypothesis: Some relationships between word meanings and comprehension. In P. J. Schwanenflugel (Ed.), *The psychology of word meanings*. (pp. 157–186). Hillsdale, NJ: Erlbaum.

Stahl, S. A., & Fairbanks, M. M. (1986). The effects of vocabulary instruction: A model-based meta-analysis. *Review of Educational Research, 56*(1), 72–110.

Stahl, S. A., & Vancil, S. J. (1986). Discussion is what makes semantic maps work. *The Reading Teacher, 40*, 62–67.

Stanovich, K. E. (1986). Matthew Effects in reading: Some consequences of individual differences in the acquisition of literacy. *Reading Research Quarterly, 21,* 360–407.

Stanovich, K. E. (2000). *Progress in understanding reading: Scientific foundations and new frontiers.* New York: Guilford Press.

Teale, W. H. (1984). Reading to young children: Its significance for literacy development. In H. Goelman & A. Oberg & F. Smith (Eds.), *Awakening to literacy* (pp. 110–121). Portsmouth, NH: Heinemann.

Trabasso, T. (1981). On the making of inferences during reading and their assessment. In J. T. Guthrie (Ed.), *Comprehension and reading: Research reviews* (pp. 56–76). Newark, DE: International Reading Association.

White, T. G., Graves, M. F., & Slater, W. H. (1990). Growth of reading vocabulary in diverse elementary schools: Decoding and word meaning. *Journal of Educational Psychology, 82,* 281–290.

Woodward, A. L. (2000). Constraining the problem in early word learning, *Becoming a word learner: A debate on lexical acquisition* (pp. 81–114). Oxford, UK: Oxford University Press.

PART II

TEACHING VOCABULARY-
LEARNING STRATEGIES

6

Teaching Prefixes
As Good as It Gets?

MICHAEL F. GRAVES

This chapter begins by placing prefix instruction in the context of vocabulary instruction more generally, explaining the particular value of prefixes, and reviewing the research literature on teaching prefixes. Following this, the chapter presents a specific method of teaching prefixes. The method includes a 4-day unit that teaches basic information about prefixes, the six most common prefixes, and a strategy for using prefixes to unlock the meanings of unknown words. The method also includes reviewing, prompting, and guiding students to independent use of the strategy in the months following that initial instruction, along with teaching additional prefixes and reviewing what has been taught in two subsequent years. The chapter concludes by asking and answering the questions of whether the knowledge we now have about prefix instruction is as good as it needs to be and how it might be improved.

In the final scene of *As Good as It Gets*, Melvin Udall, the neurotic writer of romance novels played by Jack Nicholson, finds life considerably better than it has typically been for him. He is in love with a caring and considerate woman, he has actually tried to help another human being, and he is probably as happy as he can be. Yet, although this may be as good as it gets for Melvin, we know that he is still hopelessly anxious and uncertain and that as good as it gets is a long way from as good as it ought to be. I am borrowing the film's title as my subtitle because, after considering what we know about prefix instruction and describing a specific approach to prefix instruction, I want to ask whether the knowledge we now have about prefix instruction is as good as it gets, that is, if we know as much about this small part of vocabulary instruction as we can and should know.

First, however, comes the body of the chapter. I begin by considering three basic facts about vocabulary. Next, I consider the particular value of prefixes as word elements worth teaching and research on teaching prefixes. Following that, I describe a specific approach to teaching prefixes. Finally, I discuss the extent to which our knowledge about prefix instruction is as good as it is likely to get.

THREE CRUCIAL FACTS ABOUT VOCABULARY

Research and theory reveal three particularly crucial facts about vocabulary, facts that ought to be considered when we undertake any kind of vocabulary instruction. First, vocabulary knowledge is crucial to reading comprehension (National Reading Panel, 2000; RAND Reading Study Group, 2002; Snow, Burns, & Griffin,1998) and to success in school more generally (Beck, McKeown, & Kucan, 2002; Biemiller, 1999; Petty, Herold, & Stoll, 1967). In fact, both the National Reading Panel and the RAND Reading Study Group choose to consider vocabulary as a part of comprehension.

Second, the vocabulary-learning task students face is enormous! Estimates of vocabulary size vary greatly, but my estimate based on a substantial body of recent and rigorous work (Anderson & Nagy, 1992; Anglin, 1993; Nagy & Anderson, 1984; White, Graves, & Slater, 1990) is this: The books and other reading materials used by school children include well over 100,000 different words. The average child enters school with a very small reading vocabulary, typically consisting largely of environmental print. Once in school, however, a child's reading vocabulary is likely to soar at a rate of 3,000–4,000 words a year, leading to a reading vocabulary of something like 25,000 words by the time he or she is in eighth grade and perhaps well over 50,000 words by the end of high school.

Third, there is substantial and increasing evidence that many poor children enter school with vocabularies much smaller than those of their middle-class counterparts and that having a small vocabulary is a huge obstacle to success in reading (Becker, 1977; Biemiller, 2001; Hart & Risley, 1995, 1999; National Reading Panel, 2000; RAND Reading Study Group, 2002; White et al., 1990).

Given these facts, finding effective and efficient ways to bolster students' vocabularies is essential. As I have argued elsewhere (Graves, 2000, 2002; Graves & Watts, 2002) and as the contents of this volume suggest, a comprehensive and effective vocabulary program is likely to have a number of components, including at least (1) providing children with frequent, extensive, and varied language experiences; (2) teaching individual words; (3) teaching students strategies for learning words independently; and (4) fostering word consciousness. Thus, teaching prefixes is only one small part of a vocabulary program, but it is an important part and a part we ought to be able to get right.

THE PARTICULAR VALUE OF PREFIXES

Of the three sorts of word parts that might be taught—roots, prefixes, and suffixes—prefixes are particularly worth teaching for several reasons. First, there is a relatively small number of prefixes, and they are used in a large number of words. Some years ago, Stauffer (1942) found that nearly one-fourth of the 20,000 words in Thorndike's (1932) list of 20,000 words were prefixed words. Furthermore, the 15 most frequently occurring prefixes occurred in over 4,000 words. More recently, White, Power, and White (1989) demonstrated the frequency and utility of a small number of prefixes using a newer word list, Carroll, Davies, and Richmond's *Word Frequency Book* (1971). Specifically, White and his colleagues found that the 20 most frequent prefixes were used in a total of 2,959 words. Moreover, the most frequent three prefixes, *un-*, *re-*, and *in-* (meaning "not"), accounted for 51% of this total.

Two more facts that make prefixes particularly worth teaching are that they tend to be consistently spelled and they occur at the beginning of words. Thus, they are relatively easy for students to identify. Additionally, prefixes usually have a clear lexical meaning that is attached to the base word in a straightforward way. For example, *pre-* means "before," so a *preflight check* is a check that occurs before an aircraft flies.

Of course, as White, Sowell, and Yanagihara (1989) point out, although prefixes can be particularly valuable, they do present learners with some challenges. Most notably, a number of words begin with letters that can represent prefixes but do not do so in those particular words; *reading,* for example, is not a prefixed word. Somewhat similarly, in many cases, the removal of a prefix does not leave a recognizable English word. Peeling off the *pre-* in *predict,* for example, still leaves the student with the Latin root *dict,* which is likely to be unknown. In the prefix instruction that I suggest, I follow Marchand (1969) and Stotsky (1977) and define prefixes as elements that are attached to full English words. Thus, the *pre-* in *predict*, will not be considered a prefix. Also, some prefixes have more than one meaning; for example, *in-* has the meaning "not" (as in *inaccurate*) and the meaning "in" or "into" (as in *inborn*). Finally, while prefixes tend to be consistently spelled, several of them have variable spellings, *in-*, meaning "not," also takes the forms *im-*, *ir-*, and *il-*. Thus, as with so much of what we deal with in education, prefixes present pitfalls as well as possibilities. However, I agree with White and his colleagues and with most other educators that judicious instruction can help children avoid the pitfalls and achieve the possibilities.

RESEARCH ON TEACHING PREFIXES

Although certainly not a huge body of work, there are a number of studies that deal with teaching prefixes. Here, I briefly review them. In the earliest study I have located, Otterman (1955) investigated the effects of teaching prefixes and roots to approximately 500 seventh-grade students in the Boston area. In this quasi-experiment, 10 classes served as the experimental group and 10 served as the control group. Over a 6-week period, students in the experimental group received 10 minutes of instruction on a prefix or root each day for a total of 30 lessons. Students were posttested immediately after the treatment and again 6 weeks later on ability to interpret new words containing the studied elements, spelling, visual and auditory perception, general vocabulary, reading comprehension, reading rate, and (for the delayed posttest only) recall of the meanings of the prefixes and roots. Although no significance level is given, Otterman reported that the experimental group scored significantly higher than the control group in recall of prefix and root word meanings (which were tested only on the delayed test) and spelling, and higher IQ students in the experimental group scored higher than other students on the immediate test of interpreting new words containing studied elements. No other significant gains were reported.

In a study done soon after Otterman's, Thompson (1958) taught 20 prefixes and 14 roots to 162 college students enrolled in a 10-week course titled Efficient Reading. In this single-group study, students worked with the Master Word approach developed by Brown (1949) in a series of 14 lessons. Using the Master Word approach, students studied 14 basic words, chosen because they contained 20 prefixes and 14 roots Brown deemed worth teaching, for example, *mistranscribe* and *nonextended*. Students' activities with each word included discovering the relationship between the etymology of each word part and its current meaning and examining and drilling on the various forms of each word part. Students were pre- and posttested with a 40-item multiple-choice test of their ability to recognize the meanings of the prefixes and roots, identify various forms of the prefixes and roots within words, infer the meanings of unfamiliar words through analysis of their word parts, and combine prefixes and roots to form hypothetical words. Results showed significance on all four sections of the test, with gains of 34%, 22%, 22%, and 23%, respectively.

Two decades after Thompson's study, Ess (1978) taught nine prefixes to 180 seventh-grade students in three 20- to 25-minute lessons delivered over three consecutive days. In this true experiment, 20 high-ability, 20 average-ability, and 20 low-ability students randomly selected from nine classes were randomly assigned to one of three groups—prefix instruction, whole-word instruction, or no vocabulary instruction. Teachers for the prefix and whole-word groups were supplied with directions, transparencies, and student worksheets. Students in the prefix group were taught three prefixes and given examples of several words containing the prefixes using overhead transparencies. They then completed individual worksheets that required them to recognize the meanings of the prefixes and use them to form new words and that provided them with feedback. Students in the whole-word group received similar instruction and practice but focused on the meanings of the words rather than on the prefixes. Students in the no-vocabulary group received free reading for the same amount of time that the other groups studied prefixes or whole words. Students received a pretest, posttest, and delayed posttest (3 weeks after the posttest) on the nine prefixes taught, nine high-frequency words containing the prefixes but not taught, 30 low-frequency words used during the instruction, and 12 low-frequency words not taught. Results indicated that both the prefix group and the whole-word group received significantly higher total scores than the no-vocabulary group on both the posttest and the delayed posttest, that the scores of the prefix group were significantly higher than those of the whole-word group on the test of prefixes taught, and that the scores of the prefix group were significantly higher that those of the whole-word group on the transfer words for both the posttest and the delayed posttest.

Shortly after Ess's study and as a follow-up to it, Nicol (1980) taught eight prefixes to 144 fourth-, fifth-, and sixth-grade students in three 30-minute lessons delivered over three consecutive days. In this quasi-experiment, one class at each grade level received the prefix instruction, and one class at each grade level served as the control group. Instruction for the prefix group was modeled on that used in Ess's (1978) study but was revised to provide more active involvement of students and more direct feedback from the teacher. Students received a pretest, posttest, and delayed posttest (3 weeks after the posttest) on the eight prefixes taught, 32 prefixed words used in the instruction, and 16 low-frequency words not taught. Results indicated that the two groups did not differ on the pretest, that the scores of students who received the instruction were significantly higher than those who did not on all three sections of the posttest, and that the scores of students who received the prefix instruction were again significantly higher on the delayed posttest and remained as high as they were on the immediate posttest. Results further indicated that high-, middle-, and low-ability students all profited from the prefix instruction.

Nearly a decade after Nicol's study, White, Sowell, and Yanagihara (1989) gave a brief report of a study in which a third-grade teacher in a private school enrolling Hawaiian and part-Hawaiian children taught prefixes and suffixes. In this small quasi-experimental study the teacher taught nine prefixes and a procedure for suffix removal to her top three reading groups twice weekly for 7–8 weeks. The procedure for teaching prefixes used teacher-led active teaching in which the teacher defined the concept of a prefix, taught the meaning of the nine prefixes (including some alternate meanings), and actively worked with and responded to students as they identified prefixed words in sentences and then discussed the meaning of each prefix and root in brief teacher-student dialogues. Students were posttested on a root identification test, a multiple-choice test of prefix meanings, a multiple-choice test in which they identified the meanings of prefixed words when given the meanings of base words, and a test in which they were asked to define 10 prefixed words occurring in sentence contexts. Results showed that the students who received the lessons substantially outperformed students who did not on all four tests, although no statistical tests were reported.

Slightly more than a decade after White and his colleagues' study, Baumann et al. (2002) taught prefix analysis and contextual analysis to four classes of fifth-grade students. In this quasi-experiment, one class received instruction in prefix analysis, another instruction in contextual analysis, and another instruction in both of these types of analysis in 12 50-minute lessons. The remaining class served as an instructed control group. The prefix group received one lesson on each of seven prefix families, two lessons on the prefix family *not*, and three review lessons. The teaching was designed to follow the explicit instruction model described by Pearson and Gallagher (1983) and included gradual release of responsibility (Pearson & Fielding, 1991). Each lesson followed a three-part format consisting of an introduction and examples of the lesson content; verbal explanations, modeling, and guided practice with the prefix; and independent practice with the prefix. Posttests required students to define the prefixed words taught and other words containing the prefixes, recognize the meanings of the words taught and other prefixed words, and comprehend passages containing transfer words. Delayed posttests consisted of repetitions of the first two posttests. Results indicated a significant immediate and delayed effect of prefix instruction on words taught, and an immediate effect of prefix instruction on transfer words. There was no effect of the prefix instructing on comprehension, and students were just as effective at inferring word meanings when both prefix and context instruction were provided as when only one of them was provided.

A SPECIFIC METHOD OF TEACHING PREFIXES

Taken together, these studies clearly demonstrate that prefixes can be taught and that students can use their knowledge of prefixes to unlock the meanings of novel words—at least immediately or soon after instruction. Similarly positively, the instruction in the four most recent studies—those of Ess (1979), Nicol (1980), White, Sowell, and Yanagihara (1989), and Baumann and his colleagues (2002)—has a good deal in common and thus provides very useful information for creating effective prefix instruction. Less positively, none of these studies present enough information about the instruction to enable researchers to replicate them, none of them gives teachers enough information to employ the specific teaching procedures used in their classrooms, and none of them was able to demonstrate long-term transfer. The approach presented here, therefore, is an attempt to take what seem to be the best and most practical elements of the instruction in these four studies and modify them to create a method that is more powerful, more fully described, and more likely to produce long-term transfer.

Preliminary Considerations

Several issues need to be decided before the actual teaching plan can be described. The first is that of which prefixes to teach. Here, the work of White, Sowell, and Yanagihara (1989) provides a sturdy starting point. Table 6.1, based on a table provided by White and his colleagues, shows the 20 most common prefixes found in the *Word Frequency Book* (Carroll et al., 1971). These 20 prefixes are extremely generative and together serve as tools that could assist students in unlocking the meaning of nearly 3,000 words. Should all of these be taught? Based on the fact that the first 9 prefixes on this list make up 76% of the prefixed words in the *Word Frequency Book,* White and his colleagues argue that only these 9 need be systematically taught, while the others can be taught if a convenient time emerges. Certainly, teaching 9 prefixes that represent 76% of prefixed words is a worthwhile goal. However, while the remaining 11 prefixes on the list are not as highly generative as the first 9 of them, these 11 prefixes are used in some 600 additional words. For this reason, I would make them a part of the systematic instruction.

Another issue involves the order in which to teach the prefixes. White, Sowell, and Yanagihara (1989) suggest teaching them in order of their frequency, varying that order a bit if some other consideration—for example, their occurrence in material the class is reading—suggests doing so. This seems a solid plan.

A third issue involves when to teach them. Here, White, Power, and White (1989) present frequency data showing that prefixed words are rela-

TABLE 6.1. The Twenty Most Frequent Prefixes

Prefix	Words with the prefix
un-	782
re-	401
in-, *im-*, *ir-*, *il-* (not)	313
dis-	216
en-, *em-*	132
non-	126
in-, *im-* (in or into)	105
over- (too much)	98
mis-	83
sub-	80
pre-	79
inter-	77
fore-	76
de-	71
trans-	47
super-	43
semi-	39
anti-	33
mid-	33
under-	25
TOTAL	2,959

Note. Modified from White, Sowell, and Yanagihara (1989).

tively infrequent in grade 3 and below and increasingly frequent in grades 4, 5 and 6. Based on this, White, Sowell, and Yanagihara (1989) suggest beginning instruction in grade 4. This seems to be a reasonable starting point. Additionally, half a dozen or so prefixes is a convenient number to teach in a single unit, and if instruction in the 20 most frequent prefixes is spread over grades 4, 5, and 6, neither teachers nor students are burdened with too much prefix instruction at one time, and review is a natural part of the program.

A General Approach to Instruction

The general approach that has been used in most attempts at teaching prefixes is explicit instruction (Pearson & Gallagher, 1983), and this is the approach suggested here. The components of explicit instruction have recently been listed by Duke and Pearson (2002, pp. 208–210):

- An explicit description of the strategy and when and how it should be used.
- Teacher and/or student modeling of the strategy in action.

- Collaborative use of the strategy in action.
- Guided practice using the strategy with gradual release of responsibility.
- Independent use of the strategy.

Overhead transparencies have played a major part in several of the studies, and they are used in the instruction described here. They serve two particular functions: They focus students' attention, and they free teachers from the task of writing on the board and in doing so let them better attend to students and their presentation.

A good deal of comprehension strategy instruction has included what Rosenshine and Meister (1994) refer to as "concrete prompts," brief summaries of the actions students undertake in using the strategies. In the approach suggested here, students are given a set of concrete prompts, and these are prominently displayed on a poster that is frequently referred to during the instruction and that remains up after the instruction.

The instruction described here includes elements from all four of the most recent studies (Baumann et al., 2002; Ess, 1979; Nicol, 1980; White, Sowell, & Yanagihara, 1989) that, as I have noted, have a good deal in common. However, because I have the most information on Nicol's approach (a 150-page master's thesis), hers is the largest influence on the approach. The instruction also follows the three-part framework employed by Baumann and his colleagues: an introduction and examples of the lesson content; verbal explanations, modeling, and guided practice; and independent practice. Additionally, the approach includes one component that has not been a part of previous studies—deliberate and systematic review.

Day 1: Introduction, Clarification, Motivation, and Overview

On day 1, the teacher introduces the concept of prefixes and the strategy of using prefixes to unlock the meanings of unknown words, attempts to motivate students by stressing the value of prefixes, and gives students an overview of the unit. As Stotsky (1977) has shown, there has been a good deal of confusion about prefixes and prefix instruction, and thus it is particularly important to be sure that students understand just what prefixes and prefixed words are.

To alert students to what they will be studying and as a continuing reminder throughout the prefix unit, on the first day of instruction the teacher puts up a poster advertising the instruction, perhaps something like "Prefixes—One Key to Building Your Vocabularies."

Then the teacher might say something like this: "Over the next few days, we're going to be looking at how you can use prefixes to help you figure out the meanings of words you don't know. If you learn some common prefixes and how to use your knowledge of these prefixes to understand words that contain those prefixes, you're going to be able to figure out the meanings of a lot of new words. And, as you know, figuring out the meanings of words you don't know in a passage is an important step in understanding the passage."

Next, the teacher asks students what they already know about prefixes, reinforcing correct information students provide and gently suggesting that any incorrect information they give is not quite on target. The purpose here is to get students thinking about prefixes and to get them actively involved in the session. However, it is critical that student have a clear understanding of prefixes, and for this reason the teacher follows the discussion with a presentation supported by an overhead transparency. Below is the transparency, which the teacher reads aloud to students.

- A prefix is a group of letters that goes in front of a word. *Un-* is one prefix you have probably seen. It often means "not."
- Although you can list prefixes by themselves, as with *un-*, in stories or other things that we read, prefixes are attached to words. They don't appear by themselves. In *unhappy*, for example, the prefix *un-* is attached to the word *happy*.
- When a prefix is attached to a word, it changes the meaning of the word. For example, when the prefix *un-* is attached to the word *happy*, it makes the word *unhappy*, which means "not happy."
- It's important to remember that, for a group of letters to really be a prefix, when you remove them from the word, you still have a real word left. Removing the prefix *un-* from the word *unhappy* still leaves the word *happy*. That means it's a prefix. But if you remove the letters *un* from the word *uncle*, you are left with *cle*, which is not a word. This means that the *un-* in *uncle* is not a prefix.

This is a lot for students to remember—too much, in fact. For this reason, the teacher constructs a shortened version of these points on a "Basic Facts about Prefixes" poster, puts that up next to the poster advertising the unit, and tells students that the poster will stay up for them to refer to throughout the unit and even after that.

At this point, the teacher asks students if they know any additional prefixes, being generally accepting of their answers, but (assuming that some responses are incorrect) noting afterwards that some of the elements given are not actually prefixes and that the class will continue to work on what is and what is not a prefix as the unit progresses.

Finally, the teacher introduces the three prefixes for study the next day—*un-* (not), *re-* (again), and *in-* (not)—putting them on an overhead, asking students to copy them down, and asking students to each bring in a word beginning with one of the prefixes the next day.

Day 2: Instruction on the First Three Prefixes

At the beginning of the session, the teacher refers to the "Basic Facts" posters, briefly reminding students what prefixes are, where they appear, and why it is important to know about them. Then, the teacher calls on some students to give the prefixed words they have located, jotting those that are indeed prefixed words on the board, and gently noting that the others are not actually prefixed words and that they will discuss them later.

After this, the teacher begins the standard instructional routine for teaching prefixes and prefix removal. I am suggesting this standardized routine for three reasons First, there is experimental evidence that it works. It is basically the one validated in Nicol's (1980) study with some additions from Baumann and his colleagues (2002). Second, using the same routine for teaching all six prefixes means that students can soon learn the procedure itself and then concentrate on learning the prefixes and how to work with them. Third, the routine suggested can serve as a model teachers can use in creating a complete set of materials for teaching prefixes and the strategy of prefix removal and replacement.

Next, the teacher tells students that today they will be working with the three prefixes introduced the day before and how to use them in unlocking the meanings of unknown words. The three prefixes are *un-*, meaning "not"; *re-*, meaning "again"; and *in*, also meaning "not." In teaching these three prefixes, the teacher will use several types of materials—transparencies introducing each prefix, worksheets with brief exercises requiring use of the prefix just taught, transparencies of these worksheets, exercise sheets requiring additional use and manipulation of each prefix, and review sheets on which students manipulate the three prefixes and the words that were used in illustrating the prefixes for the day. On the back of the worksheets, exercise sheets, and review sheets are answer keys so that students can immediately check their efforts.

Each introductory transparency presents one prefix, illustrates its use with two familiar words and two unfamiliar words, and uses each of the four words in a context-rich sentence. Below each sentence, the word and its definition are shown. And below these sample sentences is a fifth sentence, which gives students a root word and requires them to generate the prefixed form of the word. The introductory transparency for the prefix *re-* is shown in Figure 6.1.

Instruction begins with the teacher displaying the first sentence on the introductory transparency and leading students from the meaning of the familiar prefixed word to the meaning of the prefix itself, as illustrated below:

TEACHER: If Tom were asked to rewrite a test, what must he do?
STUDENTS: He has to take it over. He has to take it again.

THE PREFIX *RE-*

1. Tom was asked to *rewrite* his spelling test because his writing was so messy that the teacher couldn't read it.

   rewrite—to write again

2. Carmen couldn't wait to *replay* the video because she found it really exciting.

   replay—to play again

3. After the heavy doors were battered by the enemy, the soldiers rushed to *refortify* their stronghold.

   refortify—to make strong again

4. When her letter was returned by the Post Office, JoAnne had to *readdress* it.

   readdress—to put a new address on a letter

5. If *commence* means "begin," then *recommence* means _____.

FIGURE 6.1. Introductory transparency for the prefix *re-*.

TEACHER: That's correct. Using your understanding of the word *rewrite*, what is the meaning of the prefix *re-?*

STUDENTS: Again. A second time. Over again.

The process is repeated with the next three sentences on the transparency. With some prefixes, students are likely to be able to volunteer the response without difficulty. With others, they may need further prompting, in which case the teacher rephrases the sentence to add more clues. If students are still unable to respond after the prompting, the teacher gives the definition. After going through the first four sentences on the *re-* introductory overhead, the teacher presents the fifth sentence, which defines the unknown root word and asks students to define the prefixed word.

After completing introductory instruction on the first prefix, students individually complete their check sheets, while a student volunteer completes the check sheet on a transparency. Part of a check sheet is shown in Figure 6.2. As soon as students complete their check sheets, the volunteer puts the transparency on the overhead so that all students receive immediate feedback on their work. If the volunteer has made an error, the teacher corrects it at this time.

These same procedures are then completed with the two remaining prefixes for the day—*un-* and *in-*. Following initial instruction on the three prefixes, the students complete a review sheet and immediately receive feedback by checking the answers on the back of the sheet. Part of a review sheet is shown in Figure 6.3. While students are completing the review sheet, the teacher monitors their work and provides assistance when requested. This concludes the second day of the unit.

CAN YOU FIND IT?

A word or word part is hidden in each line of letters below. Read the definition of the word or prefix. Then circle the word or prefix when you find it.

1. Find the prefix meaning "under" or "below."

    antidissubplegohnobitto

2. Find the word in each line that means:
    a. "underground railroad"

        shelaunomessubwaywathoning

    b. "to put under water"

        lasubmergersinthergerows

    c. "a plot beneath the main plot"

        thisenroutelesubplotrudiw

    d. "underwater boat"

        mopeitaqksubmarinetshowl

FIGURE 6.2. Part of a check sheet for the prefix *sub-*.

REVIEW SHEET ON *UN-*, *RE-*, AND *IN-*

A. Match the prefix in the first column to its meaning in the second column.
    a. *re-* _____ not
    b. *in-* _____ again
    c. *un-* _____ not

B. Complete the following sentences with a word from the list below. You will not use every word.

    rewrite   inaudible   incomplete
    reconnect   unhappy   ungrateful

1. Because Feng-Yi was in such a hurry to finish her test before the bell rang, her last answer was _____.
2. A nearly _____ cry escaped her as she hid behind the curtain.
3. Because no one could read Terry's report, he was required to _____ it.
4. It had been a long time since the two girls had seen each other, and they were really happy to _____.

FIGURE 6.3. Part of a review sheet for the prefixes *un-*, *re-*, and *in-*.

Day 3: Review, the Prefix Strategy, and the Remaining Three Prefixes

Day 3 begins with the teacher reviewing the basic facts about prefixes on the poster. Then students complete a review sheet on the three prefixes taught the previous day and immediately correct their work.

Next comes another crucial part of the instruction—instruction in the prefix strategy. The teacher introduces the strategy by telling students that now that they have worked some with the strategy and understand how useful prefixes can be in figuring out the meanings of unknown words, the teacher is going to teach a specific strategy for working with unknown words. The teacher titles the procedure "Prefix Removal and Replacement," emphasizing that they are using a big name for an important idea.

The teacher then puts up the following transparency, which is reproduced on a prominently displayed "Prefix Removal and Replacement Strategy" poster, and talks students through the procedure with one or two sample prefixed words.

THE PREFIX REMOVAL AND REPLACEMENT STRATEGY

When you come to an unknown word that may contain a prefix:

- Remove the "prefix."
- Check that you have a real word remaining. If you do, you've found a prefix.
- Think about the meaning of the prefix and the meaning of the root word.
- Combine the meanings of the prefix and the root word, and infer the meaning of the unknown word.
- Try out the meaning of the "unknown" word in the sentence, and see if it makes sense. If it does, read on. If it doesn't, you'll need to use another strategy for discovering the unknown word's meaning.

Following this explicit description of the strategy and modeling of its use, the teacher tells students that they will continue to work on learning the meanings of prefixes and learning to use the strategy today, tomorrow, and in future review sessions. The teacher then points out to students that they now have two posters to refer to when they come to an unknown word that may contain a prefix—the "Basic Facts" poster and the "Prefix Strategy" poster. Finally, the teacher teaches and reviews the remaining three prefixes (*dis-, en-,* and *non-*) using procedures and materials that exactly parallel those used on day 2. This concludes the third day of the unit.

Day 4: Review of the Information about Prefixes, the Prefix Strategy, and the Prefixes Taught

Day 4 begins with the teacher reviewing the four facts about prefixes, again using the "Basic Facts" poster in doing so. As part of the review, the teacher asks students a few questions about these facts to be sure they understand them and answers any questions students have.

Next, the teacher reviews the prefix removal and replacement strategy using the "Prefix Strategy" poster. After this, the teacher continues with the explicit instruction model, first modeling use of the strategy with two of the six prefixes taught and then collaboratively using the strategy in a whole-class session with two more of the six prefixes. After this, the teacher divides students into small groups and provides guided practice by having the groups use the strategy with the final pair of prefixes. The teacher also has some of the groups share their work and their findings, thus providing guided practice.

As the final activity of the initial instruction, small groups of students work together on a quiz. The quiz requires them to state the four facts about prefixes, state the steps of the prefix removal and replacement strategy, and give the meanings of the six prefixes taught. As soon as students complete the quiz, they correct the quiz in class so that they get immediate feedback on their performance and hand the corrected quizzes in so that the teacher has this information to plan reviews.

REVIEWING, PROMPTING, AND GUIDING STUDENTS TO INDEPENDENCE

At this point, the instruction is far from complete. If we really want students to remember what a prefix is, recognize and know the meanings of some prefixes, and use the prefix removal and replacement strategy when they come to unknown words in their reading, then reviewing what has been taught, prompting students to use the strategy in materials they are reading, and generally continuing to nudge then toward independence are crucial.

By reviewing, I mean formal reviews. It would seem reasonable to have the first review about a month after the initial instruction, a second review something like two months after that, and a third review, if it seems necessary, several months after that. Each review might last 30–45 minutes. Two somewhat conflicting considerations are important in undertaking these reviews. The first is that it does no good and in all probability does some harm to spend time "teaching" students things they already know. Thus, if at the beginning of a review it is apparent that students already know the material, the review should be very brief. The second consideration is that we need to do our best to ensure that all students understand prefixes and the prefix removal and replacement strategy. It is not enough that only average or better readers "get it."

By prompting, I simply mean reminding students about prefixes and the prefix strategy at appropriate points. Thus, when students are about to read a selection that contains some unknown prefixed words, the teacher might say something like "In looking through today's reading, I noticed some pretty hard words that begin with prefixes. Be on the lookout for these, and if you don't know them, try using the prefix strategy to figure out their meanings." This sort of prompting should probably be fairly frequent, for it can do a lot to move students toward independent use of the strategy.

Instruction in Additional Prefixes and Additional Review and Prompting

As I noted earlier, it seems reasonable to teach the 20 most frequent prefixes over a 3-year period. Thus, following the frequency list presented in Table 6.1, the prefixes in- ("in" or "into") through fore- might be taught in fifth grade, and the prefixes de- through under- might be taught in sixth grade. Such instruction would be similar to that used with the initial six prefixes—with one very important exception. Students will have already been taught the basic facts about prefixes and the prefix removal and replacement strategy; work on those matters is review and can be briefer than the initial instruction.

Finally, reviewing and prompting is still important during fifth and sixth grades. Again, two reviews—cumulative reviews of all the prefixes taught as well as the basic facts about prefixes and the prefix strategy— seem likely to be sufficient. And, again, it is important to keep in mind that the goal is to ensure that all students know the prefixes and can use the strategy without boring students by teaching them what they already know.

AS GOOD AS IT GETS?

At this point I will return to my opening question, asking whether the knowledge we now have about teaching prefixes is as good as it gets—or perhaps I should say as good as it could get and needs to be. The answer is a decided "no." To be sure, we know a lot. We have a clear concept of what prefixes are. We know which prefixes to teach. We have half a dozen studies that show that prefixes can be taught and that students can learn a strategy that will enable them to use their knowledge of prefixes to unlock the meanings of unknown prefixed words—at least in the short run. And we have half a dozen partial models of effective prefix instruction.

So, what *don't* we have? What isn't as good as it could get and needs to be? The answer is "a lot." To begin with, we have only partial models of instruction. Because of the limits of journal space, we have no complete models of instruction—nothing like complete sets of materials and procedures that researchers wishing to replicate an approach or teachers wishing to use an approach in their classes can readily obtain. Thanks to recent technological advances, this problem is now rather easily and inexpensively solvable. Complete sets of instructional procedures and materials can be put on the Internet for teachers or researchers to use.

The other hugely important thing we lack is evidence of meaningful long-term transfer—evidence that students can use their knowledge of prefixes and a prefix strategy to unlock the meanings of unknown words 6 months, a year, or more than a year after instruction. In fact, we have little evidence even for immediate transfer. This problem, I suspect, is related to the fact that we have no long-term studies that employ systematic review. Only with such review is it likely that students will internalize their knowledge of prefixes and a strategy for using prefixes in unlocking the meanings of unknown words and use this knowledge in their day-to-day reading. This problem is not easy to solve. It requires long-term studies, which are difficult to do, expensive, and may not yield the sorts of rewards that make them attractive to researchers. Moreover, once long-term initial studies are done, they need to replicated, another expensive process and one that yields even fewer professional rewards for researchers. Beyond replication, studies that hone and fine-tune already validated procedures are needed. It will absolutely not do, in my judgment, to have independent groups of researchers reinvestigate a topic every 10 years or so basing their new studies on the very incomplete knowledge about the instruction used in previous studies that is presently available.

Several years ago, the National Research Council (1999) outlined a plan for systematic long-term research on improving student learning, proposing that a period of 15 years of systematic instructional research is the minimal commitment likely to prove successful. That report received little discussion from reading researchers, and such a lack of response was predictable because the National Research Council is not, in the minds of most reading researchers, the appropriate group to determine educational research policy. However, unless we devise long-term and carefully coordinated plans of research that make the specifics of the instruction employed public, systematically build on existing knowledge, and carefully hone that knowledge over time, what we presently know about prefix instruction, as well as what we know about other aspects of literacy instruction, is likely to remain as good as it gets.

REFERENCES

Anderson, R. C., & Nagy, W. E. (1992). The vocabulary conundrum. *American Educator*, Winter, 14–18, 44–47.

Anglin, J. M. (1993). Vocabulary development: A morphological analysis. *Monographs of the Society for Research in Child Development, 58*(10, Serial No. 238).

Baumann, J. F., Edwards, E. C., Font, G., Tereshinski, C. A., Kame'enui, E. J., & Olejnik, S. (2002). Teaching morphemic and contextual analysis to fifth-grade students. *Reading Research Quarterly, 37,* 150–176.

Beck, I. L., McKeown, M. G., & Kucan, L. (2002). *Bringing words to life: Robust vocabulary instruction.* New York: Guilford Press.

Becker, W. C. (1977). Teaching reading and language to the disadvantaged: What we have learned from field research. *Harvard Educational Review, 47,* 518–543.

Biemiller, A. (1999). *Language and reading success.* Cambridge, MA: Brookline Books.

Biemiller, A. (2001). Teaching vocabulary: Early, direct, and sequential. *American Educator, 25*(1), 24–28, 47.

Brown, J. I. (1949). Reading and vocabulary. *Word Study, 24,* 1–4.

Carroll, J. B., Davies, P., & Richmond, B. (1971). *The American Heritage Word Frequency Book.* Boston: Houghton Mifflin.

Duke, N. K., & Pearson, P. D. (2002). Effective practices for developing reading comprehension. In S. J. Samuels & A. E. Farstrup (Eds.), *What research has to say about reading instruction* (3rd ed., pp. 203–242). Newark, DE: International Reading Association.

Ess, H. K. (1978). *The transfer value of teaching prefixes to increase vocabulary.* Unpublished master's thesis, University of Minnesota, Minneapolis.

Graves, M. F. (2000). A vocabulary program to complement and bolster a middle-grade comprehension program. In B. M. Taylor, M. F. Graves, & P. van den Broek (Eds.), *Reading for meaning: Fostering comprehension in the middle grades* (pp. 116–135). New York: Teachers College Press.

Graves, M. F. (2002). *Vocabulary instruction.* Minneapolis: University of Minnesota. Paper prepared for the Minnesota Reading Excellence Act project.

Graves, M. F., & Watts, S. M. (2002). The place of word consciousness in a research-based vocabulary program. In S. J. Samuels & A. E. Farstrup (Eds.), *What research has to say about reading instruction* (3rd ed., pp. 140–165). Newark, DE: International Reading Association.

Hart, B., & Risley, T. R. (1995). *Meaningful differences in the everyday experiences of young American children.* Baltimore: Brookes.

Hart, B., & Risley, T. R. (1999). *The social world of children learning to talk.* Baltimore: Brookes.

Marchand, H. (1969). *The categories and types of present-day English word formation.* Munich, Germany: Beck.

Nagy, W. E., & Anderson, R. C. (1984). How many words are there in printed school English? *Reading Research Quarterly, 19,* 304–330.

National Reading Panel. (2000). *Report of the National Reading Panel: Teaching children to read.* Bethesda, MD: National Institute of Child Health and Human Development.

National Research Council. (1999). *Improving student learning.* Washington, DC: National Academy Press.

Nicol, J. A., Graves, M. F., & Slater, W. H. (1984). *Building vocabulary through prefix instruction.* Unpublished paper, University of Minnesota, Minneapolis.

Otterman, L. M. (1955). The value of teaching prefixes and root words. *Journal of Educational Research, 48,* 611–616.

Pearson, P. D., & Fielding, L. (1991). Comprehension instruction. In R. Barr, M. L. Kamil, P. Mosenthal, & P. D. Pearson (Eds.), *Handbook of reading research* (Vol. II, pp. 815–860). New York: Longman.

Pearson, P. D., & Gallagher, M. C. (1983). The instruction of reading comprehension. *Contemporary Educational Psychology, 8,* 317–344.

Petty, W., Herold, C., & Stoll, E. (1967). *Knowledge about the Teaching of Vocabulary.* Urbana, IL: National Council of Teachers of English.

RAND Reading Study Group. (2002). *Reading for understanding: Toward an R&D program in reading comprehension.* Santa Monica, CA: Rand Education.

Rosenshine, B., & Meister, C. (1994). Reciprocal teaching: A review of the research. *Review of Educational Research, 64,* 479–531.

Snow, C. E., Burns, M. S., & Griffin, P. (Eds.). (1998). *Preventing reading difficulties in young children.* Washington, DC: National Academy Press.

Stauffer, R. G. (1942). A study of prefixes in the Thorndike list to establish a list of prefixes that should be taught in the elementary school. *Journal of Educational Research, 35,* 453–458.

Stotsky, S. L. (1977). Teaching prefixes: Facts and fallacies. *Language Arts, 54,* 887–890.

Thompson, E. (1958). The "Master Word" approach to vocabulary training. *Journal of Developmental Reading, 2,* 62–66.

Thorndike, E. L. (1932). *The teacher's word book of 20,000 words.* New York: Teachers College Press.

White, T. G., Graves, M. F., & Slater, W. H. (1990). Growth of reading vocabulary in diverse elementary schools: Decoding and word meaning. *Journal of Educational Psychology, 82,* 281–290.

White, T. G., Power, M. A., & White, S. (1989). Morphological analysis: Implication for teaching and understanding vocabulary growth. *Reading Research Quarterly, 24,* 283–304.

White, T. G., Sowell, J., & Yanagihara, A. (1989). Teaching elementary students to use word-part clues. *The Reading Teacher, 42,* 302–308.

7

The Developing Vision
of Vocabulary Instruction

ROBERT J. MARZANO

A new vision of K–12 vocabulary instruction emerges if one examines the nature of words and the nature of word knowledge from the perspective of four topics: (1) reference, (2) modes of representation, (3) levels of knowledge, and (4) indirect versus direct instructional approaches. That vision includes the use of wide reading with an emphasis on students learning self-selected words from context; direct instruction in subject-specific vocabulary, including general terms as well as terms signifying specific persons, places, things, and events; and multiple exposure to words with structured activities to facilitate elaboration of linguistic and imagery-based representations.

Vocabulary instruction is usually discussed within the context of its strong relationship with reading comprehension (e.g., Anderson & Freebody, 1981; Beck, McKeown, & Omanson, 1987; Graves, 1989; Kame'enui, Dixon, & Carnine, 1987; Mezynski, 1983; Nagy & Herman, 1987). Additionally, the correlation between vocabulary and general reading ability appears to be sizeable throughout the K–12 spectrum (Anderson & Freebody, 1981; Mezynski, 1983; Stanovich, Cunningham, & Feeman, 1984). While it is certainly true that correlational evidence is much more plentiful than experimental evidence, there is a growing body of evidence that vocabulary knowledge is a causal determinant of differences in reading ability in general and comprehension specifically (Stahl & Fairbanks, 1986; Stanovich, 1986).

Given the perceived importance of vocabulary, it is interesting how little attention has been paid to something as basic as articulating the defining characteristics of a vocabulary term. More specifically, there appears to be no standard definition as to what constitutes a vocabulary item. Most discussions of vocabulary explicitly or implicitly communicate the message that vocabulary terms and words have a tautological relationship. A vocabulary term is synonymous with a word. Yet, this relationship offers little help, since words are not well defined either within the vocabulary literature. In fact, it seems to be the case that the answer to the question, What is a word?, depends on the perspective from which it is asked. As Baumann, Kame'enui, and Ash (2003) note: "So what is a word? Well, it depends. It depends on your purpose for asking the question and your view of thought and language" (p. 754). Similarly, Ruddell (1994) explains: "What does it mean to know a word? When is a word known? How and in what way are polysemous words known? How many words does one need to learn? The short answer to all these questions is 'We're not sure' " (pp. 418–419).

The lack of precision or agreement about the nature of vocabulary terms plays havoc with research and theory in vocabulary. For example, the problems for vocabulary research and theory created by the slippery nature of words are evidenced in the research on the size of vocabulary for students at different age or grade levels. In his review of the research on vocabulary size, Graves (1986) noted that estimating the vocabulary size of students at various age or grade levels is not a new endeavor. He explains that 35 studies were published between 1891 and 1960. Estimates of vocabulary size for first graders ranged from 2,562 to 26,000 words and for university graduate students from 19,000 to 200,000 words.

Clearly, the lack of precision about the nature of vocabulary does not serve the art and science of vocabulary instruction. I believe that a careful examination of the nature of words and, by direct extension, vocabulary terms and how they are learned provides an insight into what I refer to as the *developing vision of vocabulary instruction*. As the name implies, it is developing because all aspects of that vision are not yet clear. However, it is a vision that, when fully disclosed, will display some significant differences from and advantages over what is current K–12 practice. This developing vision is illuminated by a consideration of four topics: (1) reference, (2) modes of representation, (3) levels of word knowledge, and (4) indirect versus direct instructional approaches. Briefly, the topic of reference expands our understanding of the types of terms that should be the target of vocabulary instruction. The topic of modes of representation highlights the importance of mental imagery as a factor important to vocabulary instruction. The topic of levels of knowledge addresses the need to target general levels of understanding, as opposed to deeper definitional levels of understanding, in the initial stages of vocabulary instruction. Finally, the topic of indirect versus direct instruction attests to the importance of an integrated approach that combines the advantages of wide reading and direct instruction.

REFERENCE

Within the context of reading, *reference* refers to the act of generating a mental representation of the intended information conveyed by the words in a text. The concepts of reference and word knowledge are, for all practical purposes, synonymous within the confines of a discussion of vocabulary. This is explicit in Drum and Koponak's (1987) description of a word: "A word, an acoustic configuration of speech sounds and a written rendition (more or less) of these sounds, comes or is assigned to refer to things, events, and ideas arbitrarily. There is no inherent connection between a word and its referent; a 'tree' could be called a 'drink' and vice versa" (p. 73).

The importance of reference in terms of word knowledge is also seen in descriptions of the reading process. As Just and Carpenter (1987) explain: "As a reader progresses through a text, he constructs a representation of the objects and situations the text refers to" (p. 195). The model constructed by the reader is sometimes referred to as the "referential representation." It is also referred to as the "situational model" (van Dijk & Kintsch, 1983). The same basic dynamic applies when an individual hears or reads a word in isolation, although in these instances the reader or listener does not have the benefit of cumulative contextual information.

The treatment of reference within vocabulary research is perhaps most evident in the aforementioned studies on vocabulary size. Perhaps the most well accepted study to this end is that conducted by Nagy and Anderson (1984). To compute their estimate of vocabulary found in "printed school English," those vocabulary items students encounter in the material commonly read in school, they excluded from their count derivative forms such as regular and irregular plurals, regular and irregular inflected forms, and regular and irregular comparisons and superlatives. This makes intuitive sense from the perspective of reference. The differences in meaning signaled by these forms do not greatly alter the semantic referent for the terms. Specifically, it seems reasonable that the referents to the words *run*, *running*, and *ran* are for all practical purposes identical in the context of vocabulary knowledge. We might conclude, then, that vocabulary researchers and theorists have excluded as vocabulary terms lexical items that have the same semantic referent but vary in their form due to differences in inflection, syntax, comparative forms, superlative forms, and so on.

However, Nagy and Anderson (1984) also excluded proper names in their count of words. Thus, using the Nagy and Anderson criteria, *runner* would be considered a vocabulary term, but *Carl Lewis* would not. This, too, is a common convention in vocabulary research, and it seems to be consistent with Vygotsky's (1962) notion that a word is a label for a class of referents as opposed to a single referent: "A word does not refer to a single object, but to a group or to a class of objects. Each word is therefore already a generalization" (p. 6). Where the word *runner* has a variety of referents, the term *Carl Lewis* has only one. Just and Carpenter (1987) explain that a term that refers to a particular object is called a *singular term* while a term that refers to a class is called a *general term* (p. 199). General terms have an isomorphic relationship with concepts in that *concepts* are generally considered to be classes of objects (Turner & Greene, 1977). Using this terminology, we might conclude that vocabulary researchers and theorists have traditionally limited the universe of vocabulary items to general as opposed to singular terms because the former are more conceptual in nature.

While the exclusion of terms with singular referents might be defensible from the perspective that they do not qualify as concepts, it is not defensible to exclude them from the perspective of the process of identifying the referent of words while reading. In fact, there is a good deal of evidence indicating that individuals naturally tend to particularize referents even for general terms (e.g., Anderson & McGaw, 1973; Rosch, 1975; Smith & Medin, 1981). That is, within the cognitive act of identifying the referent of a word, all terms seem to be treated as singular terms. To illustrate, when individuals hear the word *bird*, for example, they tend to think in terms of a specific type of bird (e.g., a robin) or a stylized prototype of a bird as opposed to the general characteristics that one would associate with the concept *bird*. Unless the surrounding context specifically directs readers, they will think of a specific type of bird or stylized prototype when reading a sentence such as *The bird landed on the ground*. In short, even with generalized terms, individuals employ fairly specific referents. Just and Carpenter (1987) note: "The referential representation probably contains information about the perceptible properties of the particularized instantiation. For example, the referential representation of *dog* may include a representation of a particular dog, including its perceptible properties" (p. 201).

From the perspective of reference, then, there is good reason to include specific terms along with general terms in a list of important vocabulary items. This would be a departure from current practice and tradition, both of which would dictate that a general term like *state* would be included in a vocabulary list, but a specific term like *Colorado* would not.

The perspective of reference also expands the notion of vocabulary terms beyond a single word. That is, the process by which the referents of some word combinations are accessed appears to be the same as the process by which the referents of single words are accessed (Just & Carpenter, 1987; Potter & Faulconer, 1979). This is the case with word combinations that are so commonly used together that they function as a single lexical item. Some word combinations become compounds with repeated use (*heartbeat, landslide*). Others do not. However, even when word combinations are not expressed as compounds, many function as single units in terms of reference (*drummer boy, food poisoning, killer shark*). Linguists have identified a variety of types of these word combinations that include subject and verb combinations (e.g., *bee sting*), verb and object combinations (*book review*), verb and noun combinations (*diving board*), verb and adverb combinations (*custom built*), and so on (see Quirk, Greenbaum, Leech, & Svartvik, 1972).

In summary, the perspective of reference dramatically expands the universe of vocabulary terms since it blurs the distinctions between single-word general terms like *whale,* multi-word general terms like *killer whale,* and singular terms like *Shamu.* Consequently, from the perspective of reference the terms *whale, killer whale,* and *Shamu* would all qualify as vocabulary items.

Implications for Vocabulary Instruction

An implication of the preceding discussion is that the target lexicon for vocabulary instruction should be greatly expanded to include terms that are both general *and* singular. Such a list would, by definition, include proper nouns and phrases. This is consistent with E. D. Hirsch's (1987) notion of a "national vocabulary" (p. 139) where he identified 4,552 items about which students should have at least a passing knowledge. His list included both general terms (e.g., *vice-president*) and specific terms (e.g., *Spiro Agnew*). While I do not agree with Hirsch's list (see Marzano, Kendall and Gaddy, 1999, for a discussion), I agree with the basic sentiment that words and word combinations with singular as well as general references should be included in vocabulary lists.

MODES OF REPRESENTATION

It is safe to say that vocabulary researchers and theorists have traditionally addressed the nature of vocabulary from a predominately linguistic perspective. That is, the assumption has been that word knowledge involves meaning expressed in language form. At first glance it might appear that such a perspective is the only viable one possible. Indeed, word knowledge is frequently defined in terms of "critical attributes" (see Smith & Medin, 1981) or "semantic features" (see Katz & Fodor, 1963), both of which are linguistically based. The tacit principle, then, that appears to be underlying some aspects of vocabulary research and theory is that the linguistic modality is the primary mode of representation, if not the sole method of representation.

It is certainly the case that information in permanent memory is represented linguistically. Typically, these representations are assumed to have a propositional structure (see Kintsch, 1974, 1979; Kintsch & van Dijk, 1978; van Dijk, 1980) or a production structure (Anderson, 1983), which conform roughly to declarative and procedural knowledge (Paris, Lipson, & Wixson, 1983). While these linguistic structures are certainly a critical aspect of vocabulary knowledge, so too is another form of representation, a nonlinguistic form that is referred to as dual coding theory (Paivio, 1971, 1991; Sadoski, 1983, 1985; Sadoski & Paivio, 1994). Sadoski & Paivio (1994) have argued for the explanatory power of the dual coding theory (DCT) of storage:

> A basic premise of DCT is that all mental representations retain some of the concrete, original qualities of the external experiences from which they derive. These experiences can be linguistic or nonlinguistic. Their differing characteristics develop two separate mental systems, one specialized for representing and processing language (the verbal system) and one for processing information about nonlinguistic objects and events (the nonverbal system). The latter is frequently referred to as the imagery system because its functions include the generation and analysis of mental images in various modalities derived from the senses (visual, auditory, etc.). The verbal and nonverbal systems are separate but connected and can function independently or through a network of interconnections. (p. 584)

DCT purports that the verbal system, as described above, is made up of *logogens* (i.e., propositions and productions in another vernacular) and *imagens* (i.e., mental images). Logogens and imagens are theoretical constructs, yet are assumed to have corresponding neurological structures. The modality and size of logogens and imagens can vary. Discrete units within each system are combined and recombined into larger units. To illustrate, within the imagery system, the mental image of a *swimming pool* can represent an imagen, yet this might be made up of more atomistic elements (e.g., a specific part of the pool or its surrounding area). Of importance to the discussion here is that imagens are central to word knowledge; that is, when individuals access their word knowledge, they activate both logogens and imagens for that word.

In summary, the perspective of modes of representation expands our understanding of word knowledge to include an imagery system as well as a linguistic system.

Implications for Vocabulary Instruction

One major implication of DCT to vocabulary instruction is that having a linguistic description or definition for a word is not necessarily the end goal. Rather, one can make a case that a robust understanding of a vocabulary term would include both a definition or description of the major features of the word's referent (i.e., related logogens) and images of these features (i.e., imagens). This implication has some support in experimental research. For example, in a meta-analysis, Powell (1980) reported that imagery-based techniques for vocabulary instruction had an average effect size of 1.15 when compared with techniques in which students repeated or rehearsed a definition. Additionally, imagery-based instructional techniques had an effect size of .56 when compared with techniques in which students generated their own examples or definitions. DCT would explain the effectiveness of imagery-based instructional strategies as a natural consequence of the manner in which vocabulary knowledge is stored in permanent memory.

LEVELS OF WORD KNOWLEDGE

The third topic that informs the developing vision of vocabulary instruction is that of levels of word knowledge. The notion that words can be known at different levels is somewhat obvious and well accepted (Graves, 1984; McKeown & Beck, 1988). However, the different levels at which a word can be known are not so obvious, and there is no universally accepted model. As early as 1965, Dale proposed four stages of knowing a word: (1) never saw it before, (2) has heard it but doesn't know what it means, (3) recognizes it in context and knows generally what it has to do with, and (4) knows it well.

Stahl (1985, 1986) proposed three levels of word knowledge: association, comprehension, and generation. Knowledge of a word at the *association level* means that when presented with a word students can make accurate associations even though they might not understand the meaning of the word. Knowledge of a word at the *comprehension level* means that students understand the commonly accepted meaning of the word. Knowledge of a word at the *generation level* means that students can provide the target word in a novel context. Kame'enui, Dixon, and Carnine (1987) identify three levels of word knowledge: full conceptual knowledge, partial conceptual knowledge, and verbal association knowledge. *Full conceptual knowledge* is "the ability to recognize uninstructed examples of concepts as examples, and to discriminate them from similar examples drawn from other concepts" (p. 133). *Partial conceptual knowledge* allows for some minor misconceptions or some missing characteristics. *Verbal association knowledge* is the simple pairing of labels with meanings.

Probably one of the most interesting aspects of the phenomenon of differential levels of word knowledge is that words do not have to be known at a deep level to be useful to an individual. In fact, when we encounter a word, we initially access the surface-level characteristics first. This was demonstrated in an early experiment by Collins and Quillian (1969) who posited that an individual's knowledge of a word is organized in a hierarchic fashion. The top-level knowledge for the word *canary* might include the facts that it is yellow and frequently sings. At the next level down might be more general characteristics associated with all birds, such as: it has wings, it can fly, and it has feathers. At an even more general level would be characteristics associated with all animals, such as: it has skin, it eats, and it breathes.

If it is true that information closest to the top of the hierarchy is the most available, then people should remember the top-level information more quickly than the bottom-level information. Collins and Quillian (1969) tested this hypothesis by providing subjects with sentences like the following: *Canaries are yellow. Canaries can fly. Canaries breathe.* Subjects were asked to determine whether the information in the sentence was true or false. Time taken to validate the accuracy of a sentence was considered an indication of the information's place within the hierarchy. The study's finding supported the hierarchic hypothesis. Similar findings have been reported by Just and Carpenter (1987).

In summary, the perspective of levels of word knowledge indicates that there are many layers of meaning involved in understanding a vocabulary term, and the top layers are made up of very general characteristics that might be thought of as common knowledge regarding a term. Yet, even this relatively superficial level of understanding renders a term useful.

Implications for Vocabulary Instruction

One implication of the research on levels of word knowledge is that a definition might not be the best initial goal when new words are being learned. Given the evidence that initial word learning addresses top-level schema, it would appear that presenting students with complete and complex definitions to words that are, in fact, new to them probably does not facilitate learning. Rather, the initial target of student learning should be to obtain a sense of these top-level features.

Another implication is that complete word knowledge might not be necessary for all words that students learn. Stated differently, complete knowledge of vocabulary terms might not be the end game for all vocabulary terms. For some terms, the target of instruction might be that students have an accurate, albeit incomplete, understanding that would form the foundation on which students might build a deeper understanding through repeated interactions with the words. Citing a personal communication with Isabel Beck as the genesis of their comments, Nagy and Herman (1987) make the following case for instruction that is aimed at surface-level knowledge:

> . . . although a strong case can be made for rich, knowledge-based vocabulary instruction, one should not underestimate the possible benefits of less intensive instruction. . . . One should not underestimate the value of any meaningful encounter with a word, even if the information gained from that one encounter is relatively small. (pp. 31–32)

INDIRECT AND DIRECT APPROACHES TO VOCABULARY DEVELOPMENT

The fourth topic that informs the developing vision of vocabulary instruction is a contrast of two seemingly disparate approaches to vocabulary development. Specifically, if one were to read the extant research and theory over the last two decades, it would be fairly easy to build a case that there are two distinct philosophies regarding the best approach to vocabulary development. One philosophy might be referred to as *wide reading*, and the other might be referred to as *direct instruction*.

Wide Reading

Having students read widely as a way of enhancing their vocabulary knowledge makes good intuitive sense; the more students read, the more vocabulary terms they acquire from context. In fact, some theorists assert that wide reading is the primary way of enhancing vocabulary (Sternberg, 1987). This position is difficult to dispute. Stanovich (1986) has discussed in detail how vocabulary knowledge is both a cause and consequence of effective and voluminous reading. The more children read, the more words they learn; this, in turn, makes reading easier and consequently increases the chances that they will read more. In his studies of first graders, Allington (1984) found that the total number of words read during a week of school reading sessions ranged from a low 16 for one child who was classified as a poor reader to a high of 1,933 for a child classified as a good reader. Commenting on these findings, Stanovich (1986) noted: "The average skilled reader reads approximately three times as many words in the group reading sessions as the average less skilled reader" (p. 380). Similarly, Nagy and Anderson (1984) estimated that

> the less able and motivated children in the middle grades might read 100,000 words a year while the average children at this level might read 1,000,000. The figure for the voracious middle grade reader might be 10,000,000 or even as high as 50,000,000. If these guesses are anywhere near the mark, there are staggering individual differences in the volume of language experience, and, therefore, opportunity to learn new words. (p. 328)

If the figures supporting wide reading were not impressive enough, those supporting the futility of trying to teach all words are. To illustrate, Nagy and Anderson (1984) estimated that the number of words in "printed school English" (i.e., those words students in grades 3–9 will encounter in print) is about 88,500. Obviously, it would be impossible to teach this many words one at a time. Stahl and Fairbanks (1986) summarized this position in the following way: "Since a vocabulary teaching program typically teaches 10 to 12 words a week or about 400 a year, of which perhaps 75% or 300 are learned, vocabulary instruction is not adequate to cope with the volume of new words that children need to learn and do learn without instruction" (p. 100).

Given the futility of teaching individual words, Nagy and Herman (1987) proved the following logic for wide reading as the sole vehicle for developing vocabulary:

> If students were to spend 25 minutes a day reading at a rate of 200 words per minute for 200 days out of the year, they would encounter a million words of text annually. According to our estimates, with this amount of reading, children will encounter between 15,000 and 30,000 unfamiliar words. If 1 in 20 of these words is learned, the yearly gain in vocabulary will be between 750 and 1,500 words. (p. 26)

Programs that facilitate wide reading for students have been in place for decades (Hunt, 1970). Many of those programs utilize the name of Sustained Silent Reading (SSR) or a variant of it such as Free Voluntary Reading (FVR), Uninterrupted Sustained Silent Reading (USSR), and Positive Outcomes While Enjoying Reading (POWER). In its simplest form, an SSR program is one in which students—and quite often teachers—read silently for about 10–20 minutes from books of their choice.

Direct Vocabulary Instruction

The arguments put forth regarding the utility of wide reading are based, in part, on the assumption that students will learn some percentage, albeit small, of the words they encounter in their reading. As intuitively appealing as this argument seems, research has not supported it totally. In fact, Beck and McKeown (1991) argue that there is little evidence to support the advisability of relying on context as the vehicle for vocabulary development: "Research spanning several decades has failed to uncover evidence that word meanings are routinely acquired from context" (p. 799). At best, it is an unreliable vehicle for vocabulary development greatly influenced by external factors. To illustrate, Swanborn and de Glopper (1999) report that the chances of learning a word from context are mediated by the ability level of students, the grade level of students, and the density of the text. A study by Jenkins, Stein, and Wysocki (1984) demonstrated this point most directly. Jenkins et al. found that to adequately learn a new word in context without instruction students must be exposed to the word about six times before they have enough experience with the word to ascertain and remember its meaning. These findings are consistent with those reported by Stahl and Fairbanks (1986), who noted that multiple exposures to words produce a better understanding of those words (although Stahl and Fairbanks do not identify an optimum number of exposures).

If multiple exposures are necessary for vocabulary development, then wide reading has a built-in impediment. Specifically, word frequency studies indicate that most words appear very infrequently in written material. More than 90% of the words students will encounter while reading occur less than once in a million words of text; about half occur less than once in a billion words (Nagy & Anderson, 1984). Thus, the encounters students have with new words in their reading are, for the most part, isolated, single encounters that will not produce enough exposure to learn the new words. All of this supports the advisability of direct vocabulary instruction as a complement to wide reading, particularly instruction in subject-specific terms.

Many vocabulary development programs utilize vocabulary lists of high-frequency words, words that commonly appear in the written language (Carroll, Davies, & Richman, 1971; Harris & Jacobson, 1972). These high-frequency lists typically do not focus on the vocabulary from academic subject areas taught in school, but these are the very words that should be the focus of instruction in a vocabulary development program designed to enhance academic achievement. This was demonstrated in the meta-analysis by Stahl and Fairbanks (1986). They found that instruction in general words typically found in high-frequency word lists had an average effect size of .30 on students' comprehension of content. However, when the words taught to students are words they will encounter in the reading passages used in the study, the effect size was .97.

Research at Mid-continent Research for Education and Learning (McREL) has produced a viable set of subject matter terms and phrases. Specifically, as a result of analyzing state and national standards documents, Marzano et al. (1999) identified 6,700 terms that are critical to the understanding of 14 different subject areas. To illustrate the nature of those words, consider a few mathematics terms and phrases within the general category of *probability* that are appropriate for students in grades 6–8: *experiment, odds, theoretical probability, tree diagram, simulation*, and *experimental probability*.

In summary, the indirect and direct approaches to vocabulary instruction represent two philosophies sometimes thought of as competing. The indirect approach assumes that incidental exposure to terms in the context of reading is sufficient to provide the reader with an understanding of some new terms. If the amount of reading is extensive enough, the cumulative effect of this incidental learning is substantial. The direct approach assumes that multiple exposures are necessary to adequately learn new terms. This requires planned instructional interventions to ensure the quantity and quality of these exposures.

Implications for Vocabulary Instruction

There are at least four aspects of the preceding discussion that have direct implications for vocabulary instruction. First, the number of academic terms, at least as identified by Marzano et al. (1999), is small enough to make direct instruction feasible. If students were to receive instruction in about 18 words per week over the course of their K–12 schooling, they would be exposed to all 6,700 terms covering 14 subject areas. Of course, the number of terms directly taught to students could (and probably should) be greatly reduced if selected subject areas were targeted (e.g., mathematics, science, language arts, and social studies).

Second, by definition, these terms are the ones students will most probably encounter in their subject matter classes. Recall Stahl and Fairbanks's (1986) finding that instruction in words that are encountered in reading produced an effect size of .97. Lists of subject matter terms, then, represent a corpus of words that can potentially provide more than twice the impact on students' comprehension of subject matter knowledge than what might be expected from instruction in the more general high-frequency word lists.

Third, direct instruction should ensure that students have multiple exposures to words. One-shot approaches to direct vocabulary instruction might provide more opportunity for students to learn words than a single encounter of a new word in context, but a single exposure to a word through direct instruction appears insufficient. It would seem, then, that direct vocabulary instruction should seek to ensure that students encounter words multiple times, ideally adding to and elaborating on their understanding of words with each iteration.

Fourth, there is no obvious reason why direct vocabulary instruction and wide reading cannot work in tandem. To illustrate, students might be involved in a program of wide reading like SSR or some variant of it. However, one of the central features of the wide reading program would be for students to identify words they find intriguing from their personal reading, determine the meaning of these words from context, and then record both the words and their constructed meanings in some form of personal vocabulary notebook. Periodically, students might interact with one another to discuss the words they selected, why they considered those words interesting, the meanings they constructed, and so on.

The self-selection and group interaction components of this process have been found to be effective. For example, Fisher, Blachowitz, Costa, and Pozzi (1992) examined the effects on 5th and 7th grade students of self-selecting words and working in cooperative groups to determine the meanings of those words. One of their findings was that students tended to choose words that were fairly difficult. They also found that the group interaction impacted the amount of time students spent studying words as well as the strategies they employed to determine and verify the meaning of the selected words. Self-selection of words and social interaction are also aspects of the Vocabulary Self-Collection Strategy (VSS) (Haggard, 1982; Ruddell, 1993). As reported by Ruddell (1994), studies of VSS versus traditional approaches with high school students indicate that the VSS condition "increased collaborative time in the classroom and that students took ownership and enjoyed being in a position of self-determination in the vss condition. . . . Students in the vss condition scored higher on short-term tests administered at the end of . . . the experimental treatment" (p. 436).

AN OUTLINE OF THE DEVELOPING VISION OF VOCABULARY INSTRUCTION

Considered together, the four topics discussed in this chapter paint a fairly clear picture of what I call the developing vision of vocabulary instruction. It is a view that has been tacit in the research and theoretical literature, I assert, but has not been articulated in its totality to date. Specifically, the developing vision implies that a comprehensive program of K–12 vocabulary development would contain the following elements:

1. Students would be engaged in wide reading about subject matter content and content of their choice. As one aspect of their wide reading, students would be asked to identify new terms that are of interest to them, attempt to determine the meanings of those words from context, and keep a record of those self-selected terms and their constructed meanings.
2. Students would receive direct instruction in terms that are critical to their understanding of academic content. Such terms would not be limited to general terms but would also include proper nouns signifying specific persons, places, things, and events that are critical to the understanding of academic content.
3. The goal of 1 and 2 would be for students to develop linguistic descriptions of the top-level information for these terms along with associated images.
4. Students would be encouraged to elaborate on and refine their understanding of new words. These elaborations would include linguistics components (e.g., descriptions of addition and revisions) as well as nonlinguistic components (e.g., use of mental images, pictures, symbols, and the like). The purpose of such activities would be to provide students with multiple encounters with their self-selected terms as well as the terms for which direct instruction was provided. It would also be used to facilitate the creation of linguistic and nonlinguistic representations.

To illustrate how these elements might be implemented, consider a hypothetical middle school that employs all four. At a set time each day, all students, teachers, and administrators read from a book of their own choosing. A standing assignment for all students is to identify words of interest to them from their individual reading and try to determine the meanings of these words from context. These words and the initial guesses as to their meanings are recorded in each student's spiral notebook dedicated to vocabulary. Occasionally, at the conclusion of sustained silent reading time, students share their self-selected words with one another. Students are also provided time to verify the meanings of their words by consulting a dictionary or thesaurus.

During regular class time, teachers present a few selected content-specific terms. In science, selected terms taught directly include *meiosis* and *mitosis*. In social studies, selected terms include the *Battle of Shiloh* and the *Battle of Gettysburg*. In mathematics, selected terms include *matrix* and the *Pythagorean Theorem*. These terms are not presented in a didactic definitional fashion. Rather, information about each is presented in the form of descriptions, examples, and stories. For example, information about the important characteristics of *meiosis* is provided orally to students in the form of a brief description, as opposed to a definition. A brief story is told about the *Battle of Gettysburg*. A physical example of a *matrix* is presented along with a brief explanation.

Students do not record these characteristics, stories, and examples in a verbatim fashion. Rather, they translate the teacher's presentation into their own words and share their personal accounts with one another. Additionally, they construct a nonlinguistic representation (e.g., a picture, symbol, or pictograph) representing their understanding of each term. These linguistic and nonlinguistic constructions are recorded in each student's vocabulary notebook, which is divided into sections for each subject area as well as a section for student self-selected words. Periodically students are asked to review and revise the terms in their vocabulary notebook, adding detail and correcting misconceptions. Over time, these vocabulary notebooks become a cumulative repository for each student's constructed knowledge relative to important subject area terms as well as their self-selected terms.

REFERENCES

Allington, R. L. (1984). Content coverage and contextual reading in reading groups. *Journal of Reading Behavior, 16,* 85–96.

Anderson, J. R. (1983). *The architecture of cognition.* Cambridge, MA: Harvard University Press.

Anderson, R. C., & McGaw, B. (1973). On the representation of the meanings of general terms. *Journal of Experimental Psychology, 101,* 301–306.

Anderson, R. C., & Freebody, P. (1981). Vocabulary knowledge. In J. T. Guthrie (Ed.), *Comprehension and teaching: Research reviews* (pp. 77–117). Newark, DE: International Reading Association.

Baumann, J. F., Kame'enui, E. J., & Ash, G. E. (2003). Research on vocabulary instruction: Voltaire redux. In J. Flood, J. M. Jensen, D. Lapp, & J. R. Squire (Eds.), *Handbook of research in teaching the English language arts* (2nd ed., pp. 752–785). New York: Macmillan.

Beck, I., & McKeown, M. (1991). Conditions of vocabulary acquisition. In R. Barr, M. Kamil, P. Mosenthal, & P. D. Pearson (Eds.), *Handbook of reading research* (Vol. II, pp. 789–814). New York: Longman.

Beck, I. L., McKeown, M. G., & Omanson, R. C. (1987). The effects and uses of diverse vocabulary instructional techniques. In M. G. McKeown & M. E. Curtis (Eds.), *The nature of vocabulary acquisition* (pp. 147–163). Hillsdale, NJ: Erlbaum.

Carroll, J., Davies, P., & Richman, B. (1971). *The American Heritage word frequency book.* Boston: Houghton Mifflin.

Collins, A. M., & Quillian, M. R. (1969). Retrieval time for semantic memory. *Journal of Verbal Learning and Verbal Behavior, 8,* 240–247.

Dale, E. (1965). Vocabulary measurement: Techniques and major findings. *Elementary English, 42,* 82–88.

Drum, P. A., & Konopak, B. C. (1987). Learning word meanings from written context. In M. G. McKeown & M. E. Curtis (Eds.), *The nature of vocabulary acquisition* (pp. 73–87). Hillsdale, NJ: Erlbaum.

Fisher, P. J. L., Blachowicz, C. L. Z, Costa, M., & Pozzi, L. (1992, December). *Vocabulary teaching and learning in middle school cooperative literature study groups.* Paper presented at the National Reading Conference, San Antonio, TX.

Graves, M. F. (1984). Selecting vocabulary to teach in the intermediate and secondary grades. In J. Flood (Ed.), *Promoting reading comprehension* (pp. 245–260). Newark, DE: International Reading Association.

Graves, M. F. (1986). Vocabulary learning and instruction. In E. Z. Rothkopf (Ed.), *Review of Research in Education* (Vol. 13, pp. 49–89). Washington: American Educational Research Association.

Graves, M. F. (1989). A quantitative and qualitative study of elementary school children's vocabularies. *Journal of Educational Research, 82,* 203–209.

Haggard, M. R. (1982). The Vocabulary Self-Collection Strategy: An active approach to word learning. *Journal of Reading, 27,* 203–207.

Harris, A., & Jacobson, M. (1972). *Basic elementary reading vocabulary.* New York: Macmillan.

Hirsch, E. D., Jr. (1987). *Cultural literacy: What every American needs to know.* Boston: Houghton Mifflin.

Hunt, L. C. (1970). Six steps to the individualized reading program (IRP). *Elementary English, 48,* 27–32.

Jenkins, J. R., Stein, M. L., & Wysocki, K. (1984). Learning vocabulary through reading. *American Educational Research Journal, 21*(4), 767–787.

Just, M. A., & Carpenter, P. A. (1987). *The psychology of reading and language comprehension.* Boston, MA: Allyn & Bacon.

Kame'enui, E. J., Dixon, R. C., & Carnine, D. W. (1987). Issues in the design of vocabulary instruction. In M. G. McKeown & M. E. Curtis (Eds.), *The nature of vocabulary acquisition* (pp. 129–145). Hillsdale, NJ: Erlbaum.

Katz, J., & Fodor, J. (1963). The structure of semantic theory. *Journal of Verbal Learning and Verbal Behavior, 39,* 170–210.

Kintsch, W. (1974). *The representation of meaning in memory.* Hillsdale, NJ: Erlbaum.

Kintsch, W. (1979). On modeling comprehension. *Educational Psychologist, 1,* 3–14.

Kintsch, W., & van Dijk, T. A. (1978). Toward a model of text comprehension and production. *Psychological Review, 85,* 363–394.

Marzano, R. J., Kendall, J. S., & Gaddy, B. B. (1999). *Essential knowledge: The debate over what American students should know.* Aurora, CO: Mid-continent Regional Educational Laboratory.

McKeown, M. G., & Beck, I. L. (1988). Learning vocabulary: Different ways for different goals. *Remedial and Special Education, 20,* 482–496.

Mezynski, K. (1983). Issues concerning the acquisition of knowledge: Effects of vocabulary training on reading comprehension. *Review of Educational Research, 53,* 253–279.

Nagy, W. E., & Anderson, R. C. (1984). How many words are there in printed school English? *Reading Research Quarterly, 19,* 304–330.

Nagy, W. E., & Herman, P. A. (1984). *Limitations of vocabulary instruction.* Champaign, IL: University of Illinois, Center for the Study of Reading.

Nagy, W. E., & Herman, P. A. (1987). Breadth and depth of vocabulary knowledge:

Implications for acquisition and instruction. In M. G. McKeown & M. E. Curtis (Eds.), *The nature of vocabulary acquisition* (pp. 19–35). Hillsdale, NJ: Erlbaum.

Paivio, A. (1971). *Imagery and verbal processes.* New York: Holt, Rinehart & Winston.

Paivio, A. (1991). Dual coding theory: Retrospect and current status. *Canadian Journal of Psychology, 45,* 255–287.

Paris, S. G., Lipson, M. Y., & Wixson, K. K. (1983). Becoming a strategic reader. *Contemporary Educational Psychology. 8,* 293–316.

Potter, M. C., & Faulconer, B. A. (1979). Understanding noun phrases. *Journal of Verbal Learning and Verbal Behavior, 18,* 509–522.

Powell, G. (1980, December). *A meta-analysis of the effects of "imposed" and "induced" imagery upon word recall.* Paper presented at the annual meeting of the National Reading Conference, San Diego, CA. (ERIC Document Reproduction Service No. ED199644)

Quirk, R., Greenbaum, S., Leech, G., & Svartvik, J. (1972). *A grammar of contemporary English.* London: Longman.

Rosch, E. (1975). Cognitive representation of semantic categories. *Journal of Experimental Psychology: General, 104,* 192–233.

Ruddell, M. R. (1993). *Teaching content reading and writing.* Boston: Allyn & Bacon.

Ruddell, M. R. (1994). Vocabulary knowledge and comprehension: A comprehension-process view of complex literacy relationships. In R. B. Ruddell, M. R. Ruddell, & H. Singer (Eds.), *Theoretical models and processes of reading* (4th ed., pp. 414–447). Newark, DE: International Reading Association.

Sadoski, M. (1983). An exploratory study of the relationships between reported imagery and the comprehension and recall of a story. *Reading Research Quarterly, 19,* 110–123.

Sadoski, M. (1985). The natural use of imagery in story comprehension and recall: Replication and extension. *Reading Research Quarterly, 20,* 658–667.

Sadoski, M., & Paivio, A. (1994). A dual coding view of imagery and verbal processes in reading comprehension. In R. B. Ruddell, M. R. Ruddell, & H. Singer (Eds.), *Theoretical models and processes of reading* (4th ed., pp. 582–601). Newark, DE: International Reading Association.

Smith, E. E., & Medin, D. L. (1981). *Categories and concepts.* Cambridge, MA: Harvard University Press.

Stahl, S. A. (1985). To teach a word well: A framework for vocabulary instruction. *Reading World, 24*(3), 16–27.

Stahl, S. A. (1986). Three principles of effective vocabulary instruction. *Journal of Reading, 29,* 662–668.

Stahl, S. A., & Fairbanks, M. M. (1986). The effects of vocabulary instruction: A model-based meta-analysis. *Review of Educational Research, 56*(1), 72–110.

Stanovich, K. E. (1986). Matthew effects in reading: Some consequences of individual differences in the acquisition of literacy. *Reading Research Quarterly, 21*(4), 360–406.

Stanovich, K. E., Cunningham, A. E., & Feeman, D. J. (1984). Intelligence, cognitive skills, and early reading progress. *Reading Research Quarterly, 19,* 278–303.

Sternberg, R. J. (1987). Most vocabulary is learned from context. In M. G. McKeown & M. E. Curtis (Eds.), *The nature of vocabulary acquisition* (pp. 89–106). Hillsdale, NJ: Erlbaum.

Swanborn, M. S. L., & de Glopper, K. (1999). Incidental word learning while reading: A meta-analysis. *Review of Educational Research, 69*(3), 261–285.

Turner, A. & Greene, E. (1977). *The construction of a propositional text base.* Boulder, CO: Institute for the Study of Intellectual Behavior.

van Dijk, T. A. (1980). *Macrostructures.* Hillsdale, NJ: Erlbaum.

van Dijk, T. A., & Kintsch, W. (1983). *Strategies of discourse comprehension.* New York: Academic Press.

Vygotsky, L. S. (1962). *Thought and language.* Cambridge, MA: MIT Press.

8

The Vocabulary–Spelling Connection

Orthographic Development and Morphological Knowledge at the Intermediate Grades and Beyond

SHANE TEMPLETON

As revealed through their spelling, the nature and organization of students' lexicons offer implications for spelling and vocabulary development and instruction. Specifically, investigations of the development of higher-order orthographic knowledge reveal the nature of the interaction between orthographic knowledge and morphological knowledge. This interaction reflects the fact that word parts or morphemes that share similar meanings tend to be spelled similarly. More commonly referred to as the *spelling–meaning connection* (Templeton, 1983, 1992), this interaction provides the foundation for unifying spelling and vocabulary instruction at the intermediate levels and beyond. It suggests a more theoretically and empirically grounded scope and sequence of spelling and vocabulary instruction than has traditionally been available to guide curriculum design and development.

The linguist Mark Aronoff (1994) observed that "From a teacher's point of view, *morphology is important for two major reasons: spelling and vocabulary....* Unfortunately, very little time is spent in school on systematic learning of morphology" (pp. 820–821, emphasis added). Over the years a

118

handful of educators and linguists have called for the integration of spelling and vocabulary instruction through the examination of morphology. Aronoff's observation was certainly not the first time that educators and linguists had noted a connection between morphology and spelling/vocabulary learning and instruction. Edgar Dale and his colleagues pointed out that "organizing spelling lessons to coincide with the study of morphology gives the students a contextual structure for the study of spelling" (Dale, O'Rourke, & Bamman, 1971, p. 172). Templeton (1983) described this relationship in terms of the *spelling–meaning connection* and offered a general sequence according to which morphologically related words are studied together, for example, *compete* and *competitive, autumn* and *autumnal*. More recently, Leong (2000) concluded that "there is a need for systematic and explicit teaching of word knowledge and spelling, *based on morphemic structure* and origin of words and their productive rules, from elementary grades onwards" (p. 298, emphasis added).

While embracing and celebrating the importance of a more explicit connection between morphology and the teaching of spelling and vocabulary, a line of research has accorded a central position not to morphology but rather to *spelling* or *orthographic knowledge* in the development of morphological and vocabulary knowledge. Orthographic knowledge, in other words, is advanced as the foundation for the study of morphology and vocabulary. Templeton (1979) first framed this position in terms of "the degree to which knowledge of orthographic [spelling] structure influences the psychological reality of words. . . . The question is an important one, for it is part of a broader concern involving *the way in which individuals organize information about the vocabulary of English*" (p. 255, emphasis added). This chapter will explore the implications of this position.

Although a number of educators and linguists have emphasized the desirability of connecting spelling and vocabulary, this emphasis has received little systematic attention in most intermediate classrooms—or middle and secondary classrooms, for that matter. A number of possible explanations exist, including teachers' lack of confidence in their own understanding of the spelling system and spelling instruction and lack of familiarity with the morphological aspects of language. The teachers are hardly to blame, however. They have not been provided the knowledge foundation or the type of instructional resources that support a well-grounded and systematic scope and sequence (Templeton, 2003a). With a few exceptions (e.g. Bear, Invernizzi, Templeton, & Johnston, 2000; Henry, 1989; Templeton, 1992), there has not been focused investigation of the particulars of the integration of spelling and vocabulary instruction at the intermediate grades and beyond.

The common conception of integrated spelling and vocabulary instruction is that all new vocabulary words are also studied as spelling words.

This is *not* the stance advanced here. Rather, the case will be made that students' spelling knowledge should anchor and guide the study of particular types of morphological patterns as represented in the orthography. Once the nature of these morphological patterns as they occur in the spelling of known words is understood, these patterns may be extended to unfamiliar words. Spelling knowledge provides the basis for explicit awareness and understanding of morphology, which, in turn, may guide the systematic growth of vocabulary knowledge.

MORPHOLOGY AND THE SPELLING SYSTEM
OF ENGLISH

Morphemes, or meaning elements in words, tend to be spelled consistently (Chomsky, 1970; Cummings, 1988; Venezky, 1999), and there is a growing body of research that suggests that systematic attention to this aspect of spelling—how the system visually cues word meaning and the semantic relationships among words—also supports students' vocabulary growth and understanding (e.g., Leong, 2000; Smith, 1998). For instructional purposes, Templeton (1983, 1991, 2003b) referred to this aspect of orthographic representation of morphology as the *spelling–meaning connection*: "Words that are related in meaning are often related in spelling as well, despite changes in sound" (1991, p. 194).

There is, in fact, a folk wisdom among English-speaking cultures that the system of English spelling is illogical, often accompanied by a wistful yearning for a more phonemically based system in which sounds are spelled more consistently. This *phonocentric* view (Templeton & Morris, 2000) has persisted in much of instructional practice. Spelling or orthographic systems, however, may be considered as falling along a phonemic-to-morphological continuum; English falls more toward the morphological end of this continuum but nevertheless retains a greater consistency at the level of phonemic representation than often realized (Cummings, 1988; Hanna, Hanna, Hodges, & Rudorf, 1966; Templeton, 2003a; Venezky, 1999). Spellings that appear illogical from a phonocentric perspective become quite understandable when considered from the perspective of morphology or spelling–meaning relationships: "Orthography *clarifies*, where pronunciation may obscure, relationships among words" (Templeton, 1979, p. 257). For example, the role of the "silent *g*" in *paradigm* makes sense when the word *paradigmatic* is pointed out; the spelling visually preserves the meaning relationship between the words. *Autumn* is spelled with a final silent *n* to preserve its visual identity with *autumnal*, in which the *n* is pronounced. If these words *were* spelled more in accordance with their pronunciation, the visual identity would be lost (*paradime/paradigmatic*; *autum/*

autumnal). As Venezky (1999) summarized, "Visual identity of word parts takes precedence over letter-sound simplicity" (p. 197).

ORTHOGRAPHIC KNOWLEDGE UNDERLIES SPELLING AND READING

The convergence of two lines of research—development of morphological knowledge and development of spelling or orthographic knowledge—helps to identify the point at which students may benefit from systematic instruction in morphology that explores this relationship between the spelling or visual representation of words and their meaning. A number of studies have documented the striking growth in children's derivational morphological knowledge beginning in third grade (e.g. Anglin, 1993; Carlisle, 1988; Derwing, Smith, & Wiebe, 1995; Fowler & Liberman, 1995; Leong, 2000; Mahony, Singson, & Mann, 2000). Interestingly, and importantly, students whose *spelling instructional level* (Morris, Blanton, Blanton, & Perney, 1995) is at least third grade are able to begin explicit exploration of simple derivational morphological patterns; their lexical organization and representations accommodate simple two-syllable words and enable them to apply this knowledge to encode and decode polysyllabic words (Templeton, 1992).

Perfetti (1997) observed that the process of spelling and the process of reading draw upon the same lexical representation and therefore "spelling is the purest indicator of lexical quality" (p. 30; see also Gill, 1992). Developmental spelling research (e.g. Ehri, 1997; Perfetti, Rieben, & Fayol, 1997; Templeton & Bear, 1992) offers insight into the nature and content of individuals' lexical representations—how words are represented in our mental dictionaries—as well as how this knowledge is brought to bear in both the encoding and decoding of print. The nature and content of orthographic knowledge determines the types of printed information the reader perceives and processes on the page and, therefore, the degree of rate and accuracy with which the words are read. For this reason, the work of Morris and his colleagues addressing spelling instructional level is significant (Bear, Templeton, & Warner, 1991; Ganske, 1999; Morris, Blanton, Blanton, Nowacek, & Perney, 1995; Morris, Nelson, & Perney, 1986; Morris, Blanton, Blanton, & Perney, 1995). Determining a spelling instructional level reveals the zone of proximal *orthographic* development within which students can most productively examine words and abstract spelling patterns. Thus, students are more likely to learn, retain, and apply these patterns in their writing and in their recognition of familiar words and decoding of unfamiliar words in reading. As orthographic knowledge advances, so too does the literate lexicon.

Orthographic knowledge, therefore, is placed as the linchpin of instruction in morphology and vocabulary. Beginning in the intermediate school years, a significantly larger proportion of words occurring in print than in spoken language reflect morphological processes (Aronoff, 1994; Nagy & Anderson, 1984); there is a greater type/token ratio of derivational morphological patterns (Templeton & Scarborough-Franks, 1985); and words that reflect these patterns tend to be spelled more in accordance with their meaning than with their sound (Venezky, 1999; Templeton & Scarborough-Franks, 1985). In order to have a sufficient number of examples for study that reflect these morphological processes, therefore, a student's reading and spelling instructional level should probably be at least third grade. Through reading at both independent and instructional levels, students experience a number of times words that later are selected for spelling study. The examination of known words in reading ensures that the structure or orthography of the words will more likely be learned. This, in turn, strengthens the abstraction of particular orthographic *patterns*, which in the lexicon provide an orthographic frame that guides the perception of words in reading. In this regard, Perfetti (1997) noted that attention given to spelling is of more benefit to reading than vice versa. Working within the spelling instructional level—within the zone of proximal orthographic development—affords the lexicon the optimal conditions for growth.

Given the significance of orthographic knowledge in the development of the literate lexicon, therefore, it is not surprising that a number of researchers have consistently found that older struggling readers and spellers do not process morphological information well (e.g. Leong, 2000; Smith, 1998). They do not possess the underlying lexical knowledge and organization that would support learning and retaining words that reflect these processes. More simply expressed, such students are attempting to process and remember words that are at their spelling *frustration* level (Morris, Blanton, Blanton, & Perney, 1995). Though these students may indeed study and remember how to spell new vocabulary words on a Friday test, they will most likely misspell those words when they return to online writing because their underlying orthographic knowledge will not support the retention of these words in long-term memory. This does not mean that teachers should avoid discussion of spelling–meaning relationships with such students—such "mentioning" alerts the students to the existence of these elements (Templeton, 1989)—but the systematic spelling instruction these students require will focus on simpler orthographic patterns.

A necessary preliminary, therefore, to effective integrated spelling and vocabulary instruction through the exploration of morphological features and processes is the determination of where students fall along the developmental continuum of word knowledge as determined by an assessment of spelling or orthographic knowledge (Bear et al., 2000; Bear, Invernizzi, Templeton, & Johnston, 2004; Ganske, 1999; Masterson, Apel, & Wasowicz, 2002; Schlagal, 1992). To illustrate the relationship between underlying lexical or orthographic knowledge and the acquisition of new orthographic patterns, consider the following spelling errors by three students in the same fifth-grade classroom:

	Student A	Student B	Student C
drive	driev	drive	drive
float	flote	float	float
hurry	hery	hurry	hurry
striped	stipt	stripped	striped
mental	mintul	mentle	mental
competition		computishun	compitition
amusement		imuzemint	ammusement

As revealed through his spelling errors, student A's orthographic knowledge indicates that he is sensitive to the orthographic pattern in which silent letters are used to indicate long-vowel sounds (*driev*, *flote*). His failure to double consonants at syllable junctures (*hery*) and represent past tense with –ed indicate that these features are not yet part of his orthographic knowledge. Requiring him to memorize spelling words traditionally found at fifth-grade level would lead inevitably to frustration—his orthographic knowledge is not sufficient to retain such words in long-term memory. While student A as a fifth grader may cognitively benefit from discussion of concrete Greek roots such as *therm-* and *photo-*, his word study for purposes of encoding and decoding will not include systematic examination of words that include these forms.

On the other hand, student B's spelling errors reveal that her lexical knowledge would support systematic examination of polysyllabic words, including the addition of inflectional endings to base words. She would also benefit from exploring some prefixes and simple Greek and Latin word roots and from learning a number of new vocabulary words that include these elements, though with a few exceptions such words would not be part of her spelling words.

Student C's lexical knowledge would support a more systematic and extensive exploration of spelling–meaning patterns as part of her spelling instruction (see Table 8.1), and would also benefit from the systematic exploration of a number of most frequently occurring Greek and Latin word roots in spelling and vocabulary instruction (see Bear & Helman, Chapter 9, this volume).

Much spelling and vocabulary instruction may be ineffective, in other

TABLE 8.1. Spelling and Vocabulary: General Scope and Sequence, Intermediate Grades and Beyond

Grades 3–4

Simple prefixes and base words

un- (not: *unlock*)	tri- (three: *tricycle*)
re- (again: *remake*)	dis (opposite: *dismiss*)
non- (not: *nonfiction*)	in- (not: *indecent*)
uni- (one: *unicycle*)	mis- (wrong: *misfire*)
bi- (two: *bicycle*)	pre- (before: *preview*)

Simple suffixes and base words

-y (like: *jumpy*)	-ful (full of, like: *graceful*)
-ly (like: *gladly*)	-less (without: *penniless*)
-er, -est (comparatives)	-ness (condition: *happiness*)

Grades 4–6

The spelling–meaning connection
  Consonant alternations

Silent/sounded	crumb/crumble; sign/signal
/t/ to /sh/	act/action; select/selection
/k/ to /sh/	magic/magician; clinic/clinician
/k/ to /s/	critic/criticize; politic/politicize
/s/ to /sh/	prejudice/prejudicial, office/official

  Vowel alternation and reduction

Long-to-short	crime/criminal, wise/wisdom; compete/competitive
Long-to-schwa	compete/competition, compose/composition, confide/confident
Short-to-schwa	personality/personal; legality/legal, adapt/adaptation

Grades 5–6

Greek and Latin Word Roots
  1. Most common Greek roots; for example, -*tele*- (far, distant), -*therm*- (heat), -*photo*- (light)
  2. Move to Latin roots with the aim of gaining a working understanding of a few frequently occurring roots: e.g., -*tract*- (drag, pull), -*spect*- (look), -*port*- (carry), -*dict*- (to say), -*rupt*- (to break), and -*scrib*- (to write)

Greek and Latin prefixes
  For example, *inter*- (between), *intra*- (within), *post*- (after), *pro*- (in front of, forward), *co-/com-/con*- (together), *sub*- (under), *pre*- (before), *anti*- (against)

Common Greek suffixes
  -*crat/-cracy*: rule (*democracy*—rule by the *demos*, "people")
  -*ician*: specialist in (*dietician*)
  -*ine*: chemical substance (*chlorine, Benzedrine*)
  -*ism/-ist*: belief in, one who believes (*communism/communist, capitalism/capitalist*)
  -*logy/-logist*: science of, scientist (*geology*—science of the earth, studying the earth; *geologist*—one who studies the earth)
  -*phobia*: abnormal fear (*claustrophobia*—fear of being closed in or shut in [*claus*])

(continued)

TABLE 8.1. *(continued)*

Grades 6–8

The spelling–meaning connection: Predictable spelling changes in consonants and vowels

1. /t/ to /sh/	permit/permission, transmit/transmission
2. /t/ to /s/	silent/silence
3. /d/ to /zh/	explode/explosion, erode/erosion, decide/decision
4. /sh/ to /s/	ferocious/ferocity, precocious/precocity
5. Long-to-Short	vain/vanity; consume/consumption; receive/reception; retain/retention, detain/detention
6. Long-to-Schwa	explain/explanation; exclaim/exclamation

Grade 7 and beyond

Advanced suffix study

1. -able/-ible	respectable, favorable vs. visible, audible
2. -ant/-ance	fragrant/fragrance, dominant/dominance
-ent/-ence	dependent/dependence, florescent/florescence
3. Consonant doubling and accent	occurred, permitted vs. traveled, benefited

Absorbed prefixes

1. Prefix + base word	in + mobile = immobile; ad + count = account
2. Prefix + word root	ad + cept = accept; in + mune = immune
	ad + tain = attain

words, because there is often a mismatch between the level of orthographic knowledge required and students' level of orthographic knowledge. To the degree that an individual's underlying lexical knowledge supports an understanding of morphological patterns and processes as represented in orthographic structure—the visual representation of sound and meaning—the decoding and encoding of these patterns becomes easier, more facile, and increasingly automatic.

THE NATURE AND COURSE OF STUDENTS' KNOWLEDGE OF DERIVATIONAL MORPHOLOGICAL PATTERNS IN ORTHOGRAPHY AND PHONOLOGY

Taken together with the research into students' knowledge of derivational morphology, developmental spelling research provides some guidance by which a general scope and sequence for morphologically based spelling and vocabulary instruction may be developed. Beginning exploration may be focused on what linguists term *external* derivational morphology. A number of studies investigating the development of derivational morphology have focused on this aspect (e.g., Anglin, 1993). For example, adding the suffix *-ment* to the verb *place* yields the noun *placement*; there is no change in the pronunciation of the base when the suffix is added. Much of the initial learning in derivational morphology involves this process of simple combination of morphemic elements.

As students move through the intermediate grades and beyond, however, words that reflect processes of *internal* derivational morphology are encountered with increasing frequency. These are words in which the addition of suffixes often effects phonological changes within the base or root. For example, note the different pronunciation of the letter string *defin-* in the words *define, defin*ition, *defin*itive and *-jud-* in pre*jud*ice and ad*jud*icate. Usually these words also include Greco-Latin roots that underlie most specialized or academic vocabulary (e.g., Chomsky, 1970; Corson, 1997). *Word roots* are those elements that remain at the core or "root" of the word after all affixes have been removed but which, in contrast to *base words*, usually do not stand alone as words, for example, *-dic-* ("to speak") in *dictate, predict, indict* and *-spec-* ("to look, see") in *spectator, spectacle*, and *circumspect*. The spelling–meaning connection—*words that are related in meaning are often related in spelling as well, despite changes in sound—* applies most productively to internal derivational morphological processes.

Corson (1997) observed that "morphologically related words will only be linked in the lexicon if there is a transparent semantic relationship between them" (p. 695). Before exploring the specific Greco-Latin roots and the processes that apply to them, therefore, a foundation should be established that firmly anchors this exploration in students' awareness of *familiar* words and the ways in which they reflect spelling–meaning patterns (Templeton, 2003a). Investigation of the nature, course, and complexity of the development of certain derivational morphological patterns offers guidelines for the construction of this spelling–meaning foundation. For example, older students' awareness and application of the derivational morphological processes of *vowel alternation, vowel reduction*, and *consonant alternation* in phonology and orthography have been explored (Templeton, 1979, 1992; Templeton & Scarborough-Franks, 1985).

Vowel alternation entails the phonological alternation between tense and lax (long and short) vowels in related words such as def*i*ne/def*i*nitive and comp*e*te/comp*e*titive. *Vowel reduction* is the process in which a stressed vowel in one word is "reduced"—receives the least stress—in a related word, as in comp*e*te/comp*e*tition and ment*a*lity/ment*a*l. In general, it appears that an explicit productive knowledge of vowel alternation in orthography and phonology precedes an explicit productive knowledge of vowel reduction. The straightforward explanation for this is that there are usually fewer orthographic and phonological changes involved in vowel alternation than in vowel reduction. For students beginning an explicit examination of internal derivational morphology, therefore, the less complex long-to-short alternation patterns in words such as *wise/wis*dom and *please/pleas*ant provide a logical foundation for understanding the spelling–meaning connection, and they scaffold exploration a short time later of vowel reduction patterns. At the same time that vowel alternation patterns begin to be studied, certain straightforward consonant alternation patterns may also be introduced in known words, such as the silent/sounded alternation in sign/signature and bom*b*/bom*b*ard.

As students advance through the exploration of higher-level derivational morphology, including attention to word roots in Greco–Latin vocabulary, an interesting phenomenon develops: They become more familiar with the ways in which the orthography represents derivational morphological processes than they are with how these processes map to the phonological system (Templeton, 1979, 1992; Templeton & Scarborough-Franks, 1985). Simply expressed, they can *spell* words that follow these processes more easily than they can *pronounce* the words. For older students, in other words, *written* language—orthography—provides the foundation for learning and applying derivational morphological processes in *spoken* language (Chomsky, 1970; Templeton, 1979). Orthographic knowledge, therefore, is the anchor not only for understanding internal derivational morphological processes and for strengthening semantic connections among words in students' lexicons (Rueckl & Raveh, 1999) but also for understanding how to *pronounce* words to which these processes apply.

IMPLICATIONS FOR SELECTION OF PATTERNS AND WORDS

To reiterate the position stated at the beginning of this chapter: Integrating spelling and vocabulary does not mean we assign all new vocabulary words to be spelling words as well, but that we use the spelling system to help students become aware of the ways in which spelling represents meaning. We then extend this awareness to an understanding of how these ways support the learning of spelling as well as the acquisition through analogy of unfamiliar but derivationally related words. Based on a synthesis of the developmental spelling research and the research investigating the development of derivational morphological knowledge, the following two criteria emerge for designing an integrated spelling and vocabulary curriculum: (1) the frequency of occurrence of concrete-to-more-abstract derivational morphological patterns in orthography and phonology (Templeton, 1989); and (2) the degree of semantic transparency among the words that represent these patterns (Corson, 1997; Nagy & Anderson, 1984).

Two examples illustrate these criteria. With respect to developing an awareness of the spelling–meaning connection, begin with the straightforward process discussed above of long-to-short vowel alternation (*wise/*

wisdom; sane/sanity) and the process of consonant alternation (bomb/bombard; sign/signature) because the sound changes are easily discriminable in the familiar words that illustrate the processes. Several examples of these are very likely to lead to students' first explicit realization of the role of meaning in spelling, and thus why the spelling does not change. With respect to Greek and Latin word elements, begin simply: Introduce, examine, and apply knowledge of affixes and roots using words in which the combination of these morphemes results in concrete and consistent meanings. For example, combine an affix or two with a root whose meaning is concrete, as with *in-* + *-spect-* and *in-* + *-spect-* + *-ion*.

In general, the selection and sequencing of roots depends on their frequency and utility. The issue is usually not the abstractness of the meaning of the root but the abstractness of the meaning resulting from the combination of the root with affixes, especially in the case of words that have been in the language for hundreds of years. In these instances the meaning has evolved from the literal and more concrete to the more abstract—a phenomenon that should be discussed with students. Fortunately, however, as students advance through the grades, the meanings of less frequently occurring unfamiliar words may be quite reliably inferred by analyzing the combination of affixes and roots. This is because the meanings of words that have more recently entered the language are more straightforwardly the sum of their morphemic parts. Table 8.1 presents a general scope and sequence for an integrated spelling and vocabulary curriculum. Although grounded in the lines of research discussed above, it is important to note that the sequence should not be considered as being in lock step but rather a general guide and point of reference for teachers.

Teachers may find words that reflect appropriate derivational morphological patterns and semantic transparency in Bear et al. (2000, 2004), Ganske (2000), and Fresch and Wheaton (2002). In addition, some published spelling and spelling–vocabulary programs for the intermediate and middle grades have been constructed with these criteria in mind. These criteria can guide instruction in reading or English classes at the intermediate and middle levels (Templeton, 2002), as well as in other content areas such as mathematics, science, and social studies. Teachers who are able to plan cross-curricular units are in the best position to optimize spelling and vocabulary integration. Even when this is not possible, however, teachers may be more systematic in their selection of words for study. For example, when selecting vocabulary words that represent important concepts and ideas in a content area, teachers should think about words that are related orthographically and semantically to the focus terms and which students are already likely to know but perhaps have not analyzed.

In *math*, as an example, the concept of *fraction* gets lost even for many intermediate and middle grade students in the complexities of manipulating numbers in numerators and denominators; they literally do not realize that *fraction* deals with *breaking* something down into parts. Teachers can relate the term to the word *fracture*, which has most likely been experienced by at least one student in the class, and point out that both words contain the Latin word root *fract-*, which means "to break." *Fractions*, in other words, deal with breaking things down into parts and manipulating those parts.

In science many terms are created by combining Greek and Latin roots. Science offers one of the richest domains for students' coming to appreciate the role and importance of these elements. Moreover, the meaning of the combined elements is usually very precise. Students may be asked about a *hydroplane*, the noun or the verb, and they're likely to know one or both. Then ask about a fire *hydrant*. What does it have in common with a *hydroplane*? If students do not come to the realization themselves as a consequence of teacher questioning, the teacher then points out *hydr-* in both words and tells students that it is a Greek root meaning *water*. Then move to *hydraulic* and *hydrology*.

In *social studies*, terms such as *democracy, plutocracy, monarchy*, and *oligarchy* can be related by examining their constituent parts. The confusion between *immigrant* and *emigrant* can be explained by noting the prefix in each word. *Im-* means "into"; *immigrants* migrate *into* a country. *E-* means "out"; *emigrants* migrate out of or leave a country.

The more that teachers think about relating new terms to familiar terms based on morphology or spelling–meaning criteria, the more they will make connections—and the more excited they will become as they share these connections with students. An excellent resource for word roots, accessible to students as well as teachers, is Crutchfield (1997).

INSTRUCTION

Leong (2000) observed that word study should emphasize "the hierarchical and relational aspects of constituents of words and not just the linear concatenation of subparts. . . . Knowledge of morphological structure and the attendant phonological, semantic and syntactic alternations should enhance the proficiency of readers and spellers" (p. 298). Some of the ways in which this knowledge may be enhanced have been explored in the vocabulary instruction research (e.g., Baumann, Kame'enui, & Ash, 2003). Put succinctly, students should be actively engaged in examining words from a *variety* of perspectives (Bear et al., 2000; Templeton, 2003a). The contexts in which this examination occurs include aspects of both direct instruction and student exploration. The quality and appropriate mix of these aspects most likely depends on four teacher factors: (1) a knowledge base in the form and function of English orthography, including, in particular, those features of English word morphology; (2) a general understanding of a logical instructional sequence to be followed; (3) knowledge of how to assess where students fall along a developmental continuum of word knowledge; and (4) an awareness of and facility with providing appropriate types of activities and strategies for learning words.

Direct Instruction: Examples

The examples in this section, advancing in complexity (see Table 8.1), illustrate how these factors are applied in the context of direct instruction. In the first example, the teacher models a "walk-through" in which students are first helped to become aware of the spelling–meaning connection. The teacher begins with words the students know:

> Writing the word *sign* on the board, the teacher talks about what happens when you *sign* a letter and comments, "I wonder why there's a *g* in the word *sign*." Then, the teacher mentions that we refer to someone's signed name as their *signature*, and writes the word directly underneath *sign* so that the letters *s-i-g-n* line up. "Hmmm . . . that's interesting. We hear the *g* pronounced in *signature*, even though we don't hear it in *sign*. Are these two words related in *meaning*? I wonder if that might have something to do with why the spelling *s-i-g-n* doesn't change?
>
> "Let's try a couple of other words. Several of you have taken turns writing a *column* for our class newspaper [writes the word *column* on the board]. What did we call ourselves when we wrote a column? Right, a *columnist* [writes the word directly under *column*]. That's interesting. We don't hear the *n* in *column* pronounced but we do hear it in *columnist*. Are these two words related in meaning? Might that have something to do with why the spelling didn't change?"

This type of modeling and subsequent discussion helps students revisit words they already know and makes explicit the spelling–meaning connections among these words. Students will encounter a large number of words in their reading that follow this type of pattern. While teachers should explicitly group many of these words together for instruction, because of this explicit attention, students should be more likely to notice and remember such relationships on their own.

After several long-to-short vowel alternation patterns are examined (e.g., n*a*ture/n*a*tural, st*u*dent/st*u*dy) students may explore in depth the process of vowel reduction, in which sound is not a clue to the spelling of the schwa, or least-accented vowel; misspellings such as **resadent*, **confadence*, and **oppisition* are common. Pairing appropriate base words together with their derivatives should provide a clue to the spelling of the schwa sound: re*side*/re*sident*, con*fide*/con*fidence*, op*pose*/op*position*. The awareness of the spelling–meaning connection should evolve into a strategy for learning and remembering the spelling of words: *If you're uncertain about how to spell a word, try to think of a word that is related in spelling and meaning—very often, it will provide a clue.* Remembering *columnist*, for example, will help in remembering *column*. Remembering *confide* will help in remembering *confidence*.

Once students are aware of and understand how the spelling–meaning connection functions in *known* words, this relationship can be extended to *unknown* words. In the following example, the teacher begins with words students have misspelled:

> After writing the misspellings *locle*, *presadent*, and *autum* on the board, the teacher explains that "These are some misspellings I've noticed in your writing recently. For each of them, there is a word that is similar in spelling and meaning and which will help you remember the correct spelling. Let's take the first word. [Writes *locality* on the board.] Who's heard of it? [Several hands are raised.] Any idea what it means? Or is it one of those words we've heard but we're not quite sure about the meaning? Well, it can help us with the spelling of this word [pointing to *locle*]. What do you think the base of *locality* is? Good! [Underlines *local*.] Might this give us a clue to the spelling of 'local'? That's right. You've figured me out by now! Sure, 'local' [writes *local* underneath *locality*] is related to *locality*. And what does *local* mean? [Students respond.] Good! So *locality* has to do with or describes something that is *local*, and it helps us remember the spelling of the /el/ sound in *local*. Why? We hear that strong accented second syllable in loCALity, don't we, and because words that are related in meaning are often related in spelling—that's our clue for remembering the *-al* spelling in *local*.
>
> "We've done two things. First, we've cleared up the spelling of *local*, and second, we've just expanded our vocabulary by learning the word *locality*." The teacher proceeds with the other words, discussing how a president *presides* over a country and how *autumnal* describes something that characterizes or happens in *autumn*. In each case, the teacher points out how the problematic spelling in the *known* word is explained by the sound and spelling in the *new* word: The long *i* spelling in pre*side* explains the spelling of the schwa sound in pre*sident*; the pronounced *n* at the end of *autumnal* explains the silent *n* in *autumn*. Beginning with its focus on spelling, this lesson has become a vocabulary lesson, which, in turn, has reinforced spelling. The teacher concludes with the following observation:
>
> "You know what's neat about all of this? More and more often, you're going to notice words when you *read* that you don't know but which remind you of words you *do* know because of their similarity in

spelling. This similarity in spelling is a very important clue to the meaning of an unknown word, because, as we've learned, words that are related in meaning are often related in spelling as well. Knowing *local*, for example, would help you with *locality*; knowing *autumn* helps you with *autumnal*."

In contrast to earlier developmental levels, in which unfamiliar words are used sparingly as part of spelling study, at this level unfamiliar words may indeed be part of spelling study—provided, as in the cases of *preside*, *locality*, and *autumnal*—they are orthographically and semantically related to the familiar words.

Exploring internal derivational morphological processes as they apply in base words and derivatives should lay a secure foundation for exploring these processes as they apply to word roots. The consistent spelling of word roots is the key to identifying them and studying how they function within words; students' understanding of spelling–meaning relationships extends to perceiving the kinship among words that at first glance may appear quite different.

The following example illustrates the "introduce, examine, apply" instructional strategy for word roots referred to earlier (Bear et al., 2004; Templeton, 1997).

Beginning with a brief discussion in which the teacher reviews how base words and prefixes or suffixes combine, the teacher moves on to an introduction of the concept of word roots: "In literally thousands of words, there is a 'root' that prefixes and suffixes attach to. This word root is the most important part of the word, but unlike a base word it usually can't stand alone as a word. Let's check one out." [Points to the words *inspect*, *inspection*, and *spectator* written on the board.]

"Let's think about the words *inspect* and *inspection*. What do you do when you *inspect* something? [Student responds, describing how you "look real close at something."] Good! So, what would an *inspection* be? [Inspecting something.] All right! Now, let's think about *spectator*. What does a *spectator* do? [Watches something.] Good; a spectator watches or *looks* at something, like at a game. Now, these three words all have *spect* in them. Is *spect* a word? You're right; it isn't, but it's a very important part of each of these words. We call *spect* a word root; it comes from Latin and means 'to look.' Let's *us* look at these words and think about how the root works in each one.

"*Inspect* has the prefix *in-*, meaning 'into,' so when we put *spect* together with *in-* [pointing to *spect* and then to *in-*] we get 'to look into.' And with *inspection*, we have the *–ion* suffix, which means 'the act of doing something'—in this case [pointing to *ion*, then to *spect*, then to *in*] 'the *act* of *looking into*.'

"Now let's think about these words [writes *dictate, dictation, pre-dict* on the board]. What's the same in these three words? [Students reply that they all have d-i-c-t in them.] Right! Those letters spell the word root. Take one minute and talk to your partner about the meaning of each word and what you think that root might mean. [Students' responses indicate they have a sense of "talking."] Very good! When you dictate something, you are talking or speaking; you can 'dictate' a 'dictation,' a written record of what you've said. 'Dict' comes from a Latin word that means 'to say or speak.' That certainly makes sense in the words *dictate* and *dictation*, but what about *predict*? Remember what *pre-* means? [Student responds 'before.'] Okay! So, let's put *dict*, meaning 'to say or speak' together with *pre*, meaning 'before,' and we literally get the meaning 'to say or speak before.' Do you see how that works—when you predict something will happen, you are *saying* that it will happen before it occurs?"

The teacher then writes the following sentence on the board, containing the unfamiliar word *contradict*: *No matter what Eric says, his little brother always contradicts him.* She engages the students in a discussion of what they know about this word (the root *dict* and what it means) and how it might help them determine the meaning of the word in the context of the sentence and what they know about younger brothers and sisters. Through a number of such examples, the teacher helps students develop the understanding of how a knowledge of word roots can usually help them get an approximate meaning of an unfamiliar word. They can then check this approximate meaning in the context of the sentence, paragraph, or even entire text to determine if it makes sense.

The following example illustrates how a teacher walks students through an exploration of *prefix assimilation*, or absorbed prefixes. This feature of spelling has wide applicability and is remarkably consistent but is conceptually more advanced, depending upon an awareness of and familiarity with more advanced derivational morphological relationships:

The teacher asks the students if they've ever wondered why the prefix *in-* winds up being spelled so many different ways; when they look it up in the dictionary they find that it is also spelled *il-, im-,* and *ir-*. "What's going on here?" The teacher continues by discussing the word *immobile* and its meaning with the students, telling them the word was chosen because a number of them have spelled it and similar words with only one *m*.

"In the dictionary, we see that *immobile* is made up of the prefix *in-* and the word *mobile*—literally, 'not mobile.' Why did it change? Why don't we still have the word *inmobile*?

"Try saying the word *inmobile*. Now say *immobile*. Which word is easier to pronounce? Now think about it: Our tongue and lips have to move around more in order to pronounce *inmobile*. With *immobile*, however, there's less movement going on. Now try it with *immortal*. That's easier to say than *inmortal*, right? And for the same reason—it's easier to pronounce than *inmortal*.

"Let's try another one. If something is 'not legible,' do we say it is 'inlegible'? No, we say it is 'illegible' instead. How about if someone is 'not responsible'; do we say they are 'inresponsible'? Right! We say 'irresponsible' instead. Why? Right, because it's easier!

"Let's look at the words *immobile*, *illegible*, and *irresponsible*. In each word, the spelling of the prefix changed from *in-*. Why did *in-* change to *im-* in *immobile*? Why did it change to *il-* in *illegible*? Why did it change to *ir-* in *irresponsible*? [The teacher gets the students talking about this; it may be helpful to write additional examples such as *illegal* and *irreversible* for students to consider.] The teacher leads the students to the realization that the spelling of the *n* in *in-* changed to match the spelling at the beginning of the base word.

"This process began a long time ago. We say that the sound of the *n* was 'absorbed' into the sound at the beginning of the word the prefix was added onto. So, when *in-* is spelled *im-*, *il-*, or *ir-*, we say it has been 'absorbed.' Let's try this out: How would you spell the word that means 'not measurable'? 'Not logical'? 'Not rational'?"

Later, after students have explored other prefixes and how they have been "absorbed" into base words (e.g. *ad-* + *count* = *account*; *ad-* + *locate* = *allocate*; *con-* + *respond* = *correspond*), the teacher will explore what happens when the prefixes are added to word roots, for example, *ad-* + *tract* = *attract* and *con-* + *mit* = *commit*. In each case, it is important to talk explicitly about how the meaning of the word parts—base word or word root and prefix—combine to result in the meaning of the word. For example, "What happens when you are *attracted* to someone? The word *attracted* contains the root *tract*, meaning 'draw or pull,' and the absorbed prefix *at-* was originally *ad-*, meaning 'to or toward.' So, when you are *attracted* to someone you are 'pulled toward' them!"

Student Exploration

When teachers are helping students develop an inquisitive attitude toward words and their structure, students are motivated to compare and contrast words, looking for patterns that apply to larger families of words. *Word sort* activities, in which words are categorized according to sound, spelling, and meaning criteria (Bear et al., 2004; Ganske, 2000), are particularly effective. Teachers may establish categories according to which students sort words, and students may establish their own criteria (Bear et al., 2004; Templeton, 2002). For example, students may sort words according to common word roots, type of sound/spelling alternation pattern, or other conceptual categories. Once students become aware of and understand how *absorbed prefixes* work, for example, they often become intrigued in keeping lists of words with assimilated prefixes (the example above of *ad-* results in a list including *appear, aggression,* and *accord*). Students may also be encouraged to set up and maintain *word study notebooks* (Bear et al., 2000), in which new words they encounter in their reading are entered along with the sentence in which they occurred, appropriate dictionary definition, and any related words that occur to the student that share structural features with the target word.

CONCLUSION

As this chapter has suggested, there is now better understanding of how the relationship between spelling and vocabulary may be more systematically addressed. There is, of course, a need for sustained longitudinal research investigating the effects of the type of integrated spelling and vocabulary approach advanced in this chapter, but the argument may be made that the convergence of research discussed in this chapter may have reached a critical threshold, strongly suggesting the promise of such an approach. Moreover, this approach should be part of an overall instructional context for vocabulary development that emphasizes sensitivity to words such as that described, for example, in Beck, McKeown, and Kucan (2002) and Graves and Watts-Taffe (2002). There now exists the potential for considerably more students to develop that excitement, curiosity, and inquisitiveness about words that characterize the true wordsmith—with payoffs not only in better spelling and vocabulary knowledge but, because of that knowledge, perhaps more efficient and insightful reading and writing as well.

REFERENCES

Anglin, J. M. (1993). Vocabulary development: A morphological analysis. *Monographs of the Society for Research in Child Development, 58*(10, Serial No. 238).
Aronoff, M. (1994). Morphology. In A. C. Purves, L. Papa, & S. Jordan (Eds.), *Encyclopedia of English studies and language arts* (Vol. 2, pp. 820–821). New York: Scholastic.
Baumann, J. F., Kame'enui, E. J., & Ash, G. E. (2003). Research on vocabulary instruction: Voltaire redux. In J. Flood, D. Lapp, J. R. Squire, & J. M. Jensen (Eds.), *Handbook of research on teaching the English language arts* (2nd ed., pp. 752–785). Mahwah, NJ: Erlbaum.
Bear, D., Invernizzi, M., Templeton, S., & Johnston, F. (2000). *Words their way: Word study for phonics, spelling, and vocabulary development* (2nd ed.). Upper Saddle River, NJ: Merrill/Prentice-Hall.
Bear, D., Invernizzi, M., Templeton, S., & Johnston, F. (2004). *Words their way:*

Word study for phonics, spelling, and vocabulary development (3rd Ed.). Upper Saddle River, NJ: Merrill/Prentice-Hall.

Bear, D. R., Templeton, S., & Warner, M. (1991). The development of a qualitative inventory of higher levels of orthographic knowledge. In J. Zutell & S. McCormick (Eds.), *Learner factors/teacher factors: Issues in literacy research and instruction* (Fortieth yearbook of the National Reading Conference; pp. 105–110). Chicago, IL: National Reading Conference.

Beck, I. L., McKeown, M. G., & Kucan, L. (2002). *Bringing words to life: Robust vocabulary instruction.* New York: Guilford Press.

Carlisle, J. F. (1988). Knowledge of derivational morphology and spelling ability in fourth, sixth, and eighth graders. *Applied Psycholinguistics, 9,* 247–266.

Chomsky, C. (1970). Reading, writing, and phonology. *Harvard Educational Review, 40,* 287–309.

Corson, D. (1997). The learning and use of academic English words. *Language Learning, 47,* 671–718.

Crutchfield, R. (1997). *English vocabulary quick reference: A comprehensive dictionary arranged by word roots.* Leesburg, VA: LexaDyne.

Cummings, D. W. (1988). *American English spelling.* Baltimore: Johns Hopkins University Press.

Dale, E., O'Rourke, J., & Bamman, H. (1971). *Techniques of teaching vocabulary.* Palo Alto, CA: Field Educational Enterprises.

Derwing, B. L., Smith, M. L., & Wiebe, G. E. (1995). On the role of spelling in morpheme recognition: Experimental studies with children and adults. In L. B. Feldman (Ed.), *Morphological aspects of language processing* (pp. 3–27). Hillsdale, NJ: Erlbaum.

Ehri, L. C. (1997). Learning to read and learning to spell are one and the same, almost. In C. A. Perfetti, L. Rieben, & M. Fayol (Eds.), *Learning to spell: Research, theory, and practice across languages* (pp. 237–269). Mahwah, NJ: Erlbaum.

Fresch, M., & Wheaton, A. (2002). *Teaching and assessing spelling.* New York: Scholastic.

Fowler, A. E., & Liberman, I. Y (1995). The role of phonology and orthography in morphological awareness. In L. B. Feldman (Ed.), *Morphological aspects of language processing* (pp. 157–188). Hillsdale, NJ: Erlbaum.

Ganske, K. (1999). The Developmental Spelling Analysis: A measure of orthographic knowledge. *Educational Assessment, 6,* 41–70.

Ganske, K. (2000). *Word journeys: Assessment-guided phonics, spelling, and vocabulary instruction.* New York: Guilford Press.

Gill, J. T. (1992). The relationship between word recognition and spelling. In S. Templeton & D. R. Bear (Eds.), *Development of orthographic knowledge and the foundations of literacy: A memorial Festschrift for Edmund H. Henderson* (pp. 79–104). Hillsdale, NJ: Erlbaum.

Graves, M. F., & Watts-Taffe, S. M. (2002). The place of word consciousness in a research-based vocabulary program. In A. E. Farstrup & S. J. Samuels (Eds.), *What research has to say about reading instruction* (3rd ed., pp. 140–165). Newark, DE: International Reading Association.

Hanna, P. R., Hanna, J. S., Hodges, R. E., & Rudorf, H. (1966). Phoneme–grapheme correspondences as cues to spelling improvement. Washington, DC: United States Office of Education Cooperative Research.

Henry, M. K. (1989). Children's word structure knowledge: Implications for decoding and spelling instruction. *Reading and writing, 1,* 135–152.

Leong, C. K. (2000). Rapid processing of base and derived forms of words and grades 4, 5 and 6 children's spelling. *Reading and Writing: An Interdisciplinary Journal, 12,* 277–302.

Mahony, D., Singson, M., & Mann, V. (2000). Reading ability and sensitivity to morphological relations. *Reading and Writing: An Interdisciplinary Journal, 12,* 191–218.

Masterson, J. J., Apel, K., & Wasowicz, J. (2002). *SPELL: Spelling performance evaluation for language and literacy.* Evanston, IL: Learning by Design.

Morris, D., Blanton, L., Blanton, W. E., Nowacek, J., & Perney, J. (1995). Teaching low-achieving spellers at their "instructional level. *Elementary School Journal, 96,* 163–178.

Morris, D., Blanton, L., Blanton, W., & Perney, J. (1995). Spelling instruction and achievement in six classrooms. *Elementary School Journal, 96,* 145–162.

Morris, D., Nelson, L., & Perney, J. (1986). Exploring the concept of "spelling instructional level" through the analysis of error-types. *Elementary School Journal, 87,* 181–200.

Nagy, W., & Anderson, R. C. (1984). How many words are there in printed school English? *Reading Research Quarterly, 19,* 304–330.

Perfetti, C. A. (1997). The psycholinguistics of spelling and reading. In C. A. Perfetti, L. Rieben, & M. Fayol (Eds.), *Learning to spell: Research, theory, and practice across languages* (pp. 21–38). Mahwah, NJ: Erlbaum.

Perfetti, C. A., Rieben, L., & Fayol, M. (Eds.) (1997). *Learning to spell: Research, theory, and practice across languages.* Mahwah, NJ: Erlbaum.

Reuckl, J. G., & Raveh, M. (1999). The influence of morphological regularities on the dynamics of a connectionist model. *Brain and Language, 68,* 110–117.

Schlagal, R. (1992). Patterns of orthographic development into the intermediate grades. In S. Templeton & D. R. Bear (Eds.), *Development of orthographic knowledge and the foundations of literacy: A memorial Festschrift for Edmund H. Henderson* (pp. 31–52). Hillsdale, NJ: Erlbaum.

Smith, M. L. (1998). *Sense and sensitivity: An investigation into fifth-grade children's knowledge of English derivational morphology and its relationship to vocabulary and reading ability.* Unpublished doctoral dissertation. Cambridge, MA: Harvard University.

Templeton, S. (1979). Spelling first, sound later: The relationship between orthography and higher order phonological knowledge in older students. *Research in the Teaching of English, 13,* 255–264.

Templeton, S. (1983). Using the spelling–meaning connection to develop word knowledge in older students. *Journal of Reading, 27,* 8–14.

Templeton, S. (1989). Tacit and explicit knowledge of derivational morphology: Foundations for a unified approach to spelling and vocabulary development in the intermediate grades and beyond. *Reading Psychology, 10,* 233–253.

Templeton, S. (1991). Teaching and learning the English spelling system: Reconceptualizing method and purpose. *Elementary School Journal, 92,* 183–199.

Templeton, S. (1992). Theory, nature, and pedagogy of higher-order orthographic development in older students. In S. Templeton & D. R. Bear (Eds.) *Development of orthographic knowledge and the foundations of literacy: A memorial Festschrift for Edmund H. Henderson* (pp. 253–277). Hillsdale, NJ: Erlbaum.

Templeton, S. (1997). *Teaching the integrated language arts* (2nd ed.). Boston: Houghton Mifflin.

Templeton, S. (2002). Effective spelling instruction in the middle grades: It's a lot more than memorization. *Voices from the Middle, 9,* 8–14.

Templeton, S. (2003a). Spelling. In J. Flood, D. Lapp, J. R. Squire, & J. M. Jensen (Eds.), *Handbook of research on teaching the English language arts* (2nd ed., pp. 738–751). Mahwah, NJ: Erlbaum.

Templeton, S. (2003b). Spelling instruction. In J. Guthrie (senior editor), *Encyclopedia of Education* (2nd ed., pp. 2302–2305). New York: Macmillan.

Templeton, S., & Bear, D. R. (Eds.) (1992). *Development of orthographic knowledge and the foundations of literacy: A memorial Festschrift for Edmund H. Henderson.* Hillsdale, NJ: Erlbaum.

Templeton, S., & Morris, D. (2000). Spelling. In M. Kamil, P. Mosenthal, P. D. Pearson, & R. Barr (Eds.). *Handbook of reading research* (Vol. 3, pp. 525–543). Mahwah, NJ: Erlbaum.

Templeton, S., & Scarborough-Franks, L. (1985). The spelling's the thing: Older students' knowledge of derivational morphology in phonology and orthography. *Applied Psycholinguistics, 6,* 371–189.

Venezky, R. L. (1999). *The American way of spelling: The structure and origins of American English orthography.* New York: Guilford Press.

9

Word Study
for Vocabulary Development
in the Early Stages
of Literacy Learning
Ecological Perspectives and Learning English

DONALD R. BEAR
LORI HELMAN

The selection of word study activities to teach phonics, vocabulary, and spelling is effective when the activities match students' instructional levels. This chapter presents a series of word study activities for emergent, beginning, and transitional learners that is based on the social and perceptual ecologies of students' language experiences and their growing knowledge of written language. Word study activities such as concept sorts with pictures and words are highlighted to demonstrate how students at various literacy levels and from a variety of language backgrounds acquire new vocabulary in the classroom.

What does it take to help students acquire a reading and writing vocabulary? One student, Eric, is confused when he gets to the word *promise* in his reading because he doesn't know what that means. Katie gets stuck because she reads mostly grade-level materials that are too hard for her, missing on average about 15 words per every 100. Alex spells using a one-sound, one-letter principle, yet his weekly spelling list features long vowel patterns and homophone pairs he does not know. Rosa decodes her text but cannot understand its meaning. Mismatches abound in early literacy instruction, and these disparities work against the beginning reader's vocabulary development.

The ongoing instructional decisions educators make are key to students' literacy development. Janusz Korczak helps us consider the delicate balance between valuing what students bring to our literacy classrooms and supporting their new learning: "A child is a butterfly over the seething whirlpool of life. How can one give it steadiness without weighing down its flight; how can it be tempered without tying its wings?" (Kulawiec, 1989, p. 181).

Students come to school to join in the stream of literacy development. For educators to provide instruction that supports and steadies students' vocabulary development, several questions must be answered. We discuss these questions briefly here and elaborate throughout the chapter.

- *What are students' oral and written vocabularies?* Students' knowledge of vocabulary is reciprocal between spoken and written forms of language.
- *What oral language resources do students bring to literacy?* Students' spoken knowledge of language is created through oral interactions, and it is in the oral arena that they acquire their foundational vocabularies.
- *What written language resources do students bring to oral language development?* Students' knowledge of written language includes their knowledge of how words and characters are spelled, their orthographic knowledge.
- *What are students' exposure to and experiences in reading and writing?* Students' exposure and experiences frame their understandings about written language and their roles as learners.
- *What do students read accurately and automatically?* When students read and write words or characters easily, they have greater resources to acquire a meaning vocabulary. As students understand more complex orthographic features, their strategies to learn vocabulary expand.
- *How does literacy support vocabulary development?* Students' orthographic knowledge fosters understandings and generalizations about language systems, including vocabulary, syntax, and phonology.

Vocabulary and literacy growth are contextualized in students' social and psychological ecologies. With many English language learners acquiring oral and written languages at the same time, it is essential to understand the unique language qualities and literacy experiences that influence their vocabulary growth. Our discussion of literacy is framed by the stages of development described by Edmund Henderson and his students (Henderson, 1990; Templeton & Bear, 1992; Templeton & Morris, 2000) and ecological models of social and perceptual learning (Bronfenbrenner & Evans, 2000; Gibson, 1979). The goal of this chapter is to help educators choose vocabulary activities that build on school-aged students' language experiences and their growing perceptions of written language. By matching learners to appropriate word study activities, teachers encourage students to join the stream of literacy learning and not get swept under in a "whirlpool" of mismatches between what is taught and what they are able to learn.

THE SYNCHRONY OF LITERACY LEARNING

In written language development, we have observed a synchrony in literacy learning that is highly related to students' *orthographic knowledge*, the knowledge they have of how words are spelled (Bear, Invernizzi, Templeton, & Johnston, 2004; Ehri, 1998; Perfetti, 1997). Students' orthographic knowledge is like an engine that drives literacy development, particularly in the early periods of literacy development. During this time, we focus on word study instruction for we know that when word recognition and spelling are quick and easy, fluent reading, writing, and thinking about the material are possible. The synchrony of development means that word study instruction is reciprocal: Instruction in reading improves writing and spelling. Phonics, spelling, and vocabulary instruction are interrelated and support one another, as illustrated in Figure 9.1.

Given the central role that orthographic knowledge plays in literacy learning, the three layers of the orthography are presented across the top of the figure as the *sound/alphabet*, *pattern*, and *meaning* layers. Underneath the layers of the orthography you can see the first three of the five stages of reading and spelling (Bear & Templeton, 2000). Students' progress through these three layers and stages has been observed in a variety of languages (Henderson, 1992; Shen & Bear, 2000).

In this chapter, we discuss the layers of orthographies, the early stages of literacy development, and related word study activities with an emphasis on vocabulary learning. Templeton (Chapter 8, this volume) explores vocabulary learning among upper-level students in the most advanced two stages. We begin by examining ecological models of learning that allow us to explore the questions posed at the beginning of this chapter. We then move on to discuss the types of word study activities that make sense to students who come into our classrooms with varying language backgrounds.

Layers of the Orthography: Sound/Alphabet → Pattern → Meaning
Emergent / Emergent
Pre-K to middle of first grade
    Concept sorts with vocabulary focus
    Phonemic awareness
    Language play for rhythm, rhyme, and alliteration
    Alphabet or character recognition
    Tracking (concept of word)

   Beginning/Letter Name–alphabetic
   Kindergarten to middle of second grade
       Beginning and final consonants, consonant digraphs, and blends
       Develop word banks of sight words from rereading familiar texts
       Explore new vocabulary from readings
       Short-vowel families, short vowel sound similarities
       Examine the CVC (consonant–vowel–consonant) pattern across vowels

   Transitional/Within-word pattern
   First grade to middle of fourth grade
       Compare and contrast vowel patterns
       Homophones and homographs for vocabulary
       Concept sorts in content areas
       Integration of vocabulary, grammar, and spelling
       Students refer to dictionaries to clarify meaning

FIGURE 9.1. Stages of reading, writing, and spelling; grade ranges and types of word study activities.

ECOLOGICAL MODELS OF LEARNING

The study of orthographic knowledge and development is enhanced by an ecological perspective because it brings students' experiences from the social ecology (Bronfenbrenner & Evans, 2000) of oral and written languages to the analysis of students' psychological ecology (Gibson, 1979). Students' psychological ecology is composed of *orthographic invariants*, their unconscious or tacit understandings of how words are spelled. This tacit knowledge is the sign of well-learned behaviors and paves the way for new learning opportunities. The social ecology as applied to literacy is a series of language and literacy experiences that work in relationship to students' knowledge of orthographic invariants. Figure 9.2 illustrates the relationship between language exposure and experience and the stages of literacy development. Five social qualities of students' instructional exposure can predict change and growth in literacy: *duration, frequency, interruption, timing of interaction*, and *intensity of the experience*. Instruction is most effective when it is specific to the needs of the person, "the nature of the immediate, 'face-to-face' environmental *context*" (Bronfenbrenner & Evans, 2000, p. 119).

In Figure 9.2, literacy development is on the *x*-axis. Given the tacit and automatic way word recognition functions, learning about the orthography is described as a procedural language activity that follows the social ecological principle that development occurs "through processes of progressively more complex reciprocal interaction" (Bronfenbrenner & Evans, 2000, p. 117). The complexity in the development of orthographic knowledge is seen in the progression of the three overlapping layers: sound/alphabet, pattern, and meaning. With sufficient participation in literacy activities, invariants in the orthography are internalized at a tacit level. It can be seen for the English language learner described in Figure 9.2 that oral language development in the first language precedes written language development. The student has more exposure and experience in the first oral than in the second oral language, and this student has had greater exposure to written materials in the second language than in the first. This is true for many students who learn the meanings of words at the same time they are learning to read the words.

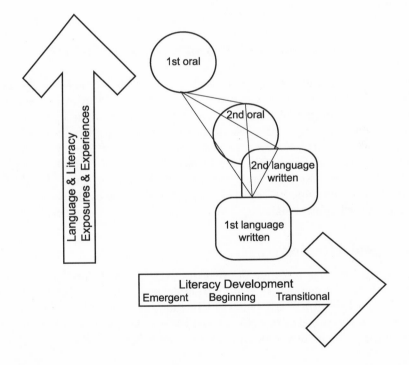

FIGURE 9.2. Oral and written language exposures and experiences, and the literacy development of a second-language learner.

Another scenario is the student who has had greater exposure to writing in the first language. This student knows more about the invariants common to both written languages, and, compared to the student represented in Figure 9.2, the boxes for both written languages would shift to the right, and the box for the first written language would be ahead of the second written language.

As was noted earlier, orthographic knowledge is central to learning written words and enriches vocabulary learning from text. Students learning another language can use their orthographic knowledge to support their vocabulary learning at the same time they acquire basic literacy skills and basic oral language skills. Many perceptual invariants occur across writing systems and can facilitate the learning of a new language. Thus, developing orthographic knowledge through word study activities supports vocabulary, phonics, and spelling growth.

In the following section, the invariants that students learn when they are in particular stages of literacy development are presented. The invariants of *directionality, articulation, beginning–end–middle,* and *abstraction of patterns* in orthographies are discussed along the developmental continuum.

DEVELOPMENTAL WORD STUDY ACTIVITIES

Each stage of literacy development is characterized by an increasingly complex understanding of how words are constructed. Students internalize invariants about the orthography at each stage and then build on this knowledge to make greater sense of the novel structures they see when they read. In this section, we describe the characteristics of literacy learners at each developmental stage, share examples of their reading and writing behaviors, and present word study activities that match learners' needs. The consideration of students' social and perceptual ecologies shows us specific practices for English language learners at these three levels of development.

Emergent Literacy

The emergent stage is a time of great discovery about print. The emergent learner begins to distinguish writing from drawing and book language from regular conversation. Early behaviors include pretend reading of books using memorized patterns or made-up stories and the use of scribbles or various shapes to write down ideas. Learners internalize several key concepts:

1. Writing is different from picture drawing.
2. The letters of the alphabet have characteristic shapes.

3. We write from left to right in English.
4. The language of books often has its own vocabulary and syntactic rhythm.

As children progress through the emergent stage, they refine their scribbles to become more letter-like in form. Their writing often begins to take on a logographic form, with a letter or group of letters pictorially representing a word. By the end of the emergent stage, most students have memorized several sight words. These words are a resource pool to begin to make letter–sound connections. Words are written by connecting the most salient sound (typically the beginning sound) with a related letter.

During the emergent stage, learners demonstrate a tacit awareness of the distinctive sounds in their oral languages. Early emergent learners notice phonological, or sound, properties of words in addition to their use and meaning. The phonological awareness abilities of rhyming, hearing beginning and ending sounds in words and, later, full segmentation are important skills that begin to develop at this time. Emergent learners recognize that words can be broken into a series of sounds and that these sounds can be represented by letters of the alphabet. This understanding develops in conjunction with the acquisition of concept of word, the ability to point accurately to a familiar text, and thus make the one-to-one connection between written and spoken words or characters (Morris, 1993).

Emergent Literacy Activities

The kinds of vocabulary and word study activities that are critical for emergent readers include listening to and engaging with the language of books; developing oral language and categorization skills through sorting activities and accompanying conversations; hearing the rhythm and rhyme of language through stories, poems, and chants; working with the sounds of oral language through guided phonemic awareness activities; and learning about the alphabet.

Hearing the language of books and having opportunities to engage in conversations that feature these words expand students' oral vocabularies and background knowledge. Teachers choose engaging and not-too-difficult narrative and expository texts, check periodically for comprehension by asking students to talk about what they heard, make predictions about what they will hear next, and discuss and clarify key vocabulary, all while maintaining the flow of the story. In read-alouds, constructive questioning leads to fruitful discussions. Students add new words to their oral vocabularies when they listen to books read aloud as long as they are not trying to learn too many vocabulary words at once. Students also internalize vocabulary orally when they use the language of books in classroom activities such as retelling stories, acting out key events in creative dramatics, and discussing ideas and connections to their world.

Sorting by concepts is a powerful platform for students to learn word meanings. In concept sorts, students take collections of objects or pictures and group them according to like attributes. We may sort as a whole class, such as when we sort shoes by various features; we may sort with a small group of students; or we may guide students as they sort individually or with partners in a parallel fashion. As the process of sorting is introduced, we demonstrate and describe the reason we are categorizing the objects as we go (Nielsen-Dunn, 2002). We begin by sorting dualistically—those that belong to a category and those that do not. For instance, in a food picture sort, we may classify pictures into those items that students have eaten and those that they have not. Later these same pictures may be sorted into the more complex categories of vegetables, meats, breads, and so forth.

Concept sorts provide the content to which students can attach new oral vocabulary. A previously unknown food such as *asparagus* can be learned in a concept sort where there is meaningful context with visual support. We advance students' vocabularies and verbal reasoning by talking about the way they sort. This, in turn, gets them ready for sorting the same pictures by sound qualities.

Rhythm, rhyme, and alliteration in text support emergent learners by drawing children's attention to common words and sounds. For example, in his story *Jamberry*, Bruce Degen (1983) creatively uses the word *berry* to encourage students to hear and experience the flow of language patterns. Students listen to and repeat rhythmic and playful text such as "Quickberry! Quackberry! Pick me a blackberry!" The rhythm and rhyme of a passage can also carry the student into new word learning. In the traditional nursery rhyme "*Jack and Jill went up the hill to fetch a pail of water. Jack fell down and broke his crown, and Jill came tumbling after*" the word *crown* is often chanted before its meaning is understood. Students gain new vocabulary as the rhyme's meaning is explored through discussions of pictures and dramatizations. Rhythmic text also helps students as they begin to match oral to written vocabulary.

Emergent learners develop an awareness of common sound properties of words—rhyming chunks, beginning sounds, and how many sounds are in a word. Guided in-class activities not only support a budding phonemic awareness, they provide an opportunity to hear, work with, and discuss a variety of new words. For example, if students are asked to identify which words sound the same at the beginning among *rose*, *rabbit*, and *house*, we create an opportunity to hear, speak, and define these words in a classroom setting.

Learning about letters is critical in leading emergent readers to the alphabetic principle. Knowledge of the letters of the alphabet provides emergent learners with the beginning symbols they use to understand and express themselves in the world of print (Johnston, Invernizzi, & Juel, 1998). Knowing the beginning sounds of words provides early learners with a scaffold to categorize and remember sight words. Listening to alphabet books and brainstorming words that begin with each letter of the alphabet also provide a surge of new vocabulary words into the burgeoning academic discourse of emergent learners. Many opportunities to reread familiar text and write at their developmental level provide a contextual application of the alphabetic principle.

Emergent Activities for English Language Learners

If a student has literacy skills in a home language, certain invariants can be easily transferred while others may need to be relearned for the new language. For example, a Russian speaker and middle to late emergent reader will understand that the text is to be read from left to right and will develop knowledge about how letters represent sounds in the words we say. Thus, a beginning level of phonemic awareness transfers to English from the home language. Some of the specific graphemes will need to be relearned in the English orthographic system, however, because they are shaped distinctly or represent different sounds than those used in Russian. For example, the /p/ sound is represented by P in English and П in Russian.

For students approaching English reading and writing tasks without literacy in their primary language, several areas will provide additional challenge. Developing phonemic awareness in English is more difficult for second-language learners who do not have an extensive oral language vocabulary in the new language. Phonemic awareness is built on numerous experiences hearing and speaking the words in a language. *Bed, ball, boy,* and *bag* are perceived to share the same beginning sound after they have been heard in conversation and their articulatory features have been experienced in practice. Second-language learners have more limited experiences hearing, saying, and playing with the phonological qualities of the oral vocabulary of English. Earlier we discussed the social ecology of an English learner who is acquiring a written and oral vocabulary simultaneously. For emergent learners in this situation, it will be critical to explicitly teach words orally, so that their articulatory features can be experienced physically.

Students who are learning English can conceptually sort a group of objects into a variety of groups without knowing all of their names. The sort is a way for students to attach labels to the pictures or objects, thus developing an oral vocabulary. This bank of oral vocabulary will, in turn, be material students use to classify words by common beginning sounds. Sound sorts would be meaningless, however, if the pictures could not be named. Oral vocabulary needs to be at least one step ahead of the content of literacy activities, even if that means the vocabulary needed is being learned moments before the picture sort. Teachers need to assess students' oral language knowledge to see what pictures need to be taught before a sort.

Equally critical for emergent learners from other language backgrounds are opportunities to learn the English alphabet and connect the letters to new words that are being acquired orally. Sound boards that show the letter–sound correspondences all on one page with explicit and concrete picture cues are especially supportive of English learners (Bear et al., 2004). Simple alphabet books that we use in teaching the alphabet simultaneously teach useful vocabulary. Building an alphabet with some of the vocabulary from their home language—including names of important people in their school and home lives and meaningful labels in their world—gives students the raw material to perceive oral and written invariants in the new language.

Beginning Literacy

Learners in the beginning stage of literacy apply their understandings of letter–sound correspondences to words they read and write, and their bank of automatically retrievable sight words grows dramatically. A number of key perceptual invariants are formed during this time when students focus on salient sound–symbol relationships.

One key perceptual invariant is the reliance on articulation, the way sounds are made in the mouth, when they spell and read using sound–symbol relationships; this is true across written languages including Chinese and Spanish (Bear, Templeton, Helman, & Baren, 2003; Shen & Bear, 2000). For example, students misspell the *dr* in *drive* with JR because both are articulated in a similar fashion (Read, 1971), and the /jr/ is an easier sound to make and spell. In the area of vowels, students spell short vowels with the letter whose name is closest to the point of articulation; for example, students at this stage often spell short *i* sounds with an *e* because the letter name *e* feels closest to the short *i*.

Another invariant acquired by beginning readers is the perceptual attention to the beginning, end, and then the middle of words and possibly to characters in nonalphabetic scripts. In the late emergent and early beginning stages, students spell and sound out the salient features, and in English this is often the first sound. The next most salient feature in English is usually the ending sound. By the middle of this stage, readers acquire a full phonemic representation and spell nearly every sound in words. Thus, this perceptual invariant is observed in the way sight words are learned. In text, students identify and acquire sight words at the beginning and end of easy and familiar sentences and two-phrase lines.

Beginning Literacy Activities

Texts for beginning readers contain repeated phrases, sight words, a controlled vocabulary, and words that allow students to use phonic understandings they have already made (Brown, 1999). Through numerous rereadings of instructional level materials, students enlarge their sight vocabularies. For the letter-name alphabetic speller, writing time is a deliberate and often time-consuming process of sounding out words and attaching related letters. Thus, each writing period becomes a phonemic-segmentation event as well (Vernon & Ferreiro, 1999).

The words students sort are nearly always words that they know the meaning of and words that they can read. Word study activities begin with contrasts of beginning consonants, consonant digraphs, and easy blends. Students go on to make observations about rhyming, onset and rime, and word families (e.g., *cat*, *mad*, *fan*) in picture and word sorts. In picture sorts, they compare word families and compare sounds across vowels.

Sight words are acquired slowly and steadily at first. For word study, sight words are collected from familiar texts and written on 1" × 2" cards and tracked carefully, usually over 2–3 months. By this time, students' word banks have 50 words in them, and students use the word banks to hunt for words that begin, end, or sound the same in the middle. With 100–150 sight words, word banks are discontinued, and students use teacher-made sorts, as illustrated in Figure 9.3 (Bear, Invernizzi, Templeton, & Johnston, 2001). This is now possible because we can predict with good accuracy what words students can read. Students study each short vowel and begin the study of the pattern layer with the primary short vowel pattern in English, the consonant–vowel–consonant (CVC) pattern words. Students often go on word hunts in familiar texts to collect words that follow this pattern.

Reading enlarges students' vocabularies during this stage when they sound out short vowels in English and encounter words they may not know. Additionally, these words may not be easily recognizable by their pictures—for example, the pictures of the *mat* and *van* in Figure 9.3. Words that are highly decodable (e.g., *fin*, *mug*, *peg*, and *bun*) may not be known. We notice differences in the breadth and depth of students' vocabularies that may not have been clear before. Preteaching the pictures and the words is necessary for many students, and not just English language learners. We tie the new vocabulary to an experience or chant, for example, experience with *pegs* in a coat closet, *pegs* in games, *pegs* in holding tools in the custodian's office, *pegs* in a rhyme or song (e.g., "pegs for you and me").

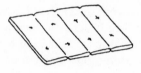

mat cat
bat hat

pan fan can
man van

FIGURE 9.3. Word family *-at* and *-an* picture and word sort.

Beginning Literacy Activities for English Language Learners

A primary concern for English language learners is the relationship between the sounds of their home language and those of English. Learning a new oral vocabulary requires the learner to be understood and to understand the sounds of English. Where common phonemes and phoneme positioning exist, hearing and saying specific sounds should not be a problem. Where there are differences between the home language and English, however, students may have difficulty learning the sound–symbol code for sounds that are not distinctive. For instance, students from Spanish-speaking backgrounds may have difficulty with the sounds at the beginning of the following words: *den, juice, rope, van, zipper, shell, thick,* and *treasure.* These sounds do not exist in Spanish. English language learners at the beginning stage of reading may have difficulty hearing and saying the short vowel sounds because these sounds are not present in many other languages, yet they represent the most common syllable pattern in English. Students who do not discern the difference between vowel sounds (such as between *pig* and *peg*) may take more time to learn the phonic regularities of English. Confusions between Spanish and English are commonly observed, as in the substitution of the flapped *r* of Spanish for the /d/ in English, for example, the spelling of BER for *bed.* The difficult-to-hear sound of /sh/ for Spanish speakers is often spelled CH or simply C. And with the scarcity of words that begin with *w* in Spanish, students may hunt for words that mimic the glide sound /w/, such as the *u* followed by another vowel. For example, we assume that a student used her knowledge of the Spanish word *buen* to spell *when* as BUEN.

Attaching a letter to one of these sounds requires conscious oral attention and explicit teaching. In the same vein, many sounds do not position themselves in similar ways in different languages. In Spanish, few consonants are allowed to end a word, so it may be difficult for a Spanish-speaking student to accurately encode the final sounds in words such as *card, girl, chirp, gasp, most,* and *mask.* This example features a comparison between English and Spanish. Given the many languages students have in our classrooms, the more we know about their social ecologies the better we can assess the similarities and differences between students' home languages and English, and then provide specific instruction to help them see through differences and break the code.

Phonics and vocabulary instruction can use words from students' first languages as they transition to English. For example, when we study the /g/ sound we may use a word in Spanish, like *gato* (cat) because students may know just a few words in English that begin with the /g/ sound. In discussions of our sorts, students learn vocabulary from one another; English-only and English language learners both observe that *gato* in Spanish is *cat* in English. Word and picture sorts teach phonics and vocabulary simultaneously. Several instructional strategies support the English learner: the use of hands-on manipulatives; the socially interactive nature of the activities; the use of language and sharing of knowledge between proximal partners; and the orthographic learning that comes from discovering patterns in spoken and written words.

Vocabulary learning becomes more abstract during this stage, as when students' sight words feature function words such as *had* or *at*, two common words beginning readers acquire. Knowing that English learners need to practice the phonic patterns they are learning in connected text, how can teachers enhance the use of decodable or controlled-vocabulary materials? Once again, vocabulary development is key. We discuss and preview unknown words with English learners using visuals whenever possible. Books are reviewed to eliminate those containing idiosyncratic vocabulary not worthy of extended in-class learning time. Syntactic patterns are listened to and discussed, echo-read, and chanted until they take on a natural rhythm.

The language experience dictations of beginning readers provide valuable material for rereading, and the hands-on experiences that are the subject of the dictation provide context-rich opportunities to learn new vocabulary. This authentic form of creating reading material also provides us with an assessment of students' oral language resources. When students dictate their language experiences, oral language development works hand in hand with its written production. For students who are just learning English, bilingual readers that contain dictations written in both the home language and in English are very helpful. If we are not bilingual, these are created with the help of an aide, parent, or older student who can record the dictation in the student's first language.

Transitional Literacy

Transitional readers are like the Wright brothers of reading: They have just gotten off the ground; they do not have much altitude; they do not travel far; and it does not take much to bring them down. Transitional readers approach fluency and use some expression in their reading, and gradually during this stage they swap oral reading for silent (Bear & Templeton, 2000). Early transitional readers tackle easy chapter books, like books in the *Frog and Toad* series (e.g., Lobel, 1979), and by the end of this stage students read longer chapter books, such as the *Amber Brown* series (Danziger, 1997).

With increased reading speed, transitional readers cover more text with more complicated syntactic structures, which makes reading a more abundant source of vocabulary development. During this stage they learn the meaning of many single-syllable words from what they read. For example, words like *blip* or *twine* may be easy words to read, but they are unfamiliar words to many students. Context helps students to clarify the meaning of these and similar words.

Transitional readers examine the patterns in English, beginning with the spelling of long vowel patterns. This is when they begin to "use but confuse" (Invernizzi, Abouzeid, & Gill, 1994) the way long-vowel words are spelled, for example, NALE for *nail*, FLOUT or FLOTE for *float*. Instead of just a letter-by-letter analysis of words, students have the power in their orthographic knowledge to directly perceive most single-syllable words.

Transitional Activities

Word study activities begin with picture and word sorts that contrast long and short vowels, and then students study the common long-vowel patterns first with one vowel and then across vowels. This word study is followed by an examination of complex and ambiguous vowel patterns that include *r*, *l* and *g* influenced patterns. By the middle of this stage, students study difficult high-frequency words.

Toward the end of this stage, students examine homophones and homographs and how the meaning layer interacts with spelling patterns. Students enjoy making lists of homophones and pairing them, and you can see here how word study is integrated across reading, writing, and spelling. Consider the discussions of vocabulary and spelling when we study homophone pairs such as *threw/through*, *hear/here*, and *one/won*. To clarify the spelling we discuss the words in phrase and sentence contexts and focus on meaning and linguistic function, for example, *threw the ball/through the door*. Less frequent homophones such as *suite/sweet*, *peak/peek/pique*, and *fowl/foul* further enlarge the speaking and reading vocabularies of students. In addition, contractions such as *they're*, *it's*, and *let's* create homophones which are analyzed for meaning and grammatical function. In such cases, the spelling, vocabulary, and grammar studies become integrated for optimal student understanding.

In small groups, students create charts of words they have sorted and categorize them by pattern and meaning, and they display these charts around the room and add to them as a center activity. Students develop a thirst for dictionaries during this time as they search to clarify the meanings of homophones and homographs. They are challenged to understand what dictionaries say about these words that look or sound alike but have different meanings. In games such as *Homophone Rummy* (Bear et al., 2004), students cluster homophones, test out each word's meaning, and connect it to the appropriate spelling. These types of sorts, word hunts, and games begin to focus on the meaning layer of the orthography, where students learn about the way spelling reflects the meaning system (see Templeton, Chapter 8, this volume).

Concept sorts continue to play an important role in vocabulary development, for now students take the vocabulary from the content areas to deepen their conceptual knowledge. In content sorts, students sort words by attributes. Next, names are attached to summarize the attributes, and these are often key terms from the textbooks, usually the words in bold. Students research the text when a summary label for a category cannot be found. Finally, students write these labels on word cards and copy the sorts into their word study notebooks. An in-class follow-up activity is for students to create a bulletin board with the content vocabulary relating to the unit of study. For example, while studying *electricity*, a concept sort may involve those materials that conduct a charge versus those that don't. Students may sort words or pictures of water, metal, wood, glass, plastic, and so forth as conductors or nonconductors. If the name for an object such as *wire* is not known, then the students will need to research formally or informally to label it. A chart of materials with their labels is posted in the room to support vocabulary review and content knowledge understanding.

Transitional Literacy Activities for English Language Learners

English language learners in the transitional stage of reading are often who we think of when teachers ask the question: "Why is it that so many English language learners can read the words but do not comprehend?" This observation may arise from the apparent discrepancy between students' word knowledge and language comprehension. English language learners in this stage are often in the intermediate grades, and they have been around enough words in print to memorize many sight words. Compared to their vocabulary knowledge and comprehension, word recognition and spelling scores may be relatively strong. Thus, a multifaceted approach that focuses on word meanings and syntactical understanding, along with the development of word analysis skills, is critical for English language learners at this time.

Many activities already presented are not only important but become essential for learners from other language backgrounds. For English learners, homophones may need to be addressed at the most basic levels, for example, comparing the meaning and spelling of *to, two*, and *too*. Content area concept sorts and classroom charts and vocabulary word banks are critical supporting aids for learning the new content vocabulary presented in lessons. Concept sorts are a way for students to demonstrate their understanding of material even before they have mastered all of the new vocabulary words. These sorts are also an informal assessment that indicates what concepts and vocabulary are unclear to English language learners.

Another activity that helps to grow students' vocabularies and gives us information about their language resources is content area dictations (Bear

& Barone, 1998). After a teacher or classmate reads a part of a text to one to three students, or after students observe a presentation or participate in an experiment or field trip, the teacher types what students dictate as they recall what they remember from the reading or experience. Working with one to three students who have difficulty reading the text at an instructional level, the teacher or a classmate reads part of a text to students, perhaps from one bold heading to another. The students then dictate a summary of what they recall as the teacher types on a word processor. In this way, students use the content language right away, and they also have a piece of text that is readable and understandable. We find that after several rereadings, many of the new vocabulary terms become familiar to students, and this brings discussions, reading, and writing closer to students' instructional levels.

Consider carefully the role of pronunciation in word study activities. Word study lessons that examine the alphabet and pattern layers at times may turn into pronunciation lessons. When we find ourselves focusing too heavily on pronunciation, we make a mental note and turn back to the content of the word study lesson. Each has its place, but it is easy to think that we are conducting a reading lesson when, in fact, we are working on pronunciation, a speaking skill that does not have to be in place for students to learn the basic orthographic invariants they need to know. Students do not need to pronounce the words the way their teachers might, but rather they need to understand conceptually the consistency in sound and spelling across the short vowels, and then they will be ready for instruction on the long vowels. There are times when students' pronunciations result in confusions in meaning. Without letting pronunciation dominate a lesson, vocabulary instruction can show students that the way they say a word may have a different meaning to listeners. Likewise, words they may spell by the way they are pronounced may not have the meaning they had intended. Occasionally making these clarifications can be embarrassing, so we are tactful in pointing out students' unintended meanings.

Throughout transitional literacy we study students' social and perceptual ecologies to develop word study lessons that draw attention to features that are confusing. When we notice students' confusions—possibly based on the sound or pattern systems of their own first language—we create sorts that highlight and clarify the differences between the two languages.

FINAL THOUGHTS

The questions we asked about vocabulary learning at the beginning of this chapter are addressed when we contextualize learning in students' social and perceptual ecologies and literacy instruction is matched to these circumstances. It is in the ecological realm where we ask: How often are students in the stream of language and literacy? Strong literacy learning is created by the quality of the *exposure* students have; they require numerous experiences with comprehensible language and texts. If this exposure is minimal, then they will not have adequate experiences to learn the oral or written vocabulary they need. Literacy blocks and tutoring programs in the primary grades go a long way toward ensuring that there is adequate *duration* of instruction. Daily teaching ensures that there is adequate *frequency*. The depth of teachers' instructional practices ensures *intensity*. There are two other qualities of exposure to concentrate on: *consistency* of instruction over a long period of time and the *timing* of instruction. To address these two aspects, we ask: What do students know about words? We want to know their backgrounds relating to both the oral and written forms of language. It is only by answering this question that we discover how literacy can be used to support vocabulary learning.

Many word study activities to teach vocabulary have been presented here for the early stages of literacy learning. We have seen how the process of picture and word sorting by concepts requires students to use language to organize and explain their ideas and categories. The success of our teaching is based on students' exposure to specific vocabulary and orthographic structures at specific times in their development. The exact word study activities may be less important than making sure that there is the match between *what* and *when* we teach. Vocabulary instruction that builds on learners' oral and written word knowledge, that is integrated with how students perceive orthographic invariants, and that provides the necessary exposure steadies students as they move forward in the developmental stream of literacy.

ACKNOWLEDGMENTS

The research described in this chapter was supported in part by a grant under the Reading Excellence Act (REA) program, PR/Award Number S338A010001, administered by the Office of Elementary and Secondary Education, United States Department of Education. The contents of the report do not necessarily represent the position, policies, or endorsement of the Reading Excellence Act Program, Office of Elementary and Secondary Education, the United States Department of Education, or the federal government.

REFERENCES

Bear, D. R., & Barone, D. (1998). *Developing literacy: An integrated approach to assessment and instruction.* Boston: Houghton Mifflin.
Bear, D. R., Invernizzi, M., Templeton, S., & Johnston, F. (2001). *Words their way:*

An interactive resource [computer software]. Columbus, OH: Merrill/Prentice-Hall.

Bear, D. R., Invernizzi, M., Templeton, S., & Johnston, F. (2004). *Words their way: Phonics, spelling and vocabulary instruction, K–8* (3rd ed.). Columbus, OH: Merrill/Prentice-Hall.

Bear, D. R., Templeton, W. S., Helman, L. A., & Baren, T. (2003). Orthographic development and learning to read in different languages. In G. Garcia (Ed.), *English learners: Reaching the highest level of English literacy* (pp. 71–95). Newark, DE: International Reading Association.

Bear, D. R., & Templeton, S. (2000). Matching development and instruction. In N. Padak, T. Rasinski, J. Peck, B. W. Church, G. Fawcett, J. M. Hendershot, et al. (Eds.), *Distinguished Educators on Reading: Contributions that have shaped effective literacy instruction* (pp. 334–376). Newark, DL: International Reading Association.

Bronfenbrenner, U., & Evans, G. W. (2000). Developmental science in the 21st century: Emerging questions, theoretical models, research designs and empirical findings. *Social Development, 9,* 115–125.

Brown, K. J. (1999). What kind of text—for whom and when? Textual scaffolding for beginning readers. *The Reading Teacher, 53,* 292–307.

Danziger, P. (1997). *Amber Brown Boxed Set.* New York: Scholastic.

Degen, B. (1983). *Jamberry.* New York: Harper & Row.

Ehri, L. C. (1998). Grapheme–phoneme knowledge is essential for learning to read words in English. In J. L. Metsala & L. C. Ehri (Eds.), *Word recognition in beginning literacy* (pp. 3–40). Mahwah, NJ: Erlbaum.

Gibson, J. (1979). *The ecological approach to visual perception.* Boston: Houghton Mifflin.

Henderson, E. H. (1990). *Teaching spelling* (2nd ed.). Boston: Houghton Mifflin.

Henderson, E. H. (1992). The interface of lexical competence and knowledge of written words. In S. Templeton & D. Bear (Eds.), *Development of orthographic knowledge and the foundations of literacy: A memorial Festschrift for Edmund H. Henderson* (pp. 1–30). Hillsdale, NJ: Erlbaum.

Invernizzi, M., Abouzeid, M., & Gill, J. T. (1994). Using students' invented spelling as a guide for spelling instruction that emphasizes word study. *Elementary School Journal, 95,* 155–167.

Johnston, F. R., Invernizzi, M. A., & Juel, C. (1998). *Book Buddies: Guidelines for volunteer tutors of emergent and early readers.* New York: Guilford Press.

Kulawiec, E. (1989). "Teachers and Teaching: "Yanoosh Who-o-o?": On the Discovery of Greatness." *Harvard Educational Review, 59,* 362–366.

Lobel, A. (1979). *Frog and Toad Together.* New York: Harper Collins.

Morris, D. (1993). The relationship between children's concept of word in text and phoneme awareness in learning to read: A longitudinal study. *Research in the Teaching of English, 27,* 133–154.

Nielsen-Dunn, S. (2002). *Picture this! Picture sorting for alphabetics, phonemes, and phonics.* San Diego, CA: Teaching Resource Center.

Perfetti, C. A. (1997). The psycholinguistics of spelling and reading. In C. A. Perfetti, L. Rieben, & M. Fayol (Eds.), *Learning to spell: Research, theory and practice across languages* (pp. 21–38). Mahwah, NJ: Erlbaum.

Read, C. (1971). Preschool children's knowledge of English phonology. *Harvard Educational Review, 41,* 1–34.

Shen, H., & Bear, D. R. (2000). The development of orthographic skills in Chinese children. *Reading and Writing: An Interdisciplinary Journal, 13,* 197–236.

Templeton, S., & Bear, D. R. (1992). Summary and synthesis: "Teaching the lexicon to read and spell." In S. Templeton and D. R. Bear (Eds.), *Development of orthographic knowledge and the foundations of literacy: A Memorial Festschrift for Edmund Henderson* (pp. 33–352). Hillsdale, NJ: Erlbaum.

Templeton, S., & Morris, D., (2000). Spelling. In M. Kamil, P. Mosenthal, P. D. Pearson, & R. Barr (Eds.), *Handbook of Reading Research* (Vol. 3, pp. 525–543). Mahwah, NJ: Erlbaum.

Vernon, S. A., & Ferreiro, E. (1999). Writing development: A neglected variable in the consideration of phonological awareness. *Harvard Educational Review, 69*, 395–415.

10

Unlocking Word Meanings
Strategies and Guidelines for Teaching
Morphemic and Contextual Analysis

ELIZABETH CARR EDWARDS
GEORGE FONT
JAMES F. BAUMANN
EILEEN BOLAND

Contextual and morphological cues provide readers useful, powerful information for determining word meanings, and instructional research indicates that teaching students to employ context and morphology can enhance their independent vocabulary learning. Drawing from the extant literature and several recent intervention experiments we have conducted, we present (1) a theoretical and empirical rationale for teaching morphemic and contextual analysis, (2) strategies and guidelines for teaching morphemic and contextual analysis, and (3) ideas for how teachers can integrate instruction in morphemic and contextual analysis.

Graves (2000) has argued that a comprehensive vocabulary development program should include four components: engaging in wide reading, teaching individual words, teaching word-learning strategies, and fostering word consciousness. Research indicates that each component contributes to children's and adolescents' vocabulary growth.

- *Engaging in wide reading.* Vocabulary grows by reading independently (Nagy, Anderson, & Herman, 1987; Swanborn & de Glopper, 1999), by listening to texts read aloud (Elley, 1989), and through exposure to enriched oral language (Dickinson, Cote, & Smith, 1993).
- *Teaching individual words.* Students learn word meanings when vocabulary is taught directly and explicitly through a variety of instructional strategies (Baumann, Kame'enui, & Ash, 2003; Beck & McKeown, 1991; Blachowicz & Fisher, 2000; Stahl & Fairbanks, 1986).
- *Teaching word-learning strategies.* Students learn words independently when they are taught strategies for determining the meanings of words by analyzing morphemic and contextual clues (Buikema & Graves, 1993; Fukkink & de Glopper, 1998; Tomesen & Aarnoutse, 1998; White, Sowell, & Yanagihara, 1989; Wysocki & Jenkins, 1987).
- *Fostering word consciousness.* Vocabulary develops when students engage in playful language activities (Anderson & Nagy, 1992; Beck & McKeown, 1983) and develop word awareness or metacognitive knowledge (Beck, McKeown, & Omanson, 1987; Graves & Watts-Taffe, 2002; Nagy & Scott, 2000; Watts & Graves, 1996; see Chapters 11–13, this volume).

In this chapter, we focus on Graves's (2000) third component: teaching word-learning strategies. We address how teachers can teach students to use morphemic and contextual analysis to determine the meanings of unknown words. Other components of Graves's four-part vocabulary development program are addressed elsewhere in this volume. We begin by providing a theoretical and empirical rationale for teaching morphemic and contextual analysis. Next, we present strategies and guidelines for teaching morphemic and contextual analysis. Finally, we offer ideas for how teachers can integrate instruction in morphemic and contextual analysis.

WHY TEACH MORPHEMIC AND CONTEXTUAL ANALYSIS?

Definitions

Morphemic analysis, which is also referred to as *structural analysis*, involves deriving the meaning of a word by examining its meaningful parts (morphemes), such as word roots, prefixes and suffixes, and inflected endings. Instruction in morphemic analysis as we conceptualize it involves teaching students to (1) disassemble words into roots and affixes (*indecipherable* = *in-* + *decipher* + *-able*); (2) acquire the meanings of roots and affixes (*in-* = not; *decipher* = to decode or understand; *-able* = able to do so); and (3) reassemble the meaningful parts to derive word meanings (*indecipherable* = to not be able to decode or understand something). Morphemic analysis involves the use of intraword linguistic information to derive a word's meaning.

Contextual analysis involves inferring the meaning of a word by scrutinizing surrounding text, which includes syntactic and semantic linguistic cues provided by preceding and succeeding words, phrases, and sentences. Instruction in contextual analysis involves teaching students to identify and employ generic and specific types of context clues. Contextual analysis involves interword linguistic information to infer a word's meaning.

Rationale for Instruction in Morphemic and Contextual Analysis

Based on an analysis of vocabulary in materials students encounter in school, Nagy and Anderson (1984) asserted that "for every word a child learns, we estimate that there are an average of one to three additional related words that should also be understandable to the child" (p. 304). They qualified this estimate, however, by stating that this kind of vocabulary growth depends upon "how well the child is able to utilize context and morphology to induce meanings" (p. 304). In other words, students skilled in morphemic and contextual analysis have the potential to increase their vocabulary breadth and depth substantially.

Given the logic for teaching students to use morphology and context, it has been standard for curriculum developers to include lessons on morphemic and contextual analysis in reading and language arts instructional materials (Beck, McKeown, McCaslin, & Burkes, 1979; Blachowicz & Fisher, 2000; Durkin, 1978–1979; Ryder & Graves, 1994), and curriculum guidelines at the state (e.g., California Department of Education, 1999) and national (e.g., National Institute for Literacy, 2001) level recommended instruction in morphemic and contextual analysis. Strategies for teaching morphemic and contextual analysis are also commonly included in works designed to help teachers expand students' reading vocabulary (Blachowicz & Fisher, 2002; Bromley, 2002; Dale & O'Rourke, 1986; Johnson, 2001; Johnson & Pearson, 1978).

Research on Teaching Morphemic and Contextual Analysis

Instruction in morphemic analysis appears to be appropriate for students in grades 4 and above (Nagy, Diakidoy, & Anderson, 1993; White, Power, & White, 1989). Although classic instructional studies were limited methodologically or were inconclusive (Hanson, 1966; Otterman, 1955; Thompson, 1958), more recent research suggests that students can be taught various morphemic elements as means to derive the meanings of novel words (Graves & Hammond, 1980; Nicol, Graves, & Slater, 1984; White, Sowell, & Yanagihara, 1989; Wysocki & Jenkins, 1987). Likewise, early research on teaching contextual analysis was equivocal (Askov & Kamm, 1976; Hafner, 1965; Sampson, Valmont, & Allen, 1982), but more recent studies have revealed that context clue instruction enhances students' vocabulary growth (Buikema & Graves, 1993; Carnine, Kame'enui, & Coyle, 1984; Fukkink & de Glopper, 1998; Jenkins, Matlock, & Slocum, 1989; Patberg, Graves, & Stibbe, 1984; Sternberg, 1987).

Dale and O'Rourke (1986) argued that "students need to make use of context clues in relation to other methods of vocabulary study [that include] the process of word formation by means of roots, prefixes, suffixes, and compounds" (p. 72). Tomesen and Aarnoutse (1998) reported that grade 4 Dutch students who were taught morphemic and contextual analysis were able to derive the meanings of unfamiliar words, but there has been little English-language research examining the combination of instruction in both morphemic and contextual analysis.

We addressed this need by conducting two studies with grade 5 students in diverse U.S. public elementary school classrooms. In our first experiment (Baumann et al., 2002), we provided students instruction in either morphemic analysis only (MO), contextual analysis only (CO), or a combination of morphemic and contextual analysis (MC). Results revealed that students who received MO or MC instruction were more adept at deriving the meanings of unfamiliar morphemically decipherable words than were CO students or those in an instructed control group. Similarly, students in the CO or MC group were more skillful at inferring the meanings of unfamiliar words in context than were MO or control students. There were no group differences on a comprehension measure, and students were generally just as effective at determining word meanings when the morphemic and contextual analysis instruction was provided in combination (MC) as when the instruction was provided separately (MO or CO). We concluded that instruction in morphemic and contextual analysis can positively influence independent vocabulary learning but not necessarily comprehension of texts containing contextually and morphologically decipherable words.

In a follow-up study (Baumann, Edwards, Boland, Olejnik, & Kame'enui, 2003), four grade 5 teachers provided 78 students combined instruction in morphemic and contextual analysis (MC) that was embedded within social studies lessons, and four other teachers provided 79 students instruction in key textbook vocabulary (TV) from the social studies lessons. Teachers taught 25 45-minute daily lessons on the Civil War using the social studies textbook, which included 15-minute vocabulary lessons. Using vocabulary from the textbook, MC teachers taught students morphemic and contextual analysis strategies and how to use them in an integrated fashion; TV teachers used various established vocabulary instructional techniques to teach key textbook vocabulary directly. Results revealed that TV students learned the key textbook vocabulary and MC students learned to apply morphemic and contextual analysis to determine the meanings of novel words on immediate or delayed measures. As in the prior study, there were no group differences on a comprehension measure and tests of content learning. We concluded that morphemic and contextual analysis instruction can be integrated effectively to promote students' vocabulary growth.

In summary, there exist a theoretical rationale and empirical evidence for teaching morphemic and contextual analysis. We now turn to instructional strategies and guidelines for teaching morphemic and contextual analysis separately and in an integrated fashion.

TEACHING MORPHEMIC ANALYSIS

Definitions

The key instructional elements of morphemic analysis are roots and affixes. A *root* is "the basic part of a word that usually carries the main component of meaning and that cannot be further analyzed without loss of identity" (Harris & Hodges, 1995, p. 222). Roots can stand alone as words, which are referred to as *free morphemes* or simply *root words* (*car, run, blue*). Roots can also be meaningful parts of words that cannot stand alone, and they are referred to as *bound morphemes* and often take the form of Latin or Greek roots (*scribe* as in *transcribe* and *inscribe*).

An *affix* is "a bound (nonword) morpheme that changes the meaning or function of a root or stem to which it is attached" (Harris & Hodges, 1995, p. 5). Affixes that come before a root are called *prefixes* and alter meaning (*un*happy, *over*heat). Affixes that follow roots are called *suffixes* and come in two varieties. *Inflectional suffixes*, or simply *inflections*, change the form of a word but not its speech part; these include verb forms (jump, jump*ed*, jump*ing*), plurals (cow, cow*s*), and comparatives and superlatives (bright, bright*er*, bright*est*). *Derivational suffixes* are like prefixes in that they alter a word's meaning (kind*ness*, elect*ion*, wash*able*).

Which Morphemic Elements to Teach

We recommend teaching common affixes and roots (Irwin & Baker, 1989; Johnson & Pearson, 1978; White, Sowell, & Yanagihara, 1989). Graves and Hammond (1980) argued that prefixes are worth teaching because they are relatively few in number and most have consistent meanings and spellings. White, Sowell, and Yanagihara (1989) reported that 20 prefixes account for 97% of prefixed words that appear in school reading materials (Carroll, Davies, & Richman, 1971), and four (*un-*, *re-*, *in-*, *dis-*) accounted for 58% of all prefixes. To promote instructional efficiency, we recommend that teachers begin instruction with the most common prefixes (see Graves, Chapter 6, this volume).

We also recommend that teachers spend time teaching derivational suffixes because, like prefixes, they are fairly regular in meaning and can lead to useful word building and vocabulary expansion. Because inflectional suffixes do not alter a word's root meaning (e.g., the meaning of the root word *jump* in *jumps, jumped,* and *jumping* is basically unchanged), they are not as helpful in deriving word meanings, so we recommend less instructional emphasis on them.

After exploring a number of affixes, students may be ready to delve into the meanings of Greek and Latin roots. Instruction in these roots should be sequenced according to the abstractness of their meaning, from concrete to more abstract. Bear, Invernizzi, Templeton, and Johnston (1996) suggest introducing Greek roots before Latin roots because their meaning is more apparent and the way in which they combine with other elements is more understandable. Latin roots, which are more abstract, can be presented later.

Guidelines for Teaching Morphemic Analysis

Now that we have defined terms and considered which morphemic elements to teach, we present four guidelines for teaching morphemic analysis.

• *Guideline 1: Provide explicit instruction in how morphemic analysis works.* Students must be able to disassemble words into roots and affixes and learn how parts function together to construct word meanings. Research demonstrates the effectiveness of explicit instruction in morphemic analysis (Graves & Hammond, 1980; White, Sowell, & Yanagihara, 1989; Wysocki & Jenkins, 1987). Explicit instruction is necessary because "a number of studies (e.g., Sternberg & Powell, 1983; O'Rourke, 1979) provide evidence that even many high school students are unaware that decomposing words into their parts can help with deriving their meanings" (Stahl, 1999, p. 45). Therefore, the teacher's task is to help students learn to locate meaningful parts of unfamiliar words to derive their meanings.

Baumann et al. (2002) explicitly taught the prefix *sub-* following four steps:

1. Root words (e.g., *zero, soil, conscious*) were presented on a transparency, and student volunteers read them and discussed their meanings.

2. The teacher presented an overlay that attached the prefix (*sub-*) to the root words. Students were asked to read the words with the prefix attached, to define them, and to try to derive their meanings.
3. The teacher explained the meaning of the prefix (*sub-* = under, below) and discussed how this prefix altered the meaning of the words.
4. Students practiced deriving the meanings of additional *sub-* words on a handout.

• *Guideline 2: Use word families to promote vocabulary growth.* Nagy and Anderson (1984) propose teaching word families, which include a root word and its derived forms (e.g., *cycle, monocycle, bicycle, tricycle, cyclist*). One advantage of teaching words as families is that, if students know the meaning of the root or most frequent derivative in a family, this knowledge can serve as a bridge to less common or familiar forms. Furthermore, teaching words as families calls attention to word-formation and word-analysis processes that relate the different members of a family (see Templeton, Chapter 8, this volume). Therefore, students are more likely to use semantic relationships when learning unfamiliar words independently. Another benefit of covering a family of words is that it familiarizes students with the types of changes in meaning that often occur among related words, thus preparing them to deal with cases in which the semantic relationships among morphologically related words are not as obvious (e.g., *transparent, apparent, appear*).

• *Guideline 3: Promote independent use of morphemic analysis.* The number of prefixes, suffixes, and Latin and Greek roots is enormous, so it is not feasible to teach all elements directly. Therefore, teachers need to promote and encourage independent learning of affix and root meanings so that students can expand their word learning beyond instructional time.

One way to foster independent growth is by showing students how to use a word study notebook during independent reading time. Bear et al. (1996) describe six steps for using word study notebooks: "1. Collect the word. 2. Record the word and sentence. 3. Look at word parts and think about their meaning. 4. Record related words. 5. Study the word in the dictionary, and record interesting information. 6. Review" (p. 336).

Blachowicz and Fisher (2002, pp. 193–195) reference Lindsay (1984), who suggests that students create their own "affixionary," which is an alphabetical listing of affixes with one entry per page. Each affix is defined and followed by words that include the affix with sentence examples for each. Prefixes and suffixes may be kept separately. A similar notebook could be used for Latin and Greek roots. Affixionaries can be initiated as a teacher-led group activity but later become an independent activity (e.g., during self-selected reading).

We recommend that teachers display charts that list prefixes, suffixes, and roots along with their meanings and examples of words containing the word parts. Although students may recognize a morphemic element in an unknown word, they may not be able to recall the meaning of the affix or root, so lists serve as a quick reference for students.

• *Guideline 4: Enhance students' awareness that morphemic analysis does not always work.* Although using morphemic analysis can be a useful strategy, there are occasions when it does not work. White, Sowell, and Yanagihara (1989) discussed three prefix pitfalls. First, some prefixes are not consistent in meaning (e.g., *in-* means both *not* and *into*). Second, sometimes the removal of what appears to be a prefix leaves no meaningful root (e.g., *intrigue*) or a word that is not related in meaning to the whole word (e.g., *invented*). Third, if students only consider word-part clues, they may be misled about the true meaning of a word (e.g., *unassuming* may be analyzed as *not supposing* instead of *modest*). Suffixes can be confusing as well. As pointed out by Schmitt (2000), "Someone having a special skill is a *specialist*, a person who is pragmatic is a *pragmatist*, but a person who acts on stage is an *actor* not an *actist*" (p. 61).

There are pitfalls to learning Latin and Greek roots as well. Nagy and Anderson (1984) state that they are "highly skeptical of approaches to vocabulary that proceed on an etymological or historical approach to word meanings, approaches which feign that words such as *dialect, collect,* and *intellect* have some basic meaning in common" (p. 326). Additionally, Shepherd (cited in Nagy and Anderson, 1984) found that knowledge of Latin roots is not strongly related to knowledge of the meanings of words containing such roots. Despite these pitfalls and limitations to morphemic analysis, we believe that instruction is still warranted because of the evidence supporting its efficacy.

TEACHING CONTEXTUAL ANALYSIS

Which Context Clues to Teach

Although context clues may involve graphic, pictorial, or typographic information, we focus on two types of linguistic context clues: syntactic and semantic. *Syntactic clues* involve using word order, which is potentially powerful because English is a highly positional language. In other words, English relies heavily on word order to convey a message in that the position of a word in a sentence affects the word's meaning as well as the meaning of the sentence. Changing word order may consequently alter meaning or even destroy it, by and large (Durkin, 1981). *Semantic clues* involve the use of meaning-based information in a text that enables a reader to infer the sense of a word or at least limit alternate meanings

(Johnson & Pearson, 1978). Building on prior descriptions and syntheses of context clues (Dale & O'Rourke, 1986; Drum & Konopak, 1987; Johnson & Pearson, 1978; Sternberg & Powell, 1983; Suttles & Baumann, 1991) and our own research (Baumann et al., 2002, 2003), we recommend teaching five context clue types as follows (examples from Baumann et al., 2003).

1. *Definition.* Sometimes the definition for a word is right in the sentence. For example, in the sentence *When the sun hit its zenith, which means right overhead, I could tell it was noon by the tremendous heat,* the word *zenith* is defined as *right overhead.*
2. *Synonym.* Sometimes the reader can find a familiar word that is similar in meaning to an unfamiliar word. For example, in the sentences *Captain Jackson's uniform was impeccable. In fact, it was so perfect that she always had the highest score during inspection,* the word *perfect* is a more familiar synonym for the word *impeccable.*
3. *Antonym.* Sometimes an unfamiliar word is clarified by the presentation of a word nearly opposite in meaning. For example, in the sentence *The soldier was very intrepid in battle, although the person next to him was quite cowardly,* the word *intrepid* is contrasted with the more familiar word *cowardly.*
4. *Example.* Occasionally an author provides several words or ideas that are examples of a word. For instance, in the sentence *Tigers, lions, panthers, and leopards are some of the most beautiful members of the feline family,* the words *tigers, lions, panthers,* and *leopards* are examples of the category *feline family,* or cat family.
5. *General.* Sometimes an author provides some general clues to the meaning of a word. For example, in the sentences *Martha liked attention. She wore bright-colored clothes and had an unusual hairstyle. She spoke loudly and thought she was important. People said she was ostentatious,* the words *liked attention, bright-colored clothes, unusual hairstyle,* and *spoke loudly* helped clarify the meaning of *ostentatious.*

Guidelines for Teaching Contextual Analysis

Now that we have suggested five types of context clues to teach, we turn to instructional guidelines.

• *Guideline 1: Provide instruction in how contextual analysis works.* Students need to be able to recognize context clue types and understand how interword linguistic information can provide clues to unknown words. Following are three contextual analysis instructional strategies.

1. *Cloze procedure.* In the cloze procedure (Taylor, 1953; Jongsma, 1971), students read passages in which words have been deleted either systematically (e.g., every fifth word) or by design (e.g., certain parts of speech). We recommend the latter when cloze is used to teach or practice contextual analysis, specifically deleting words that are embedded in reasonably rich context. The task is to read the passage and supply the missing words. Cloze requires readers to use their generalized knowledge of context or specific context clue types to supply appropriate or plausible words that are consistent with the passage content. Sometimes letter clues are given, making it easier for the student to determine the missing words (Emans & Fischer, 1967). For example, all consonants, the first letter only, or the first and last letters might be provided.

There are several modifications of the cloze procedure that provide teacher support and scaffold students' acquisition of contextual analysis (see Blachowicz & Fisher, 2002, pp. 31–32). In the *zip cloze* procedure, a teacher uses masking tape to cover context-rich words in a text on a chart or from a big book. After skimming the text for meaning, students predict the meanings of the masked words, and the teacher pulls (zips) the tape off to reveal the actual words. In *maze cloze*, students are provided with several word choices, only one of which fits both the syntax and semantic content of the passage. In *synonym cloze*, students are provided synonymous words or short phrases below the blank to support them in inferring the deleted words.

2. *C(2)QU.* The purpose of C(2)QU (Blachowicz, 1993) is "to present both definitional and contextual information about new words to students in a way that allows them to hypothesize about meaning, to articulate the cues that lead to the hypothesis, and to refine and use what they have learned with feedback from the group and from the teacher if necessary" (Blachowicz & Fisher, 2002, pp. 33). C(2)QU has four steps: (1) C1: Present a word in meaningful context, and ask students to predict its meaning and then justify their predictions. (2) C2: Add more context and definitional information and have students evaluate their initial predictions. (3) Q: Question students about the word's meaning, providing a definition if necessary. (4) U: Have students construct a sentence that contains the word (Blachowicz & Fisher, 2002, p. 34).

3. *Contextual redefinition.* Contextual redefinition (Readence, Bean, & Baldwin, 1998) is intended to help students learn to infer the meanings of unknown words through context. The procedure consists of five steps (Tierney & Readence, 2000, pp. 382–385): (1) Select challenging, comprehension-critical words from a reading assignment. (2) Write or select from the text a context-rich sentence for each word. Use different types of context clues (see our preceding list) for different words. (3) Present the words in isolation and invite students to offer definitions and provide explanations for each. (4) Present the words in context and invite students to infer

the meanings from context and justify their suggestions. (5) Use a dictionary to verify their hypothesized word meanings.

• *Guideline 2: Provide students metacognitive context instruction.* After students develop facility with contextual analysis, teachers can initiate lessons that involve monitoring their ability to predict and verify word meanings. Blachowicz and Fisher (2002) recommend the following procedure: "(a) *Look.* Before, at, and after the word. (b) *Reason.* Connect what they know with what the author has written. (c) *Predict a possible meaning.* (d) *Resolve or redo.* Decide if they know enough, should try again, or consult an expert or reference" (p. 27). To implement this strategy, Blachowicz and Fisher (2002, pp. 26–29) recommend that teachers select a passage with one or more difficult words and lead the students in an analysis of the text for context clues, focusing on students' ability to monitor and control their developing ability to infer word meanings from linguistic clues.

• *Guideline 3: Enhance students' awareness that contextual analysis does not always work.* Not every study supports the use of context clues as a sound strategy for identifying unfamiliar words. There is evidence to suggest that naturally occurring written contexts do not always provide very effective learning environments (McKeown & Beck, 1988). In other words, there are limits to the power and generalizability of contextual analysis (McKeown, 1985; Nagy & Herman, 1987; Schatz & Baldwin, 1986; Swanborn & de Glopper, 1999). For example, we know that not all contexts are equally rich (Beck, McKeown, & McCaslin, 1983; Nist & Olejnik, 1995); some contexts are unreliable in providing meaning clues (Baldwin & Schatz, 1985; Schatz & Baldwin, 1986); and explicit context clues are often not available in natural text (Stahl, 1999). Further, teaching context clues through contrived contexts is unlikely to transfer to natural contexts (Beck, McKeown, & Kucan, 2002). Thus, it is important to inform students that there are limits to contextual analysis and demonstrate this by providing examples of difficult words that are in context-lean environments.

TEACHING MORPHEMIC AND CONTEXTUAL ANALYSIS IN AN INTEGRATED MANNER

Why Teach Morphemic and Contextual Analysis in Tandem?

As we have shown, teaching students morphemic and contextual analysis strategies provides students several keys for unlocking the meanings of many words, and we see a place for separate instruction in morphemic and contextual analysis. Logic suggests, however, that combining instruction in morphemic and contextual strategies would be efficient and effective, and this intuition has empirical support (Baumann et al., 2002, 2003; Tomesen & Aarnoutse, 1998). Although not all unknown or low-frequency words possess morphemic elements to analyze and are situated in rich context, teaching students how to look for and use morphemic clues, context clues, or both is an effective means to provide students multidimensional, flexible strategies to infer word meanings. We now turn to how a teacher might integrate these strategies in vocabulary lessons.

How to Teach Morphemic and Contextual Analysis in Tandem

In a recent study with fifth graders, we devised a series of lessons for teaching morphemic and contextual analysis in tandem within a social studies unit on the Civil War (Baumann et al., 2003). Our primary instructional strategy was what we referred to as the "Vocabulary Rule," a whole–part–whole (i.e., context, word parts, context again) approach for integrating morphemic and context clues that is an abbreviated version of Ruddell and Ruddell's (1995) four-step sequential procedure for independent vocabulary learning. The Vocabulary Rule, which was presented on a teaching chart, stated:

> When you come to a word, and you don't know what it means, use: 1. CONTEXT CLUES: Read the sentences around the word to see if there are clues to its meaning. 2. WORD-PART CLUES: See if you can break the word into a root word, prefix, or suffix to help figure out its meaning. 3. CONTEXT CLUES: Read the sentences around the word again to see if you have figured out its meaning.

Teachers explained the steps of the Vocabulary Rule and then modeled how to apply it, thinking aloud as they demonstrated the use of the rule with excerpts from the social studies textbook or content-related texts.

Following several lessons in which we taught the generic Vocabulary Rule, we focused on specific morphemic elements and context clue types. Using our whole–part–whole approach, we used vocabulary taken directly from the textbook lessons to introduce affixes and context clue types (whole). We then taught the specific morphemic or context clue strategy using the anchor vocabulary (part). Finally, students applied the strategy by using additional textbook excerpts or conceptually similar texts (whole). In all cases, however, whether we were focusing on a morphemic or context clue element, we always had students use the Vocabulary Rule, that is, employ a context–morphemic–context strategy.

To teach morphemic analysis elements, we presented a chart that included four steps for examining words for word-part clues:

1. Look for the ROOT WORD, which is a single word that cannot be broken into smaller words or word parts. See if you know what the root means. 2. Look for a PREFIX, which is a word part added to the beginning of a word that changes its meaning. See if you know what the prefix means. 3. Look for a SUFFIX, which is a word part added to the end of a word that changes its meaning. See if you know what the suffix means. 4. Put the meanings of the ROOT WORD and any PREFIX or SUFFIX together and see if you can build the meaning of the word.

Over a series of lessons, we used this four-step approach to teach 20 different prefixes and suffixes organized into eight families, or types. For example, the prefixes *un-*, *dis-*, *in-*, and *im-* made up the "Not Prefix Family," and *-ship*, *-ness*, and *-ment* made up the "State or Quality of Suffix Family." To illustrate, when teaching the "Before, During, and After Prefix Family," we used the words *prewar*, *mid-war*, and *postwar* to explain and model how to word-build with the prefixes *pre-* (before), *mid-* (during or middle), and *post-* (after). Students then applied the strategy with additional words in short contexts (e.g., *Preheat* the oven before putting in the pizza. My cat took a *midmorning* nap.), ending with an exercise in which they used the Vocabulary Rule to determine the meanings of words in textbook excerpts. We also taught students to be aware of exceptions. We used words such as *pressure*, *midget*, and *postage* to demonstrate that not all words that appear to begin with prefixes or end with suffixes necessarily involve word parts that can be disassembled, identified, and then reassembled into a full-word meaning.

We taught five context clue types presented in the preceding section in a similar fashion. Specific context clue types were described, illustrated, and modeled using excerpts from the textbook. In the remaining lessons, we emphasized the integration of morphemic and contextual analysis strategies. For example, using a textbook excerpt on post-Civil War Reconstruction, we demonstrated how the prefix *re-* (again) and root *construction* could be used to determine the meaning of *Reconstruction*. We also pointed out that there was a synonym context clue (*rebuilding* was in the text nearby) that guided students to the meaning of *Reconstruction*. It was through this kind of integrated instruction that students learned to rely on what they had learned about roots, affixes, and context clues to determine the meaning of novel vocabulary.

CONCLUSION

During the past 20 years, many researchers have called for promoting independent vocabulary learning strategies that will enable students to access the sheer volume of vocabulary they are likely to encounter in school texts (e.g., Baumann, Kame'enui, & Ash, 2003; Nagy, 1988; Nagy & Anderson, 1984). Teaching students how to apply intraword (morphemic) and interword (contextual) cues in tandem makes sense because most vocabulary is presented in running text. Teachers should have knowledge of which morphemic elements (e.g., prefixes, suffixes, and Latin and Greek roots) and which context clues (e.g. definition, synonym, antonym, example, and general) are worth teaching. To this end, we recommend that teachers spend instructional time on the four guidelines of morphemic analyses: (1) *provide explicit instruction in how morphemic analysis works*; (2) *use word families to promote vocabulary growth*; (3) *promote independent use of morphemic analysis*; and (4) *enhance students' awareness that morphemic analysis does not always work*. Instructional time should also be spent on the three guidelines for contextual analysis: (1) *provide instruction in how contextual analysis works*; (2) *provide students metacognitive context instruction*; and (3) *enhance students' awareness that contextual analysis does not always work*. The independent word-learning strategies of morphemic and contextual analysis provide students with two keys for unlocking word meaning and should be combined to form one component of a balanced vocabulary program (Graves, 2000).

REFERENCES

Anderson, R. C., & Nagy, W. E. (1992). The vocabulary conundrum. *American Educator, 16,* 14–18, 44–47.

Askov, E. N., & Kamm, K. (1976). Context clues: Should we teach children to use a classification system in reading? *Journal of Educational Research, 69,* 341–344.

Baldwin, R. S., & Schatz, E. L. (1985). Context clues are ineffective with low frequency words in naturally occurring prose. In J. A. Niles & R. V. Lalik (Eds.), *Issues in literacy: A research perspective: Thirty-fourth yearbook of the National Reading Conference* (Vol. 34, pp. 132–135). Rochester, NY: National Reading Conference.

Baumann, J. F., Edwards, E. C., Boland, E., Olejnik, S., & Kame'enui, E. J. (2003). Vocabulary tricks: Effects of instruction in morphology and context on fifth-grade students' ability to derive and infer word meaning. *American Educational Research Journal, 40,* 447–494.

Baumann, J. F., Edwards, E. C., Font, G., Tereshinski, C. A., Kame'enui, E. J., & Olejnik, S. (2002). Teaching morphemic and contextual analysis to fifth-grade students. *Reading Research Quarterly, 37,* 150–176.

Baumann, J. F., Kame'enui, E. J., & Ash, G. (2003). Research on vocabulary instruction: Voltaire redux. In J. Flood, D. Lapp, Squire, J. R., & Jensen, J. (Eds.), *Handbook of research on teaching the English language arts* (2nd ed., pp. 752–785). New York: Macmillan.

Bear, D. R., Invernizzi, M., Templeton, S., & Johnston, F. (1996). *Words their way: Word study for phonics, vocabulary, and spelling.* Upper Saddle River, NJ: Merrill.

Beck, I. L., & McKeown, M. G. (1983). Learning words well—A program to enhance vocabulary and comprehension. *The Reading Teacher, 36,* 622–625.

Beck, I. L., & McKeown, M. G. (1991). Conditions of vocabulary acquisition. In R. Barr, M. Kamil, P. Mosenthal, & P. D. Pearson (Eds.), *Handbook of reading research* (Vol. III, pp. 789–814). New York: Longman.

Beck, I. L., McKeown, M. G., & Kucan, L. (2002). *Bringing words to life: Robust vocabulary instruction.* New York: Guilford Press.

Beck, I. L., McKeown, M. G., & McCaslin, E. S. (1983). Vocabulary development: All contexts are not created equal. *Elementary School Journal, 83,* 177–181.

Beck, I. L., McKeown, M. G., McCaslin, E. S., & Burkes, A. M. (1979). *Instructional dimensions that may affect reading comprehension: Examples from two commercial reading programs* (LRDC Publication 1979/20). Pittsburgh: University of Pittsburgh, Learning Research and Development Center.

Beck, I. L., McKeown, M. G., & Omanson, R. C. (1987). The effects and uses of diverse vocabulary instructional techniques. In M. G. McKeown & M. E. Curtis (Eds.), *The nature of vocabulary acquisition* (pp. 147–163). Hillsdale, NJ: Erlbaum.

Blachowicz, C. L. Z. (1993). C2QU: Modeling context use in the classroom. *The Reading Teacher, 47,* 268–269.

Blachowicz, C. L. Z., & Fisher, P. (2000). Vocabulary instruction. In M. L. Kamil, P. B. Mosenthal, P. D. Pearson, & R. Barr (Eds.), *Handbook of reading research* (Vol. III, pp. 503–523) Mahwah, NJ: Erlbaum.

Blachowicz, C. L. Z., & Fisher, P. (2002). *Teaching vocabulary in all classrooms* (2nd ed.). Englewood Cliffs, NJ: Merrill/Prentice-Hall.

Bromley, K. (2002). *Stretching students' vocabulary.* New York: Scholastic.

Brown, D. F. (1980). Eight Cs and a G. *Guidelines, 3,* 1–17.

Buikema, J. L., & Graves, M. F. (1993). Teaching students to use context cues to infer word meanings. *Journal of Reading, 36,* 450–457.

California Department of Education. (1999). *Reading/language arts framework for California public schools, kindergarten through grade twelve.* Sacramento, CA: Author.

Carnine, D. W., Kame'enui, E., & Coyle. G. (1984). Utilization of contextual information in determining the meaning of unfamiliar words. *Reading Research Quarterly, 19,* 188–204.

Carroll, J. B., Davies, P., & Richman, B. (1971). *The American heritage word frequency book.* Boston: Houghton Mifflin.

Dale, E., & O'Rourke, J. (1986). *Vocabulary building: A process approach.* Columbus, OH: Zaner-Bloser.

Dickinson, D. K., Cote, L., & Smith, M. W. (1993). Learning vocabulary in preschool: Social and discourse contexts affecting vocabulary growth. In D. Daiute (Ed.), *The development of literacy through social interaction* (New Directions for Child Development, No. 61, pp. 67–78). San Francisco: Jossey-Bass.

Drum, P. A., & Konopak, B. C. (1987). Learning word meanings from written context. In M. G. McKeown & M. E. Curtis (Eds.), *The nature of vocabulary acquisition* (pp. 73–87). Hillsdale, NJ: Erlbaum.

Durkin, D. (1981). *Strategies for identifying words: A workbook for teachers and those preparing to teach.* Boston: Allyn & Bacon

Durkin, D. D. (1978–1979). What classroom observations reveal about reading comprehension instruction. *Reading Research Quarterly, 14,* 481–533.

Elley, W. B. (1989). Vocabulary acquisition from listening to stories. *Reading Research Quarterly, 24,* 174–187.

Emans, R., & Fischer, G. M. (1967). Teaching the use of context clues. *Elementary English, 44,* 243–246.

Fukkink, R. G., & de Glopper, K. (1998). Effects of instruction in deriving word meaning from context: A meta-analysis. *Review of Educational Research, 68,* 450–469.

Graves, M. F. (2000). A vocabulary program to complement and bolster a middle-grade comprehension program. In B. M. Taylor, M. F. Graves, & P. van den Broek (Eds.), *Reading for meaning: Fostering comprehension in the middle grades* (pp. 116–135). Newark, DE: International Reading Association.

Graves, M. F., & Hammond, H. K. (1980). A validated procedure for teaching prefixes and its effect on students' ability to assign meaning to novel words. In M. L. Kamil & A. J. Moe (Eds.), *Perspectives on reading research and instruction.* Twenty-ninth yearbook of the National Reading Conference (pp. 184–188). Washington, DC: National Reading Conference.

Graves, M. F., & Watts-Taffe, S. M. (2002). The place of word consciousness in a research-based vocabulary program. In S. J. Samuels & A. E. Farstrup (Eds.), *What research has to say about reading instruction* (3rd ed., pp. 140–165). Newark, DE: International Reading Association.

Hafner, L. E. (1965). A one-month experiment in teaching context aids in fifth grade. *Journal of Educational Research, 58,* 471–474.

Hanson, I. W. (1966). First grade children work with variant word endings. *The Reading Teacher, 19,* 505–507, 511.

Harris, T. L., & Hodges, R. E. (Eds.). (1995). *The literacy dictionary: The vocabulary of reading and writing.* Newark, DE: International Reading Association.

Irwin, J. W., & Baker, I. (1989). *Promoting active reading comprehension strategies: A resource book for teachers.* Englewood Cliffs, NJ: Prentice-Hall.

Jenkins, J. R., Matlock, B., & Slocum, T. A. (1989). Approaches to vocabulary instruction: The teaching of individual word meanings and practice in deriving word meaning from context. *Reading Research Quarterly, 24,* 215–235.

Johnson, D. D. (2001). *Vocabulary in the elementary and middle school.* Needham Heights, MA: Allyn & Bacon.

Johnson, D. D., & Pearson, P. D. (1978). *Teaching reading vocabulary.* New York: Holt, Rinehart & Winston.

Jongsma, E. (1971). *The cloze procedure as a teaching technique.* Newark, DE: The International Reading Association.

Lindsay, T. (1984). The affixionary: Personalizing prefixes and suffixes. *The Reading Teacher, 38,* 247–248.

McKeown, M. G. (1985). The acquisition of word meaning from context by children of high and low ability. *Reading Research Quarterly, 20,* 482–496.

McKeown, M. G., & Beck, I. L. (1988). Learning vocabulary: Different ways for different goals. *Remedial and Special Education, 9,* 42–46.

Nagy, W. E. (1988). *Teaching vocabulary to improve reading comprehension.* Newark, DE: International Reading Association.

Nagy, W. E., & Anderson, R. C. (1984). How many words are there in printed school English? *Reading Research Quarterly, 19,* 303–330.

Nagy, W. E., Anderson, R. C., & Herman, P. A. (1987). Learning word meanings from context during normal reading. *American Educational Research Journal, 24,* 237–270.

Nagy, W. E., Diakidoy, I. N., & Anderson, R. C. (1993). The acquisition of morphology: Learning the contribution of suffixes to the meanings of derivatives. *Journal of Reading Behavior, 25,* 155–170.

Nagy, W. E., & Herman, P. A. (1987). Breadth and depth of vocabulary knowledge:

Implications for acquisition and instruction. In M. G. McKeown & M. E. Curtis (Eds.), *The nature of vocabulary acquisition* (pp. 19–35). Hillsdale, NJ: Erlbaum.

Nagy, W. E., & Scott, J. A. (2000). Vocabulary processes. In M. L. Kamil, P. B. Mosenthal, P. D. Pearson, & R. Barr (Eds.), *Handbook of reading research* (Vol. III, pp. 269–284) Mahwah, NJ: Erlbaum.

National Institute for Literacy. (2001). *Put reading first: The research building blocks for teaching children to read* (Publication EXR0007B). National Institute for Literacy, U.S. Department of Education. Washington, DC: Author.

Nicol, J. E., Graves, M. F., & Slater, W. H. (1984). *Building vocabulary through prefix instruction.* Unpublished manuscript, Department of Curriculum and Instruction, University of Minnesota, Minneapolis.

Nist, S. L., & Olejnik, S. (1995). The role of context and dictionary definitions on varying levels of word knowledge. *Reading Research Quarterly, 30*(2), 172–193.

O'Rourke, J. (1979, April). *Prefixes, roots, and suffixes: Their testing and usage.* Paper presented at the annual meeting of the International Reading Association, Atlanta, GA.

Otterman, L. M. (1955). The value of teaching prefixes and word-roots. *Journal of Educational Research, 48,* 611–616.

Patberg, J. P., Graves, M. F., & Stibbe, M. A. (1984). Effects of active teaching and practice in facilitating students' use of context clues. In J. A. Niles & L. A. Harris (Eds.), *Changing perspectives on research in reading/language processing and instruction.* Thirty-third yearbook of the National Reading Conference (pp. 146–151). Rochester, NY: National Reading Conference.

Readence, J. E., Bean, T. W., & Baldwin, R. S. (1995). *Content area reading: An integrated approach* (6th ed.). Dubuque, IA: Kendall/Hunt.

Ruddell, R. B., & Ruddell, M. P. (1995). *Teaching children to read and write: Becoming an influential teacher.* Needham Heights, MA: Allyn & Bacon.

Ryder, R. J., & Graves, M. F. (1994). Vocabulary instruction presented prior to reading in two basal readers. *Elementary School Journal, 95* (2), 139–153.

Sampson, M. R., Valmont, W. J., & Allen, R. V. (1982). The effects of instructional cloze on the comprehension, vocabulary, and divergent production of third-grade students. *Reading Research Quarterly, 17,* 389–399.

Schatz, E. K., & Baldwin, R. S. (1986). Context clues are unreliable predictors of word meanings. *Reading Research Quarterly, 21,* 439–453.

Schmitt, N. (2000). *Vocabulary in language teaching.* New York: Cambridge University Press.

Stahl, S. A. (1999). *Vocabulary development.* Cambridge, MA: Brookline Books.

Stahl, S. A., & Fairbanks, M. M. (1986). The effects of vocabulary instruction: A model-based meta-analysis. *Review of Educational Research, 56,* 72–110.

Sternberg, R. B. (1987). Most vocabulary is learned from context. In M. G. McKeown & M. E. Curtis (Eds.), *The nature of vocabulary acquisition* (pp. 89–105). Hillsdale, NJ: Erlbaum.

Sternberg, R., & Powell, J. S. (1983). Comprehending verbal comprehension. *American Psychologist, 38,* 878–893.

Suttles, W. C., & Baumann, J. F. (1991, December). *A review and synthesis of descriptive, theoretical, and empirical definitions of context clues: A classification scheme for researchers and practitioners.* Paper presented at the annual meeting of the National Reading Conference, Palm Springs, CA.

Swanborn, M. S. L., & de Glopper, K. (1999). Incidental word learning while reading: A meta-analysis. *Review of Educational Research, 69,* 261–285.

176 TEACHING VOCABULARY-LEARNING STRATEGIES

Taylor, W. L. (1953). Cloze procedures: A new tool for measuring readability. *Journalism Quarterly, 30*, 360–368.
Thompson, E. (1958). The "master word" approach to vocabulary training. *Journal of Developmental Reading, 2*, 62–66.
Tierney, R. B., & Readence, J. D. (2000). *Reading strategies and practices: A compendium* (5th ed.). Needham Heights, MA: Allyn & Bacon.
Tomesen, M., & Aarnoutse, C. (1998). Effects of an instructional programme for deriving word meanings. *Educational Studies, 24*(1), 107–128.
Watts, S. M., & Graves, M. F. (1996). Expanding your vocabulary program to foster word consciousness. *Wisconsin State Reading Association Journal, 40*(2), 19–24.
White, T. G., Power, M. A., & White, S. (1989). Morphological analysis: Implications for teaching and understanding vocabulary growth. *Reading Research Quarterly, 24*, 283–304.
White, T. G., Sowell, J., & Yanagihara, A. (1989). Teaching elementary students to use word-part clues. *The Reading Teacher, 42*, 302–308.
Wysocki, K., & Jenkins, J. R. (1987). Deriving word meanings through morphological generalization. *Reading Research Quarterly, 22*, 66–81.

PART III

TEACHING VOCABULARY
THROUGH WORD
CONSCIOUSNESS
AND LANGUAGE PLAY

11

Logology

Word and Language Play

DALE D. JOHNSON
BONNIE VON HOFF JOHNSON
KATHLEEN SCHLICHTING

This chapter defines eight broad categories of logology (word and language play) and presents a brief review of research related to the field. The categories are onomastics, expressions, figures of speech, associations, formations, manipulations, games, and ambiguities. The major focus of the chapter is onomastics (the study of names), a ubiquitous but often neglected resource for classroom use. Expressions and figures of speech are two other categories addressed. This chapter rests on the awareness that word play is pervasive in American English, and its understanding is essential for the production and comprehension of language. The chapter also acknowledges that the use of language play activities stimulates students' natural interest in and curiosity about language.

It Was Bears over Bulls, by a Nose.—MARINO (2001, December 2)

Selig: Baseball in a pickle.—BODLEY (2001, December 6)

The Art of Turning a Sow's Ear into a Silk Purse.—SEELYE (2002, January 13)

Don't Discount the Fat Cats Yet.—BERKE (2002, February 17)

Criminals pack more heat than officers at times.—COLE (2002, March 7)

Most Americans would agree that when students leave high school, the majority of those graduates should be able to read a newspaper. All the preceding examples are headlines from local and national newspapers. These headlines include idioms (*in a pickle*), slang (*pack more heat*), a proverb (*turning a sow's ear into a silk purse*), ambiguities (*fat cats*), and onomastics (*Bears, Bulls*). Newspaper articles also can contain a variety of language play devices. In a single *New York Times* article (Harden, 2002, March 3), *blowhard, had bitten off more than he could chew, smelled a rat, first got wind of, the lid came off,* and *spill the beans* were used.

Dmitri Borgmann (1965) introduced the word *logology* into the English language in his book *Language on Vacation*. Logology refers to all forms of word and language play that abound in English. Morice (2001) pointed out that Borgman considered logology "a body of knowledge with its own concepts, principles, and terms" (p. xii). Borgmann also founded *Word Ways: The Journal of Recreational Linguistics*, which became a forum for all types and forms of wordplay. Since 1960 wordplay has flourished. Richard Lederer's book *Anguished English* (1987) became popular after talk show host Jay Leno read from it for 8 minutes on his late-night television program. Many other books on word and language play have been published, and dozens of dictionaries of every subcategory of word play can be found in public and university libraries.

Word play, as logology is more commonly known, refers to the adaptation or use of words to achieve an effect, and it is accomplished through the manipulation of meanings, arrangements, sounds, spellings, and various other aspects of words. There are authors of children's literature (e.g., Dr. Seuss, 1990; Shel Silverstein, 1996; Roald Dahl, 1990; Jack Prelutsky, 1993) who intentionally and strategically construct and play around with words so as to engage children in playful and humorous interaction with language. Word play is not unique to American culture, but it is pervasive in American English, particularly in the category of logology called onomastics, or naming. Johnson (2001) proposed organizing types of word play into seven categories, and in this chapter we add an eighth.

THE EIGHT CATEGORIES

The eight categories of word play are:

1. Onomastics: proper names (*Bernadette*), nicknames (*Bernie*), pseudonyms (*Agatha Christie*), eponyms (*leotard*), toponyms (*paisley*), aptronyms (*D. Bonebreak, M.D.*), demonyms (*Long Islander*), place names (*Wilmington*), business names (*Curl Up and Dye*).
2. Expressions: idioms (*hold your horses*), proverbs (*Too many cooks spoil the broth*), slang (*greasy spoon*), catchphrases (*Don't call us, we'll call you*), slogans (*I Like Ike*).

3. Figures of speech: similes (*as due as the rent*), metaphors (*George is a dictionary*), hyperbole (*tons of money*), euphemisms (*between jobs*), oxymorons (*accreditation wisdom*).
4. Word associations: synonyms (*skinny–trim*), antonyms (*lively–dull*), homographs (*conduct–conduct*), homophones (*there–their*), collocations (*green grass*), coordinates (*pansy–daisy*), superordinates–subordinates (*flowers: tulips, daffodils*).
5. Word formations: affixes (*un-, -ous*), compounds (*homesick*), acronyms (*NATO*), initialisms (*FBI*), portmanteaus (*telecast*), neologisms (*twigloo*).
6. Word manipulations: anagrams (*teach–cheat*), palindromes (*star–rats*), rebuses (*2 4 T*).
7. Word games: alphabetic (*Scrabble*), alliteration (*John Jones from Janestown*), rhyming (*swift gift*), riddles, tongue twisters (*sixty sticky thumbs*).
8. Ambiguities: ambiguous words, phrases, and sentences (*fish biting off the coast*).

Logology, or word play, serves two critical roles in the home and classroom. First, it is imperative that a learner be able to interpret and produce these linguistic manipulations to completely comprehend or generate oral or written language. A primary reason that American English is so colorful is because it is laced with word-play devices. The headlines above show how widespread the use of idioms, slang, proverbs, onomastics, and ambiguity is in our everyday language. Second, from birth children exhibit a natural interest in language. They often explore and experiment with the sounds, the nuances, and the unpredictable qualities and complexities associated with language. Language can be a source of excitement and pleasure to children. As children observe and listen to others in their environment, they discover how to use language to communicate their wants, needs, and feelings. Children learn best when they have strong personal interest and are actively and interactively involved with learning. When children are having fun—when they see a purpose or direction to their learning—learning takes on a more personal, more authentic, more welcoming quality. As teachers, it is important that we incorporate word and language play activities in the classroom to stimulate, sustain, or recapture that natural interest. Some teachers recognize the value in engaging children in word-play activities. They observe the way children eagerly interact with this unique and playful aspect of language and how they revisit a familiar story, poem, or passage. Children return to a book such as *Tikki, Tikki, Tembo* (Mosel, 1968) to reread the story. They are heard during lunch, in hallways, and in bathrooms giggling over the refrain "Tikki tikki tembo—no sa rembo—chari bari ruchi—pip peri pembo" (p. 2).

Geller (1985), however, stated that, based on her observations, language learning in classrooms is too often viewed as work rather than play.

> For me, as an educator, the anomaly in this situation has been the absence of wordplay from the classroom—especially classrooms of the primary and middle elementary years. Teachers of these ages are aware of youngsters' penchant for play; however, most see no educational reason to bring it into the classroom. The question generally posed is, What does wordplay have to do with language education? or, more to the point: What does wordplay have to do with the teaching of reading and writing? (pp. 2–3)

RESEARCH REVIEW

Although wordplay has been described in books, specialized dictionaries, and periodicals, and despite its relevance to oral and written language development and maintenance, it has not received much research attention with school-aged children. A few studies have been conducted that examined acquisition and comprehension primarily of metaphors and idioms.

Ortony (1984) undertook a review of literature to answer the question of whether or not figurative language in written text was an important source of comprehension failure. He included such subcategories as similes, metaphors, irony, and other more obscure elements of figurative language. He defined figurative language as the use of language in which what is said is different from what is meant, and the type of relationship between the two accounts for the different subcategories of figures of speech. Ortony concluded that "figurative (or at least metaphorical) uses of language do not require any special cognitive mechanism" (p. 466). He argued that the greatest research need now is for research related to instructional issues. Based on his review of research literature, he offered two suggestions for including this category of word play in classroom instruction.

> It would not be unreasonable at this juncture to wonder why one should bother to introduce figurative uses of language to young children. There are at least two answers to this. First, figurative language is a powerful way of relating old knowledge to new. Second, figurative language increases the expressive power of the available linguistic resources by permitting the expression of what might otherwise be difficult or impossible to express. How else can the opera singer's voice be described, if not by the metaphorical use of some word like *thin?* And, if ships don't plow the seas, what do they do literally? (p. 467)

Ortony argued for including appropriate use of figurative language from the earliest school years rather than waiting until middle grades, as is the current practice. Several authors who can skillfully help teach young children about the use of figurative language to create lasting images in the readers' minds are Patricia Polacco (2001), Chris Van Allsburg (1985), Barbara Park (1993), and David Shannon (1998).

Teresa Labov (1992) conducted a review of studies of adolescent slang. Based on her review and a questionnaire study of 89 slang terms used by high school and college students, she demonstrated differences in slang recognition. For example, more than 90% recognized *jocks* and *cool*, but only about 6% recognized *dexters* and *motorhead*. Statistically significant differences were found for the recognition of specific slang terms by gender (e.g., *airhead* by girls), race (e.g., *homie* by African Americans), community type (e.g., *za* by suburbanites), school type (e.g., *dweebs* by private schoolers), coast (e.g., *wicked good* by East Coasters), and college year (e.g., *bag it* by college seniors).

Nippold, Uhden, and Schwarz (1997) demonstrated that language continues to develop through adolescence and into adulthood, especially in the interpretation of figurative language and expressions. Their study of low-familiarity proverbs with 353 subjects ranging in age from 13 to 79 showed this growth. Each proverb was used in a concluding sentence of a four-sentence story. The subjects read the paragraph silently and interpreted the proverb in writing. Nippold et al. noted that "performance on the task improved markedly during adolescence and into adulthood. It reached a plateau during the 20s" (p. 245).

Perhaps more studies of idiom comprehension have been reported than of any other category of logology. Studies have shown that older children comprehend more idioms than younger children and that the period between ages 7 to 11 is when idiom understanding is acquired most rapidly (Levorato & Cacciari, 1995). Other researchers have demonstrated that high-familiarity idioms such as *beat around the bush* are learned more easily than low-familiarity idioms such as *to take a powder* (Nippold & Taylor, 1995). Transparent idioms such as *to keep a straight face* are learned more easily than opaque idioms such as *talk through one's hat* (Gibbs, Nayak, & Cutting, 1989; Gibbs, 1991; Nippold & Taylor, 1995). Children of average intelligence are better at comprehending idioms than children with learning difficulties (Ezell & Goldstein, 1991). Finally, children find it more difficult to produce idiomatic expressions than to comprehend them (Levorato & Cacciari, 1995). The implications of these idiom studies are that school-aged children can and do understand idiomatic expressions, their idiomatic facility develops through the school years, and some care must be taken by teachers in their own idiomatic usage with younger or academically less able students. Marvin Terban, an author of several books on idioms (*Punching the Clock*, 1990; *Mad as a Wet Hen!*, 1987; *Scholastic Dictionary of Idioms*, 1996) teaches children about the definitions and origins of idioms as he takes an everyday part of the English language and makes it engaging and fun for students.

Holmes (1999) demonstrated that children use language play as response to literature. The fourth graders in her study used conventional language play (e.g., metaphorical proverbs) and inventive language play (e.g., rhymes and colloquialisms) in both oral and written expression in response to stories.

This chapter rests on the foundation that there are many forms and types of word play that permeate the English language. Furthermore, the use of word play generates and sustains active interest and involvement in language and language learning. Research has shown that children and adolescents can and do comprehend and use many types of figurative and expressive language. Children come to school with a language instinct and an innate preoccupation with using and manipulating language. Also, every genre of written and oral language requires an understanding of word-play devices. This ranges from newspaper headlines to television broadcasts, from descriptive literature to television talk show jokes, from magazine advertisements to children's literature. Children's writing takes on a new quality and depth as they become more familiar with and exposed to the different categories of language play.

In this chapter, we place our major focus on the category most overlooked in schools—onomastics, the study of names. In an afterword to Morice's (2001) *The Dictionary of Wordplay*, Richard Lederer wrote, "It thrums with the human passion to name" (p. 256). Eckler's (1986) *Names and Games* and Dickson's (1996) *What's in a Name?* are devoted entirely to the field of wordplay with names. There are many others, including entire dictionaries on subcategories such as eponyms and demonyms. Onomastics is the heart of our chapter on word play because it is such a rich resource for the elementary, middle, and high school classroom. We also give attention to expressions and figures of speech. Throughout the chapter, we offer strategies, activities, and resources for introducing children to these three forms of language play that encourage them to interact, create, and share their growing depth of expression.

ONOMASTICS

Onomastics is the study of names. School lessons based on onomastics are as scarce as hen's teeth, perhaps because it is human nature to take for granted what is right in front of our noses. Names are everywhere—on street signs, inside shoes, on 18-wheelers, under our desk chairs. Although it is unusual to encounter the study of names in educational materials, the business world and some academicians take the study of names seriously. There are businesses that do nothing but create names for other businesses. Sam Birger, a psycholinguist who works for Whatchamacallit, a naming firm based in Boston and San Francisco, stated, "The whole point of the

Rumpelstiltskin story is that when you have the right name for a thing, you have control over it" (Kaplan & Bernays, 1997, p. 110). Research has shown that names do influence our feelings toward a person, place, or thing (Dickson, 1996). Which eatery is more expensive? Big Belly's (an actual restaurant in Appleton, Wisconsin) or Chéz Louis? Which physician has a more pleasant bedside manner: Elmer Clodmore or Cindy Carter? Which tropical hotel is more luxurious: Sam's Sleep Tite or The Grand Waterfall? Which teacher is more strict: Ms. Melanie Brooks or Ms. Hortense Walpole? Which dog is more vicious: Killer or Fluffy? Hollywood starmakers know the importance of names. Judy Garland was born Francis Gumm, little Cary Grant was actually little Archibald Alexander Leach, and John Wayne was Marion Michael Morrison.

Land developers, too, recognize the psychology at work behind a name. We do not see names such as Black Widow Bend or Cockroach Clearing on signs for new subdivisions. Rustling Willows or Clearbrook Acres are more like it—even though there may not be a willow tree or a clear brook within 50 miles of the sites. Bryson (1994) pointed out that a property name change can increase property values by as much as 15 percent. A name might also affect enrollment in some private prep schools. There is a school north of the city of Monroe, Louisiana, that caters to fairly well-off families. The school is located on a street named *Finks Hideaway*. In every ad we have seen for the school of privilege, the street address is written as just *Hideaway*. The *Finks* has been dropped. Apparently the school leaders and parents decided that it wouldn't look or sound too impressive for their children to come from a school that is situated on a Hideaway of Finks.

First Names and Surnames

People naturally have an interest in their own names. We feel somewhat slighted or perhaps even a bit offended when someone mistakenly calls us by an incorrect name. When we receive direct mail advertisements, we feel confident throwing the material away when our names are not correct. Dictionaries of names can be found in any reference section of a good-sized bookstore. Rare are the people who pick up one of these dictionaries and do not try to locate their own first names and surnames. A *Delmore* may be disappointed that his first name means *at a marsh* whereas a *Donaldo* may relish *world leader*. Some surnames, according to Johnson (1999), "come from a patronym or father's name (e.g., *Knutson* means *son of Knut*), occupation (e.g., *Baker*), a place (e.g., *Wald* is German for *woods*), or physical characteristic (e.g., *Longfellow*)" (p. 11). She cautioned, however, that tracing the origins of some surnames can be a time-consuming task. Many names were Americanized or misspelled at immigration stations.

There certainly is no shortage of unusual names floating around. In one university faculty directory are *Drs. Sun, Moon, Askew, Smiley, Junk, Bacon, Bug, Small*, the disagreeable-sounding *Dr. Sour*, the fun-sounding *Dr. Bacchus*, and the curt-sounding *Dr. Short*. There's also a *Dr. George Washington* who does not teach history and a *Dr. Smart* who is an aptronym, which we will discuss later. Unusual names often are found in children's literature. Examples include Kevin Henkes's *Chrysanthemum*, Shel Silverstein's *Sarah Cynthia Sylvia Stout*, and Sharon Creech's characters *Salmanca Tree Hill* and *Phoebe Winterbottom*.

According to Kaplan and Bernays (1997), Lee Salk, an expert on child development, stated, "Parents who give their kids weird names are weird themselves" (p. 125). Perhaps. There are some doozies in the annals of names. Authenticated names listed by Dickson (1996) include *Leafy Beagle, Oofty Goofty Bowman, Toni Chickaloni, Orie Corn, Adeline Dingledine, Nice Go, Rains Munday, Tarzan Kush, Duel Maroon, Petway Plunk, Farce Pickle, Melon Roof, Shrubble Seeds*, and more. Some are a play on words, such as *Jerzy Kowski, Only Human*, and *Tin Cans* (p. 87). The people who carry these names probably aren't chuckling.

Eponyms

An *eponym* is a word named after a person. Eponyms can be found in nearly every category of interest. In the category *plants*, there is the *Bartlett pear* (Encoh Barteltt, 1779–1860), the *Douglas fir* (David Douglas, 1798–1834), and the *Sequoia* (Sequoya, 1770?–1843). Under *clothing* there is the *cardigan* (7th Earl of Cardigan, 1797–1868), the *leotard* (Jules Leotard, 1842–1870), and the *mackintosh* (Charles Mackintosh, 1766–1843). In the *measurement* category, we find the *Geiger counter* (Hans Geiger, 1882–1945), the *Richter scale* (Charles Richter, 1900–1985), *Fahrenheit* (Daniel Fahrenheit, 1686–1736), and *Celsius* (Anders Celsius, 1701–1744). From a cookbook we note chicken tetrazzini (Louisa Tetrazzini, 1872–1941), *peach melba* (Nellie Melba, 1861–1931), *Béchamel sauce* (Louis de Béchamel, died 1703), and *beef Wellington* (1st Duke of Wellington, 1769–1852). There are tens of thousands of eponyms in the English language. The medical profession alone claims at least 15,000 eponyms (see *http:// www.whonamedit.com*). *Alzheimer's disease* (Alois Alzheimer, 1864–1915), *Parkinson's disease* (James Parkinson, 1755–1824), and *Down's syndrome* (John Down, 1828–1896) are just three familiar medical eponyms.

Table 11.1 presents a short list of eponyms. Challenge your students to trace the story behind these and other eponyms after having them predict the eponyms' origins. Some student-friendly sources that will tell the stories are Laura Lee's *The Name's Familiar: Mr. Leotard, Barbie, and Chef*

TABLE 11.1. Eponyms

argyle	Dow Jones average	Oscar award
bibb lettuce	ferris wheel	reuben sandwich
Big Ben	frisbee	salmonella
blanket (noun)	Gallup poll	saxophone
blurb	graham crackers	schrapnel
boycott	guppy	stetson
boysenberry	macadamia nuts	Tony award
cobb salad	maverick	Venn diagram
doberman pinscher	ohm	watt

Boyardee (1999), Eugene Ehrlich's *What's in a Name? How Proper Names Became Everyday Words* (1999), and *Webster's New World Dictionary of Eponyms: Common Words from Proper Nouns* (Douglas, 1990). Although the *Webster's* is an older reference, it contains more than 800 eponyms.

Aptronyms

An *aptronym* is a name that is appropriate to the person's occupation. As mentioned above, *Dr. Smart* is a professor; thus her name is an aptronym. While looking for a telephone number, we noted an aptronym. A family named *Wood* owns a lumber company. A *New York Times* article on weekend workers (Jackson, 2002, March 10) mentioned *Ms. Heather Carb*, who is a bakery manager near Philadelphia. We skimmed the Physicians and Surgeons section of the *Yellow Pages* in a medium-sized city and found the following aptronyms: *Leslie Coffman, M.D.; Michael Caire, M.D.; Michael Hand, M.D.; Randy Head, M.D.; Terry Tugwell, M.D.;* and *John Price, M.D.* Dickson (1996) reported that past American Medical Association Directories listed the surnames of *Arms, Bones, Colon, Cure, Finger, Knee, Pill, Dose, Gauze, Heal,* and *Mesick* (p. 32). Teachers could put students into cooperative groups and assign (or have them select) an occupation. Then students could create a list of aptronyms specific to the occupation (e.g., Dentist: *Rudolph Root, Ruth Tooth*).

Demonyms

A *demonym* is a word for people who live in a particular place. A *Barabooian* is a person who resides in Baraboo, Wisconsin. Someone who lives in Fergus Falls, Minnesota is a *Fergusite*. A *Dane* lives in Denmark, and a *Florentine* hails from Florence, Italy. An indispensable book for the study of demonyms is Paul Dickson's *Labels for Locals: What to Call People from Abilene to Zimbabwe* (1997). There are some rather complex rules for creating demonyms, but Dickson stated that "people in a place tend to decide what they will call themselves, whether they be *Angelenos* (from Los Angeles) or *Haligonians* (from Halifax, Nova Scotia)" (p. x). Teachers could engage students in researching demonyms for schools, neighborhoods, communities, and states of interest. For example, one of us is an *Old Abe* who was a *Tenth Warder*, an *Eau Clairian*, and a *Wisconsin-ite*.

Toponyms

A *toponym* is a word named after a place. *Magenta* is a reddish-pink color, and it is a toponym. The rather upbeat color is named after a downbeat scene—the blood-soaked battlefield at the Battle of Magenta in Italy in 1859 (Freeman, 1997). Other toponyms include *duffel bag* (Duffel, Belgium), *sardines* (the island of Sardinia), and *paisley* (Paisley, Scotland). We suggest that you have your students look in local and large commercial cookbooks for toponyms.

Unusual Town and City Names

Each state in our country has colorful town and city names. There is a small town in Louisiana with a big name: *Transylvania*. It lies in the Mississippi delta region of the state, so the topography is flat. From miles away, travelers on the main highway can see the town's water tower with a gigantic drawing of a bat on it—just like in old Dracula movies and resembling Batman's logo. The Transylvania general store had a witty sign on its window until some town father or mother or skittish tourist convinced the proprietors to remove it. The sign said: "Welcome to Translyvania. We're always looking for new blood." Upon inquiring about the origin of the town name, the clerk in the general store told us that the name came from someone who had ancestors from Transylvania, which was a province in Romania.

Just as every word has a story behind it, every town has a story behind it. Some are amusing, some surprising. According to Gallant (1998), *Toast*, North Carolina, was a name submitted to the U.S. Post Office by a school administrator whose mind was on food. *Charm*, Ohio, was named for a charm that a local jeweler wore on his watch chain. *Only*, Tennessee, came from a store owner's preceding every price quote with "only" (e.g., "*only* ten cents, *only* a quarter"). *Snowflake*, Arizona, refers to Mr. Snow and Mr. Flake, the men who are credited with naming the town.

Table 11.2 gives a couple of examples of colorful town names in each state. ZIP codes are included in case you want your students to write to historical societies or town officials for the origins of the town names. As a

TABLE 11.2. Colorful Town Names

Brilliant, Alabama (35548)

Eek, Alaska (99578)

Carefree, Arizona (85377)

Cash, Arkansas (72421)

Cool, California (95614)

Brush, Colorado (80723)

Headquarters, Connecticut (06759)

Bakers Choice, Delaware (19946)

Picnic, Florida (33547)

Ideal, Georgia (31041)

Happy Valley, Hawaii (96793)

Bench, Idaho (83241)

Normal, Illinois (61761)

Fickle, Indiana (46041)

Gravity, Iowa (50848)

Admire, Kansas (66830)

Quicksand, Kentucky (41363)

Plain Dealing, Louisiana (71064)

Reach, Maine (04627)

Boring, Maryland (21020)

Blissville, Massachusetts (01364)

Payment, Michigan (49783)

Staples, Minnesota (56479)

Hot Coffee, Mississippi (39428)

Cash, Missouri (63534)

Circle, Montana (59215)

Superior, Nebraska (68978)

Jackpot, Nevada (89825)

Beans, New Hampshire (03595)

Deal, New Jersey (07723)

Dusty, New Mexico (87943)

Gang Mills, New York (14870)

Apex, North Carolina (27502)

Cannon Ball, North Dakota (58528)

Dent, Ohio (45211)

Boss, Oklahoma (74745)

Plush, Oregon (97637)

Bonus, Pennsylvania (16049)

Harmony, Rhode Island (02829)

Fair Play, South Carolina (29643)

Parade, South Dakota (57647)

Difficult, Tennessee (37145)

Ding Dong, Texas (76542)

Bountiful, Utah (84010)

Mosquitoville, Vermont (05042)

File, Virginia (22427)

Forks, Washington (98331)

Odd, West Virginia (25902)

Loyal, Wisconsin (54446)

Ten Sleep, Wyoming (82442)

Flea Hop, Alabama (36078)

Sourdough, Alaska (99586)

Surprise, Arizona (85374)

Greasy Corner, Arkansas (72346)

Jelly, California (96080)

Tincup, Colorado (81210)

Puddle Town, Connecticut (06022)

Shortly, Delaware (19947)

Two Egg, Florida (32423)

Social Circle, Georgia (30279)

Volcano, Hawaii (96785)

Riddle, Idaho (83604)

Roaches, Illinois (62898)

Santa Claus, Indiana (47579)

What Cheer, Iowa (50268)

Neutral, Kansas (66725)

Rush, Kentucky (41168)

Sharp, Louisiana (71447)

Strong, Maine (04983)

Cabin John, Maryland (20818)

Old Furnace, Massachusetts (01031)

The Fingerboard Corner, Michigan (49705)

Young America, Minnesota (55494)

Rich, Mississippi (38617)

Bland, Missouri (65014)

Truly, Montana (59485)

Worms, Nebraska (68872)

Contact, Nevada (89825)

Pickpocket Woods, New Hampshire (03833)

Yellow Frame, New Jersey (07860)

House, New Mexico (88121)

Idle Hour, New York (11769)

Crisp, North Carolina (27852)

Zap, North Dakota (58580)

Jumbo, Ohio (43326)

Bunch, Oklahoma (74931)

Remote, Oregon (97458)

Eighty-Four, Pennsylvania (15330)

Hope, Rhode Island (02831)

Return, South Carolina (29678)

Promise, South Dakota (57601)

Disco, Tennessee (37737)

Wink, Texas (79789)

Bonanza, Utah (84008)

Prosper, Vermont (05091)

New Store, Virginia (23901)

Mold, Washington (99115)

Joker, West Virginia (26141)

Luck, Wisconsin (54853)

Halfway, Wyoming (83113)

follow-up activity, have students look in the index of an atlas or state highway maps for more unusual names. They are plentiful.

Odonyms

Odonyms are street names. Odonyms can be quite colorful, too. Near Ruston, Louisiana, is a *Goodgoin Road* and a *Stone's Throw Road. Just Imagine Drive* is in Avon, Ohio; *None Such Place* is in New Castle, Delaware; and *Almosta Road* is in Darby, Montana (Wallechinsky & Wallace, 1993).

Dickson (1996) delineates three time periods in the naming of American streets. The first is from 1682 to 1945. William Penn is credited with numbering streets (e.g., First Street, Second Street) and using the names of trees for streets (e.g., Elm Street, Maple Street). Also during this time frame, streets were named after prominent people (e.g., Washington Street), business that was conducted on the street (e.g., Bank Street), and where the street led (e.g., Boston Street). The second era of street naming, according to Dickson, was from 1945 to 1960. Developers trying to cash in on the returning World War II veterans wishing to settle down and buy a home used enticing, relaxing type names with *Haven* or *Grove* or *Woods* in them. The third period, from 1960 to 1995, reflects streets named for a theme. If, for example, the developer was after a medieval theme, he or she might call the subdivision *Camelot* and name the streets *Castle Road, Knights' Lane,* and *Tournament Trail.* In one subdivision named *Treasure Island,* there is a *Fortune Drive, Pirate Drive, Silver Drive, Jolly Roger Drive, Captain Kidd Drive, Spyglass Drive,* and *Stevenson Drive.* The appearance of the houses in the subdivision suggest they were built during the third period of street naming. Using a local map, or by taking students on a walking tour, have them note unusual street names in the community. Have students investigate the origins of these names by checking with town clerks, city planners, or established realtors. For example, in one New Jersey community, several street names in a neighborhood are named after the developer's grandchildren.

Anemonyms

Anemonyms are the names of storms. Tornadoes are not named *Fred* or *Gwen*; blizzards are not named *Jane* or *Carlos.* Tornadoes are rated according to the *Fujita* scale (an eponym after Professor T. Theodore Fujita) and range from F0 (40 mph estimated wind speed) to F5 (300+ mph estimated wind speed). Blizzards often are referred to by the year in which they occurred (e.g., the Blizzard of '76). Among storms, only hurricanes have names. According to the National Hurricane Center (n.d.):

Experience shows that the use of short, distinctive given names in written as well as spoken communication is quicker and less subject to error than the older more cumbersome latitude–longitude identification methods. These advantages are especially important in exchanging detailed storm information between hundreds of widely scattered stations, coastal bases, and ships at sea. (*http://www.nhc.noaa.gov/aboutnames.html*)

Male names were not given to hurricanes until 1979, whereas female names have been used since 1953. Kaplan and Bernays (1997) pointed out that 39 names have been permanently retired by the National Hurricane Center. Among these are *Agnes, Bob,* and *Camille.* The names of these particularly destructive hurricanes probably would cause needless anxiety if used again. Kaplan and Bernays also noted that if the names were used again there could be confusion in insurance work and research studies. The names are selected by the World Meteorological Organization. There are different names for storms in the Atlantic (e.g., *Kate, Felix*), Central North Pacific (e.g., *Akoni, Peke*), Eastern North Pacific (e.g., *Sonia, Gil*), Western North Pacific (e.g., *Kai-Tak, Usagi*), Western Australian Region (e.g., *Emma, Daryl*), Eastern Australian Region (e.g., *Blanch, Ernie*), Northern Australia Region (e.g., *Kay, Sid*), the Fiji Region (e.g., *Atu, Drena*), the Papua New Guinea Region (e.g., *Tako, Upia*), and the Southwest Indian Ocean (e.g., *Bako, Ikala*). All the names can be found on the National Hurricane Center's website noted above. As a classroom activity, students can create names for particular storms of the type that are prevalent in their locales (e.g., blizzards in Nebraska, dust storms in Oklahoma, ice storms in Arkansas, gales in Maine) and give reasons for selecting the names.

Nicknames

Some onomasticians believe that nicknames are older than surnames. Ancient Egyptians used the nicknames *Red, Tiny, Big Head,* and *Frog,* among others (Dickson, 1996). An Athenian, Aristocles (427?–347 B.C.), had a nickname that all of us use today when we refer to him. His nickname comes from a Greek word that described Aristocles' wide forehead and shoulders (Kaplan & Bernays, 1997). We refer to the Athenian as *Plato.* Nicknames can be based on romantic partners (e.g., *Cuddles, Dumplin'*), physical features (*Shrimpie, Slim*), IQ (*Gray Matter, Featherbrain*), aspects of personality (*Skinflint, Motor Mouth*), or just clipped versions of a given name (e.g., *Willy* for *William*).

All of our Presidents have had nicknames. Some have had more than one. Andrew Johnson's nicknames were *His Accidency* and *Sir Veto.* Ronald Reagan, in addition to his childhood nickname of *Dutch,* was called the *Great Communicator* and the *Teflon President.* For a complete listing of

Presidential nicknames and how they were acquired, see Michael Shook's (1994) book *By Any Other Name.*

Big-time criminals seem to attract nicknames. Apparently folks such as FBI chief J. Edgar Hoover appreciated the nicknames because they gave clues to the crooks' identities or habits (Dickson, 1996). Examples of famous Bad Boys include Al *Scarface* Capone, Jack *Legs* Diamond, Charles *Pretty Boy* Floyd, George *Machine Gun* Kelly, and Lester *Baby Face* Nelson.

Not all well-known people with nicknames led a life of crime. Many American heroes and heroines have had nicknames, too. Harriet Tubman was called *Moses,* Clara Barton was *Angel of the Battlefield,* and Thomas Edison was *The Wizard of Menlo Park.* Nicknames abound in the entertainment and sports worlds. There's the *King* (Elvis), the *Fab Four* (The Beatles), and the *Queen of Soul* (Aretha Franklin). *Babe* (George Herman) Ruth, *Yogi* (Lawrence) Berra, and the *Iron Horse* (Lou Gehrig) are just three of many nicknames for sports notables. Sports teams, too, have nicknames. The *Hoosiers* are from Indiana University, the *Badgers* hail from the University of Wisconsin, and the *Blue Devils* from Duke University.

All states and several cities have nicknames. California is the *Golden State,* so named because of the Gold Rush; Florida is the *Sunshine State,* Georgia is the *Peach State,* and Kentucky is the *Bluegrass State.* Some origins of state nicknames are not as obvious as the aforementioned. For example, Oklahoma is known as the *Sooner State.* The nickname comes from those settlers who claimed land before the territory was officially opened. They were *Sooners* rather than *Laters.* The *Buckeye State,* Ohio, received its nickname for the numerous buckeye trees in the state.

New Orleans is the *Big Easy;* Denver is the *Mile-High City;* Dallas is the *Big D;* Nashville is *Music City, USA;* and Detroit is *Motor City.* Chicago, *Hog Butcher to the World* and the *City of Big Shoulders,* is often called by its third nickname, the *Windy City.* Although Chicago lies adjacent to Lake Michigan, the *Windy* refers to windbag politicians in the city—not to the wind speed (Shook, 1994). Groups of students can be asked to locate the nicknames of all 50 states, major cities, and people in politics, entertainment, or sports.

Pen Names

There are a variety of reasons for authors to use pen names. William Sydney Porter, for example, wanted to keep secret his having been incarcerated and so he used the pen name *O. Henry.* Other writers who were already well established sometimes used pseudonyms when departing from their usual bread-and-butter fare. Famous pen names include *Pearl Buck* (Pearl Comfort Sydenstricker), *Truman Capote* (Truman Streckfus Persons),

Agatha Christie (Agatha Mary Clarrisa Miller), *George Eliot* (Mary Ann Evans), *Dorothy Parker* (Dorothy Rothschild), *George Orwell* (Eric Arthur Blair), *Tennessee Williams* (Thomas Lanier Williams), and many more. Students may enjoy creating their own pen names for particular classroom writing assignments.

Store Names

As noted above, some companies exist just to name other businesses. A look through the *Yellow Pages* tells which businesses opt for creative names and which businesses tend to be more conservative. Hairdressers are especially creative in naming their businesses. We know of a *Kuttin Up, Smooth Operators, Shear Perfection,* and *The Clip Joint.* Independent bookstores have some clever names: *Turning Pages* (Natchez, Mississippi), *Cover to Cover* (also in Natchez), and *Tattered Cover* (Denver) are but three examples. Eateries may reflect geographical locations (e.g., *South of the Border, Pacific Delights*), a particular person (e.g., *Mama Maria's*), or the type of cuisine being served (e.g., *The Cajun Café*). Have students compile a list of unusual names for businesses in their communities. They can interview the owners of the businesses to find out how the names were chosen. Students can also design their own community and supply clever names for various businesses.

In the remainder of this chapter, we describe and exemplify expressions and figures of speech, two categories of logology with which students will have frequent contact in oral and written language. For a discussion of the remaining types of wordplay we refer you to *Wordworks: Exploring Language Play* (Johnson, 1999) and to Chapters 12 and 13 in this volume.

EXPRESSIONS

The extensive category of *Expressions* includes idioms, proverbs, slang, catchphrases, and slogans.

Idioms

An *idiom* is an expression in which the entire meaning is different from the usual meanings of the individual words. Idioms are often viewed as a single vocabulary word in concept even if they are made up of more than one word (e.g., *down in the mouth* means *sad*). As Crystal (1995) pointed out, no word in an idiomatic expression can be changed and retain the meaning of the idiom. For example, *a drop in the bucket* means a very small amount. The idiom cannot be changed to *a globule in the bucket* or *a drop in the pail.* Perhaps the most surprising thing about idioms is that many are old. Three ancient idioms include *not out of the woods yet* (circa 200 B.C.), *to eat someone out of house and home* (40 A.D.), and *in one ear and out the other* (80 A.D.). Other comparatively old idioms include *in a pickle* (1585), *to walk on eggs* (1621), and *to have bigger fish to fry* (1660).

Idioms that do not make literal sense to contemporary readers made perfectly good sense to speakers and the readers during the times in which they were coined. *To give someone the cold shoulder,* for example, can be traced to the 1800s. The idiom referred to the age-old problem of receiving unwelcome guests—usually right around meal time. The guests were given a cheap shoulder cut of unheated meat to hasten their departure. *To have something up one's sleeve* is an even older idiom (1400s) that was used before pockets were invented. Sleeves were used to keep items that we slip into pockets nowadays. We recommend the *Scholastic Dictionary of Idioms* (1996) by Marvin Terban for use with intermediate- and middle-grade students. The book contains the meanings and origins of more than 600 idioms. In the story *Junie B. Jones and a Little Monkey Business,* author Barbara Park (1993) offers students many examples of idioms. A popular idiom exercise is to have students illustrate the literal meanings of the words within an idiom. For example, children learn that *in a pickle* means *in trouble* but would draw a picture of a person inside a gherkin. In the second picture, students illustrate the figurative meaning of the idiom (i.e., to be in trouble).

Proverbs

A *proverb* is a short saying that offers guidance on how to live one's life. All cultures have proverbs because there never is a shortage of people, whether well-meaning or intrusive, who feel it necessary to provide advice to others. As with idioms, many proverbs are old and their originators have been lost with the passage of time. Examples include *familiarity breeds contempt* (40s B.C.); *out of sight, out of mind* (1200s); *easy come, easy go* (1300s); and *still waters run deep* (1400s). Some proverbs are contradictory. Examples include *the squeaky wheel gets the grease; silence catches a mouse; strike while the iron is hot; haste makes waste; the more the merrier; two's company but three's a crowd.*

The study of proverbs fits into the study of any country or people. Proverbs used by particular cultures can provide insights into their guiding principals and show learners that there usually are common human threads and shared experiences regardless of geography or background. Here are a few: *Better a patch than a hole* (Welsh proverb); *No choice is also a choice* (Jewish proverb); *When the mouse laughs at the cat, there is a hole nearby*

(Nigerian proverb); *Since the house is on fire, let's warm ourselves* (Italian proverb); *Never eat in a restaurant where the chef is thin* (Chinese proverb).

Although many familiar proverbs are old, some are fairly recent and have been created by Americans. Just three of many examples include *you can't unscramble eggs, an apple never falls far from the tree,* and *one who slings mud loses ground.* For those readers who want to investigate proverbs used in specific states in the country, a valuable resource is *A Dictionary of American Proverbs* (Mieder, Kingsbury, & Harder, 1992). Although the work is arranged according to key words (e.g., *clothes, meal, rule*), one can find proverbs used in certain states. From Louisiana comes *to know everything is to know nothing. When the outlook isn't good, try the uplook* was recorded in Illinois, and North Carolinians wisely say, *there's no beauty like the beauty of the soul.* Older students who grasp the meanings of these wise sayings will enjoy exploring books such as *Proverbs from Around the World* (Gleason, 1992) and the *International Dictionary of Proverbs* (de Ley, 1998).

Slang

Slang, according to Lighter (1994), is "an informal, nonstandard, nontechnical vocabulary composed chiefly of novel-sounding synonyms for standard words and phrases" (p. xi). Slang has gotten a bum rap. Granted, some slang is fleeting and offensive, but established slang adds variety and often amusement to our language. The importance of slang to our vocabularies has been supported by language scholars such as S. I. Hayakawa, H. L. Mencken, and Steven Pinker.

Some words that we consider "legitimate" words started off as slang and gradually worked their way into our everyday speech and writing. Examples include *number cruncher, cash cow, junk food, brown bag lunch, greasy spoon, puddle jumper, overkill, egghead, street smarts, tuckered out, wish list, sleazy, psyched up, nine-to-five, 24-7, to moonlight, low-life, high roller, goof up,* and tens of thousands more. There are slang terms that are occupation-specific (e.g., a computer *hacker*), there is rhyming slang (e.g., *fender bender*), there is repeating slang (e.g., a *no-no*), and there is slang in which only a letter has been changed (e.g., *chit-chat, wishy-washy*). A useful resource for teachers is the *Random House Historical Dictionary of American Slang* (Lighter, 1994, 1997) which, when completed, will have three volumes. The etymologies of established slang are included. Some children's books that incorporate slang include Alexandra Day's (1990, 1994) *Frank and Ernest* books, Diane Stanley's (1996) *Saving Sweetness,* and Jon Scieszka's (1989) *The True Story of the 3 Little Pigs.*

Catchphrases

Nigel Rees (1995) defined a *catchphrase* as "a phrase that has 'caught on' with the public and is, or has been, in frequent use" (p. vi). One might think that catchphrases are somewhat new expressions that have been helped along by the proliferation of contemporary media. Just as there are many old idioms, however, there also are many old catchphrases. *Avoid like the plague* was a catchphrase used during the fourth century; *eat your heart out* was used in the 1500s. A catchphrase often wears itself out through overuse. A faux pas among those in the know is to date oneself by the use of an out-of-date catchphrase. As we examined catchphrases for this chapter, we noted that the older catchphrases (e.g., the journalistic *If in doubt, strike it out*, from 1894) seem more fresh than the more recent ones (*Are we having fun yet?* from 1984). Perhaps it is the nature of catchphrases to recycle themselves so that they appear clever to generations who don't remember them the first time around. Here is a list of just a few of the thousands of catchphrases in the English language. We have grouped them according to the dates in which they became popular with large groups of people. All of these catchphrases are from Rees's (1995) *Dictionary of Catchphrases*:

> 1900: *It's all done with mirrors.* 1910: *Another day, another dollar.* 1920s: *Act your age.* 1930s: *Famous last words.* 1940s: *I don't mind if I do.* 1950s: *Be my guest.* 1960s: *Garbage in, garbage out.* 1970s: *Cry (or laugh) all the way to the bank.* 1980s: *Been there, done that.* 1990s: *Get a life.*

Slogans

A *slogan* is a type of catchphrase that is used to promote a person, group, or product (Ammer, 1989). When we think of slogans, we often think of presidential campaigns and advertisements. Some memorable presidential campaign slogans include:

> *In Hoover we trusted, now we are busted* (Franklin Delano Roosevelt, 1932); *Dewey or don't we?* (1944, Thomas Dewey); *Phooey on Dewey* (1948, Harry S Truman); *In your guts you know he's nuts* (1964, Lyndon B. Johnson, referring to Barry Goldwater); *What's wrong with being right?* (1964, Barry Goldwater); *Nixon is through in '72* (1972, George McGovern); *The Nation needs fixin' with Nixon* (1972, Richard Nixon).

There is an onslaught of others every 4 years. As election time approaches in your community and state, your students could develop a collection of slogans used in ads by candidates or proponents of issues.

In addition to advertising slogans, of which there is no shortage of examples, slogans also can be found in public service announcements. The United States Post Office promises: *We deliver.* The Boys and Girls Club says, *Support the club that beats the streets.* *Only you can prevent forest fires* is Smokey the Bear's slogan.

Divide your class into five groups. Each group can select or be assigned one of the five types of expressions: idioms, slang, proverbs, catchphrases, and slogans. The group is to compile a list of expressions in contemporary use through scanning newspapers and magazines and by listening to conversations at school and at home. The groups can report their findings to the full class.

FIGURES OF SPEECH

Figures of speech, as categorized by Johnson (2001), include similes, euphemisms, dysphemisms, oxymorons, alliteration, onomatopoeia, tongue twisters, metaphors, hyperbole, meiosis (understatement), irony, personification, and puns. Johnson states, "Figures of speech are rhetorical devices that use words in distinctive ways to achieve special effects. They make an impact that is either descriptive, shocking, political, social, upbeat, entertaining, or imaginative" (p. 152). We take a closer look at two of these categories: similes and euphemisms.

Similes

Similes are comparisons using *like* or *as*. Many familiar similes are relegated to the cliché pile, but to do so without studying their origins would be to miss out on stories that make our language captivating. We're not referring to *as thick as pea soup* or other obvious origins. Some, such as *neat as a pin*, are more difficult to figure out. For example, Johnson (1999) explained, "The simile 'neat as a pin' was recorded in the late 1700s as 'neat as a new pin.' Originally pins rusted quickly because they were made from iron wire. Only new pins were free of corrosion" (p. 171). There are other intriguing origins for *know someone like a book, fit as a fiddle, as easy as pie, as happy as a clam,* and *as easy as falling off a log. Dictionary of Colorful Phrases* (Carothers & Lacey, 1994) is an easy-to-read resource for students that contains the stories behind some of our most commonly used similes. Children's literature is laced with similes that help students see language in different ways and discover the power of words to create lasting images. David Shannon (1998), Chris Van Allsburg (1985), and Denise Fleming (1996) are well-known authors who employ similes in their colorful writing.

Euphemisms

Euphemisms are "feel good" words. A euphemism for *pain* is *discomfort*; a euphemism for *television commercial* is *message*. Many euphemisms are just plain good manners. *Passed* and *loss* are more sensitive word choices than *died*. It is especially important that students learn about the use of euphemisms because there is nothing playful about some of them. *Career change opportunity, repositioning,* and *streamlining* all mean that people will be fired. *Action entertainment* means violent entertainment. A *consideration* is a bribe. When someone is in a *re-education camp,* they are behind bars. Large hog operators in Iowa refer to their hog-waste holding pits as *lagoons.* The real estate section of any newspaper contains euphemisms such as *cozy, mint condition,* and *handyperson's special* that can be translated into more accurate descriptions of the properties—and, in the process, improve children's critical reading skills.

CONCLUSION

Almost from birth children have a fascination with words and language, and before they ever enter a classroom they exhibit natural talents for language manipulation. Teachers have the opportunity to build on children's instinctive capabilities as they stimulate and augment language acquisition through the school years. When children are actively and interactively engaged with language, they see learning as purposeful and enjoyable. Language play activities enhance this enjoyment. Through playing with words and expressions, children begin to discover and develop their own language abilities.

The English language abounds in logology—the many forms of word and language play. We recommend that teachers incorporate wordplay in their language and literacy programs. Such instruction will pay off in two ways: by generating and enhancing students' interest in language and by helping students deal with the many facets of oral and written language as listeners, speakers, readers, and writers.

REFERENCES

Ammer, C. (19899). *Fighting words: From war, rebellion, and other combative capers.* Lincolnwood, IL: NTC Publishing.

Berke, R. L. (2002, February 17). Don't discount the fat cats yet. *The New York Times,* p. WK1.

Bodley, H. (2001, December 6). Selig: Baseball in a pickle. *USA Today,* p. C1.

Borgmann, D. A. (1965). *Language on vacation.* New York: Charles Scribner's Sons.

Bryson, B. (1994). *Made in America: An informal history of the English language in the United States.* New York: Morrow.

Carothers, G., & Lacey, J. (1994). *Dictionary of colorful phrases.* New York: Sterling.

Cole, N. (2002, March 7). Criminals pack more heat than officers at times. *The News-Star,* p. A8.

Crystal, D. (1995). *The Cambridge encyclopedia of the English language.* Cambridge, UK: Cambridge University Press.

Dahl, R. (1990). *Esio trot.* New York: Penguin.

Day, A. (1990). *Frank and Ernest play ball.* New York: Scholastic.

Day, A. (1994). *Frank and Ernest on the road.* New York: Scholastic.

de Ley, G. (1998). *International dictionary of proverbs.* New York: Hippocrene Books.

Dickson, P. (1996). *What's in a name? Reflections of an irrepressible name collector.* Springfield, MA: Merriam-Webster.

Dickson, P. (1997). *Labels for locals: What to call people from Abilene to Zimbabwe.* Springfield, MA: Merriam-Webster.

Douglas, A. (1990). *Webster's new world dictionary of eponyms: Common words from proper nouns* New York: Simon & Schuster.

Eckler, R. (1986). *Names and games.* New York: University Press of America.

Ehrlich, E. (1999). *What's in a name? How proper names became everyday words.* New York: Henry Holt.

Ezell, H. K., & Goldstein, H. (1991). Comparison of idiom comprehension of normal children and children with mental retardation. *Journal of Speech and Hearing Research, 34,* 812–819.

Fleming, D. (1996). *Where once there was a wood.* New York: Henry Holt.

Freeman, M. S. (1997). *A new dictionary of eponyms.* New York: Oxford University Press.

Gallant, F. K. (1998). *A place called Peculiar: Stories about unusual place names.* Springfield, MA: Merriam-Webster.

Geller, L. G. (1985). *Wordplay and language learning for children.* Urbana, IL: National Council of Teachers of English.

Gibbs, R. W., Jr. (1991). Semantic analyzability in children's understanding of idioms. *Journal of Speech and Hearing Research, 34,* 613–620.

Gibbs, R. W., Nayak, N. P., & Cutting, C. (1989). How to kick the bucket and not decompose: Analyzability and idiom processing. *Journal of Memory and Language, 28,* 576–593.

Gleason, N. (1992). *Proverbs from around the world.* Secaucus, NJ: Citadel.

Harden, B. (2002, March 3). A far-right militia's far-fetched plot draws some serious attention. *The New York Times,* p. YNE18.

Holmes, L. A. (1999). Language play as response discourse. *Language Arts, 76*(3), 258–261.

Jackson, M. (2002, March 10). It's 5 p.m. Friday. Know where your weekend is? *The New York Times,* p. BU8.

Johnson, B. v. H. (1999). *Wordworks: Exploring language play.* Golden, CO: Fulcrum Publishing.

Johnson, D. D. (2001). *Vocabulary in the elementary and middle school.* Boston: Allyn & Bacon.

Kaplan, J., & Bernays, A. (1997). *The language of names: What we call ourselves and why it matters.* New York: Simon & Schuster.

Labov, T. (1992). Social and language boundaries among adolescents. *American Speech, 67,* 339–366.

Lederer, R. (1987). *Anguished English*. New York: Dell.

Lee, L. (1999). *The name's familiar: Mr. Leotard, Barbie, and Chef Boyardee*. Greta, LA: Pelican.

Levorato, M. C., & Cacciari, C. (1995). The effects of different tasks on the comprehension and production of idioms in children. *Journal of Experimental Child Psychology, 60,* 261–283.

Lighter, J. E. (1994). *Random House historical dictionary of American slang: Volume I, A–G*. New York: Random House.

Lighter, J. E. (1997). *Random House historical dictionary of American slang: Volume II, H–O*. New York: Random House.

Marino, V. (2001, December 2). It was Bears over Bulls, by a nose. *The New York Times,* p. BU13.

Mieder, W. S., Kingsbury, S. A., & Harder, K. B. (Eds.). (1992). *A dictionary of American proverbs*. New York: Oxford University Press.

Morice, D. (2001). *The dictionary of wordplay*. New York: Teachers and Writers Collaborative.

Mosel, A. (1968). *Tikki tikki tembo*. New York: Holt, Rinehart & Winston.

National Hurricane Center. (n.d.). *World-wide tropical cyclone names*. Retrieved February 26, 2002, from *http://www.nhc.noaa.gov/aboutnames.html*.

Nippold, M. A., & Taylor, C. L. (1995). Idiom understanding in youth: Further examination of familiarity and transparency. *Journal of Speech and Hearing Research, 38,* 426–433.

Nippold, M. A., Uhden, L. D., & Schwarz, I. E. (1997). Proverb explanation through the lifespan: A developmental study of adolescents and adults. *Journal of Speech, Language, and Hearing Research, 40,* 245–253.

Ortony, A. (1984). Understanding figurative language. In P. D. Pearson, R. Barr, M. L. Kamil, & P. Mosenthal (Eds.), *Handbook of reading research* (pp. 453–470). New York: Longman.

Park, B. (1993). *Junie B. Jones and a little monkey business*. New York: Random House.

Polacco, P. (2001). *Betty doll*. New York: Penguin.

Prelutsky, J. (1993). *It's raining pigs and noodles*. New York: Greenwillow.

Rees, N. (1995). *Dictionary of catchphrases*. London, UK: Cassell.

Scieszka, J. (1989). *The true story of the 3 little pigs*. New York: Viking.

Seelye, K. Q. (2002, January 13). The art of turning a sow's ear into a silk purse. *The New York Times,* p. WK3.

Seuss, D. (1990). *Oh, the places you'll go!* New York: Random House.

Shannon, D. (1998). *A bad case of stripes*. New York: Scholastic.

Shook, M. D. (1994). *By any other name: An informative and entertaining look at how hundreds of people, places, and things got their names*. New York: Prentice-Hall.

Silverstein, S. (1996). *Falling up*. New York: Harper Collins.

Stanley, D. (1996). *Saving sweetness*. New York: G.P. Putnam's Sons.

Terban, M. (1987). *Mad as a wet hen! And other funny idioms*. New York: Clarion.

Terban, M. (1990). *Punching the clock: Funny action idioms*. New York: Clarion.

Terban, M. (1996). *Scholastic dictionary of idioms*. New York: Scholastic.

Van Allsburg, C. (1985). *The polar express*. Boston: Houghton Mifflin.

Wallechinsky, D., & Wallace, A. (1993), *The book of lists: The '90s edition*. Boston: Little, Brown.

12

Developing Word
Consciousness

JUDITH A. SCOTT
WILLIAM E. NAGY

Word consciousness refers to the knowledge and dispositions necessary for students to learn, appreciate, and effectively use words. Word consciousness involves several types of metalinguistic awareness, including sensitivity to word parts and word order. In this chapter, we focus on the need for students to be aware of differences between conversational and written language, and of the pervasive power of word choice as a communicative tool in the latter. Specific activities for promoting word consciousness developed by a team of upper elementary teachers are described. We argue that word consciousness is not just a tool for the appreciation of literature or for effective writing but is essential for vocabulary growth and for comprehending the language of schooling.

To effectively promote vocabulary growth, teachers not only must aim to help students learn specific words (although this is often an important goal) but also must develop vocabulary knowledge that is *generative*—that is, knowledge and dispositions that will transfer to and enhance students' learning of other words as well. One part of generative vocabulary knowledge is word-learning strategies, which are discussed in Part II (Chapters 6–10) of this book. In this chapter, we focus on a different aspect of generative word knowledge, word consciousness, and on one aspect of word consciousness in particular—an awareness of the difference between the

201

conversational and written registers, and the powerful role that word choice plays in the latter. Later in the chapter, we provide examples of specific ways that teachers can promote word consciousness in their classrooms.

Vocabulary knowledge has been identified as one of five essential components of reading in recent federal documents (RAND Reading Study Group, 2002; NICHD Report of the National Reading Panel, 2000). Although teaching specific words is one important component of promoting vocabulary growth, one cannot teach students all of the words that they need to learn. Hence, as Baumann, Kame'enui, and Ash (2003) point out, teaching specific words is only one of three important instructional objectives in a comprehensive program of vocabulary instruction. The other two objectives are to "teach students to learn words independently" and to "help students to develop an appreciation for words and to experience enjoyment and satisfaction in their use" (p. 778). In recent papers, Graves and his colleague (Graves, 2000; Graves & Watts-Taffe, 2002) have advocated a four-part vocabulary program: wide reading, teaching individual words, teaching word learning strategies, and fostering word consciousness.

Although word consciousness can be thought of as one component of a vocabulary curriculum (Graves, 2000), the word *component* may suggest a compartmentalization that is not intended. We are not suggesting that word consciousness should be added as one of several different kinds of vocabulary activities, but rather that teachers need to take word consciousness into account throughout each and every day. Although developing an appreciation for words is among the most intangible of all goals in vocabulary learning (Graves, 1987), this goal is critical for both the development of conscious control over language use and the ability to negotiate the social language of schooling.

WHAT IS WORD CONSCIOUSNESS?

Word consciousness can be defined as interest in and awareness of words (Anderson & Nagy, 1992; Graves & Watts-Taffe, 2002). Despite the apparent simplicity of this definition, it is probably best to conceptualize word consciousness as a cluster of rather diverse types of knowledge and skills.

Word Consciousness as Metalinguistic Awareness

Word consciousness is first of all a type of *metalinguistic awareness*, that is, the ability to reflect on and manipulate units of language—in this case, words. However, one can make further distinctions in the types of meta-linguistic awareness that contribute to word consciousness.

Most basic may be the concept of *word* as a term referring to identifiable units in written and spoken language. Teachers in primary grades should not assume that their students have a complete understanding of this basic term. Roberts (1992) described the gradual development of this concept in kindergarten, first-, and second-grade children, finding that students' tacit knowledge of this concept remained ahead of their ability to explain it.

There are several specific types of metalinguistic awareness that may contribute to word consciousness. One is *morphological awareness*: awareness of word parts and how they contribute to the overall meaning of a word. Anglin's (1993) findings suggest that morphological awareness makes an important contribution to vocabulary growth—most obviously, to the explosive increase between first and fifth grade in the number of prefixed and suffixed words that children can explain.

Syntactic awareness is the ability to reflect on and manipulate the order of words in a sentence. It can be tested, for example, by a sentence anagram task, asking students to reassemble scrambled words back into a meaningful sentence. One way syntactic awareness may contribute to vocabulary growth is through its contribution to the process of inferring the meanings of new words from context. For example, a different set of words would fit in the blank in *He saw the _____ car* versus *He saw the car _____*. The errors of children who fail to successfully infer the correct meaning of a word in context often show a disregard for the syntactic structure of the sentence (McKeown, 1985; Werner & Kaplan, 1952).

Similarly, syntactic awareness seems to contribute to the successful use of definitions. The errors of children who fail to correctly use information in a definition often show a disregard for the structure of the definition (Miller & Gildea, 1987; Scott & Nagy, 1997).

Though *metasemantic awareness* is not a commonly used term, it should also be clear that children's ability to reflect on the meanings of words also contributes to their vocabulary knowledge and use. Knowledge of terms such as *antonym* and *synonym* is part of word consciousness, as is the ability to deal with *figurative language* and *metaphor*.

Knowledge and Beliefs about Word Learning

Word consciousness also involves knowledge and beliefs about word learning, and the various instructional practices and tools used to achieve it. That is, one can ask "What is it that teachers and students should know about word learning?" We believe that the following should be included in such a list (see Nagy & Scott, 2000, for a more complete discussion of these points):

- Word knowledge is complex: Knowing a word is more than knowing a definition.
- Word learning is incremental: It is a process that involves many small steps.
- Words are heterogeneous: Different kinds of words require different learning strategies.
- Definitions, context, and word parts can each supply important information about the meaning of a word, but each of these sources has significant limitations.

Furthermore, there are general principles of learning that have important implications for vocabulary instruction. To take a very specific example, there is a substantial body of research showing that distributed practice is more effective than massed practice for learning vocabulary, at least when it involves memorizing definitions (Willingham, 2002).

Knowledge about the nature and use of definitions is also important to vocabulary learning. Children's ability to produce definitions in conventional form shows substantial growth between kindergarten and fourth grade (Watson & Olson, 1987), but even sixth grade children's ability to understand definitions of novel words is limited in certain ways (Scott & Nagy, 1997). Fischer (1990, 1994) suggests that one reason that high school foreign language students make ineffective use of bilingual dictionaries is an overly simplistic concept of definition—that is, they simply look for cross-language synonyms. On a more positive note, Schwartz and Raphael (1985) reported benefits in word learning when students used a graphic organizer that restructured definitional information.

WORD CONSCIOUSNESS AND THE DIFFERENCE BETWEEN SPOKEN AND WRITTEN ENGLISH

So far we have presented word consciousness as a multifaceted and rather complex topic. However, we believe that there is one aspect of word consciousness that is fundamental: helping students become aware of the differences between spoken and written English and, in particular, the role that precision of word choice plays in effective writing.

In every language, there are multiple *registers*—levels or styles of usage appropriate to different situations, topics, and audiences. Although there are a variety of registers in both written and spoken English, for the purpose of this chapter, we will focus on the differences between the oral language typical of face-to-face conversation and the written language typical of books. The difference in modality (the fact that the former is spoken and the latter written) is only one of the differences between these two registers; there also are differences in vocabulary, in syntax, in the purposes for which language is used, and in the tools used to accomplish these purposes. Snow (1994) argued that the difference in modality is not the only difficulty facing children learning to read and in fact that learning to decode is far less of a problem than learning to cope with the differences in the way that the oral and written registers are used.

One of the important ways that oral and written language differ is in terms of their vocabulary. Written language typically uses a far richer vocabulary than oral language (Hayes & Ahrens, 1988). However, this difference is not because writers tend to have larger vocabularies than talkers; rather, it has to do with how oral and written language are used, and what constitutes effective communication in each. In particular, it has to do with the different role of word choice in these two registers.

Precise choice of words is not an essential skill in conversation. Careful word choice can play a role in some types of oral language, for example, in storytelling. In conversation, however, there are simply too many other factors that are more important, or at least more easily available. One can use prosody (pitch, stress, and phrasing), gesture, and facial expression to nuance the meaning of a word. In conversation, one must have strategies for getting and holding the floor, and these strategies are not dependent on the precision of word choice. In conversation, communicative effectiveness depends heavily on making use of shared beliefs, knowledge, and experiences. "You know who" can say more than a detailed description. The demands of producing and understanding speech at a relatively rapid rate also discourage the use of uncommon words (Chafe & Danielewicz, 1987).

Written language, on the other hand, is typically decontextualized. That is, when one is reading a novel, for example, there is less information offered by the context than there is when one is engaged in a conversation with a friend. The author obviously cannot point to objects in the readers' physical context and use words such as *this* or *that*. Nor can the author use gestures, facial expressions, or intonation. Nor can the author make detailed assumptions about what knowledge he or she might share with the reader (Rosenblatt, 1978). Communication is, therefore, much more dependent upon the language itself, and one of the primary linguistic tools used by writers is precision in their choice of words. In writing, therefore, unlike in conversation, word choice is one of the most important, if not the most important, tool for expressive power.

Children are familiar with the rules of conversation, but even if they have learned the mechanics of reading and writing, they are not necessarily familiar with how decontextualized language functions. They have to be

initiated into the pragmatics of written language—how it is used to effectively accomplish communicative purposes—as well as the mechanics
(Snow, 1994). If children do not understand the communicative power of
precise word choice, it is hard to see how they will come to understand the
distinctions in meanings among related words or be motivated to learn
words. Written language is an arena in which vocabulary is the currency,
but you have to know that if you are going to make the effort to invest in it.

WORD CONSCIOUSNESS AND MOTIVATION

We have already suggested that understanding the differences between
written and oral language and the expressive power of word choice in written language are foundational to word consciousness. They are also fundamental in terms of motivation. Learning words can be viewed as valuable if
you know what to do with them and if you know how to use them as tools.

One key principle of motivation is success. Students are unlikely to enjoy a task that they cannot perform adequately. On the other hand, being
able to perform a task successfully is itself a powerful motivator. Thus,
scaffolding students' success is an important factor in effective instruction.

Language, including vocabulary, is at least as emotionally laden as any
other part of the curriculum. Making a linguistic error, for example, a spelling error, can be humiliating. Not knowing what a word means or using a
word incorrectly can also pose a serious risk. Learning the literate register
is learning a new dialect of English, and dialect differences are also associated with very visceral reactions.

How does a teacher create an environment in which it is possible for a
student to take linguistic risks and in which students can achieve a level of
success high enough to motivate them to continue taking these risks? In the
remainder of this chapter, we give some examples.

PROMOTING WORD CONSCIOUSNESS
IN THE CLASSROOM

In this section, we describe activities developed during a 7-year, teacher research project called The Gift of Words (Henry et al., 1999; Scott, Asselin,
Henry & Butler, 1997; Scott, Blackstone, et al., 1996; Scott, Butler, &
Asselin, 1996; Scott & Wells, 1998; Skobel, 1998). In this project, we
found that teachers could influence word consciousness in their students,
including the perceptions that students have about the use of words with an
academic or literate tone, by providing an enriched focus on word use during reading, writing, and discussions.

The underpinning of the project was the work of Vygotsky, as developing conscious awareness and control of language was one of his central themes (Minick, 1987). Vygotsky (1978) also provided the foundation for understanding teacher and student interactions as mediated assistance, which facilitates students' learning and motivation. In this process, teachers help children become consciously aware of their use of oral and written language by controlling instruction strategically to focus attention on different aspects of reading and writing. Instruction is also mediated in that the teacher creates future contexts in which children can consciously apply what they are learning in new ways (Moll & Whitmore, 1993). In vocabulary acquisition, as in all aspects of learning, it is essential for students to be actively engaged in and to take increasing responsibility for their own learning.

Teaching Word Consciousness and Generative Knowledge of Words

The Gift of Words project grew out of the collaborative experiences and ideas from a core group of practicing elementary teachers and university participants who met and worked together for 7 years. As teachers invested time and energy in word learning strategically throughout the day, their students began to use words differently. The vocabulary-group teachers were able to develop students' willingness to experiment with words and to risk using them in new ways (Scott, Butler, & Asselin, 1996, 1997; Skobel, 1998). One teacher articulated a general agreement that she would "lay any money down that there isn't a single kid in my class . . . that isn't more aware of words" (Henry et al., 1999, p. 264). Another veteran teacher agreed, saying, "Without question, the kids were excited about words in a way that, in my teaching, I have never seen before. And, it's not that I have ignored words before; it is just that this year, [the focus] was major" (Henry et al., 1999, p. 264).

The vocabulary-group teachers chose to focus explorations with vocabulary learning in different curricular areas. A focus on vocabulary within literature circles has been described elsewhere (Scott & Wells, 1998). Four other teachers looked at vocabulary development that occurred in the context of writing. Precise understanding of words is not necessary in many situations during reading. It's relatively easy to skip over a word when you're reading. It's much more difficult to skip a word in writing, and in writing the use of different words or phrases can create a different register or tone. The motivation for learning and using words is enhanced when children are trying to express themselves in writing because they are trying to communicate with others. In writing word choice is an important tool because students are trying to convey specific thoughts or ideas to amuse their audience or to describe a setting, a character, or a chain of events. We saw word consciousness developing out of the perceived need to use words well.

Reading and writing are reciprocal processes, and modeling has been shown to be an effective instructional strategy for each. The underlying tenet of the program was that modeling word consciousness with a focus on language use in general, as opposed to a particular set of words, will help students develop a mind-set for learning to pay attention to words.

The Gift of Words project was based on the premises that (1) students need to learn to value words in order to spend the time and energy trying to learn them; and (2) both wide reading and direct instruction are important. Through wide reading, children are exposed to a variety of words and word usage. Through direct instruction and discussion, students can become more conscious of specific words, learn how these words fit with other words, and deepen their knowledge of morphology and syntax. The teachers used words encountered in stories and poems as the text for instruction to model conscious attention to language. In the development of word consciousness, they used the instructional cycle shown in Figure 12.1.

Well-written novels and poems provided the foundation for the project. Emerging writers need to study master writers, just as emerging musicians and artists study the masters in their fields. Introducing well-crafted text with rich use of vocabulary allowed students to internalize how various authors used words and provided models that could be critiqued and analyzed.

Any piece of good literature will work, but some authors paint pictures with words more aptly than others. Our teachers started by using Newbery Medal books, Children's Choices, and other novels by renowned authors such as Katherine Paterson, Avi, Jack London, Jerry Spinelli, Lois Lowry, Karen Cushman, Natalie Babbitt, and Paul Fleishman.

Books and poems read aloud to the classes became a way to analyze word use together. The following phrases, for example, were identified as

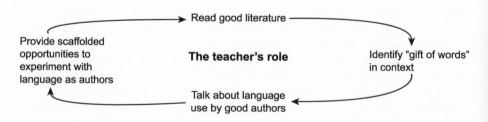

FIGURE 12.1. The teacher's role in developing word consciousness.

Gifts of Words: the phrases the author used to paint a particularly vivid picture or a descriptive phrase that added texture and tone to the writing.

- "joy jiggling inside . . . " *Bridge to Terabithia* (Patterson, 1977, p. 101)
- "The house felt as lifeless as a tomb." *The Half-A-Moon-Inn* (Fleischman, 1980, p. 10)
- "His long chin faded into an apologetic beard." *Tuck Everlasting* (Babbitt, 1975, p. 17)

The Gifts of Words phrases provided the opportunity to talk about meaning and analyze word choice. The words were not necessarily difficult or academic in tone, but attention to metaphors, similes, and descriptive language created an entry point for discussion about word meaning and word use. For instance, the teacher could relate *apologetic* to the known word *apology*, talk about noun and adjective forms, and ask students how a *beard* could be *apologetic*.

Talk about Language Use by Good Authors

An important aspect of any teaching is to take the implicit and make it explicit for students. Talking, for instance, about why you, the teacher, like a particular phrase or how the words in a good lead sentence grabbed your attention provides the metacognitive link between an author's word choice and the response of the reader. A teacher can discuss how authors make comparisons and build a sense of character in their books. The attention given to the way words are used by experienced authors can foster attention to language use in students' writing and the purposeful exploration of words.

Provide Scaffolded Opportunities to Experiment with Language as Authors

Scaffolded opportunities occur when a teacher or a more competent person helps students by giving them support when they need it and taking it away as they become more capable independent learners (Bruner, 1986; Diaz, Neal, & Amaya-Williams, 1990). The teachers provided different sets of scaffolded opportunities for their students. However, in all the classrooms, students started their explorations by borrowing phrases from the authors they were reading and inserting them in their own writing.

Baktin (1981) claimed that the word in language is half someone else's. It only becomes one's own when the speaker or writer appropriates the word, adapting it to his or her own semantic and expressive intention. This notion, called *ventriloquism* (Wertsch, Tulviste, & Hagstrom, 1993), assumes that any written or spoken utterance contains both the voice of the current speaker and the voices of those who have used the same words or patterns of discourse within the context in which the word or pattern of discourse was learned. Wertsch et al. developed this idea to address how students learn to "ventriloquate" through new social languages. They theorized that students need to actively appropriate the way that others converse in order to form changes in their own patterns of interaction. According to Wertsch et al., this occurs when students are encouraged and given the opportunity to appropriate or ventriloquate new social languages.

For many students, the language of novels constitutes a new social language. Thus, we need to provide children with a chance to learn to value and appropriate such language and make it their own. In this project, the vocabulary, phrases, and sentences found in children's literature were used as springboards that students could adapt in their own attempts to communicate in writing.

The Gift of Words Bank—a collection of rich descriptive phrases— made such phrases available for students to appropriate in their writing. Ms. Cross, a grade 5 and 6 teacher, had students collect Gift of Word phrases from their own independent reading of novels, from the novels read aloud, and from poems and short stories. Once they had an adequate collection, each student received four or five Gift of Words phrases that had been written out on long sentence strips. They categorized their phrases into action, feelings, settings, personalities, and a miscellaneous category. These were then bound together and hung on the wall. As students were writing their own stories and poems, they could borrow these collections and either insert a phrase directly into their writing or use the phrase as a model. In several of the students' stories, characters "burst out of bed as though the sheets were afire" (Fleishman, 1980, p. 1).

Students were also taught how to use the phrases analogically to fit into the context of their own story. For example, the phrase "There are more thieves than trees in a place like this," from *The Half-A-Moon-Inn* (Fleischman, 1980), became "There is more filth than clean air in a dump like this" in one student's writing. Another changed "She was a great potato of a woman" (Babbitt, 1975, p. 10) to "He was a long string bean of a man."

Another activity that developed word consciousness focused on developing possible settings for the students' stories. Ms. Cross's class discussed the importance of a good setting in a well-written story and brainstormed many different settings together. The students then picked a setting that they might use in their story. Individually, they drew or painted their setting on medium-sized tag board. When they were completed, lined paper was attached to the back, and the class circulated to write a descriptive phrase to describe each picture. Students developed setting phrases such as:

- Bright lights burst out from the tiny windows.
- The dark green grass grew taller than the house itself.
- The river flowed heavily under the lonely bridge.

The various settings were shared in authors' circles and became available for borrowing when students began to write their stories. A similar process was followed for creating characters.

For Ms. Cross, the main objective for these activities was to prepare the students to write their own stories. She commented:

> The students all told me that they would not have been able to write the stories that they did if the class bank of character cards, setting cards and Gift of Words Bank weren't there for them to use. The more talented writers were able to take their writing that much further and the struggling writers were able to feel successful because of the structured support [that] the writing scaffolds provided for them throughout the writing process. (in Scott, Blackstone, et al., 1996, p. 49)

Another teacher, Ms. Skobel, wrote:

> Improving student writing begins with examining how other authors use language effectively. Picture books, poems and novels are used as the model or the text for student learning. The first aspect of improving student writing [that] I look at is the way other authors use words effectively. Students have little difficulty recognizing the figurative language used in poems and books. It is this awareness of how words are arranged that transforms a "boring" piece into a more powerful piece, *for the reader*. It is the person who is going to read a piece that I try to encourage my students to remember, just as the author we happen to be examining at any given time has thought of their reader. Authors, like painters, try to create an image for their audience; a painter with paints, an author with words. (1998, p. 23)

Word consciousness can also be developed through the critique of texts where rich description is not a primary component of the writing. In Ms. Blackstone's class, the students commented that the author did an inadequate job of describing the characters or setting in her picture book *Snow White in New York* (French, 1986). The fifth graders then decided to rewrite the book, using drama to re-enact the scenes and enhance their writing.

The story was divided into parts and distributed to groups of students. The groups acted out the sections of the story, maintaining the basic plot while they exaggerated the actions. After each segment of the story was presented, the students brainstormed descriptions of the characters' actions and appearances that were recorded on charts. Each group then rewrote their part of the story to include more colorful and powerful language.

When writing, they referred to their experience while portraying the character in the story, as well as the words brainstormed by the group. Compiling the segments to create a class book became the final step of the project.

The writing shown in Table 12.1 indicates progress toward sophisticated writing and exploration of word use beyond what the students might have written alone. Although this is not perfect prose, the examples show how students experimented with the use of more complex language structures and vocabulary in the re-creation of the story. This story was chosen by the students, but any short story containing action, student appeal, and limited descriptive language would suffice for this activity.

Wordless picture books can also create opportunities to scaffold children's word consciousness during writing. The plot and structure of the story are given through rich visual representation. The challenge for students is the development of words and phrases that aptly describe the elements already in place.

Our teacher-research group concluded that a focus on words in general as opposed to teaching specific words was critical for creating word consciousness within their classrooms. The teachers wanted to "turn children on to words" so that they would continue to explore and use new words and phrases on their own. As students read a variety of authors' works, they paid attention to the way authors used language and developed an extended vocabulary base; the more they wrote, the more they learned how to manipulate words and phrases to express themselves in the forms of language found most often in academic settings or in literature. As they drew upon and manipulated sophisticated language, the more natural it became to incorporate these forms into their own writing and speaking.

TABLE 12.1. Sections of the Picture Book _Snow White in New York_ (French, 1986) as rewritten by Grade 5 Students

Original version	Rewritten version
"The seven jazz-men, their hearts broken, carried the coffin unsteadily up the church steps" (p. 25).	At Snow White's funeral, the seven heartbroken jazzmen, their hearts shattered, shuffled up the church steps.
"Suddenly one of them stumbled . . . " (p. 25).	Then suddenly, one of the jazzmen slipped on a rock and skidded like a car pressing on its brakes fast.
"The poisoned cherry that had been stuck in her throat was gone" (p. 26).	The casket landed on the ground with a thud, and the cherry that had been stuck in Snow White's throat burst out.

Word Consciousness and Teaching Specific Words

Although we have presented word consciousness in terms of generative vocabulary knowledge, it should be pointed out that word consciousness depends heavily on in-depth knowledge of specific words. We have suggested that understanding the power of word choice is crucial to word consciousness. However, one can only understand the power of word choice if one knows the (sometimes subtle) distinctions in meaning between the words among which one is choosing. A discussion of why one would choose *announce* versus *proclaim* in a given sentence doesn't work if the student has no sense of the difference in meaning between these two words. To help students develop this in-depth knowledge of specific words, in addition to extensive exposure to rich language, there also has to be some intensive instruction on specific words.

Intensive Instruction on Specific Words

When teaching specific words, a teacher first needs to decide which words are important to teach. Some words and phrases are new labels for known concepts (e.g., *carlin* as a word meaning *old woman*), and other words are new concepts (e.g., *photosynthesis*) (Graves, 1987). If one thinks of words as interconnected webs of meaning, hooking a new label onto a developed concept or expanding the web to include terms closely related to known words (e.g., *glance* as a form of *looking*) is much easier than creating an entirely new web to form a new concept. Direct explicit instruction may be most useful in developing understanding of a new concept or in identifying subtle differences.

In-Depth Development of New Concepts

Let us examine for a moment two examples of exemplary direct and explicit instruction from a recent study of 23 ethically diverse classrooms (Scott, Jamieson-Noel, & Asselin, 2003). In the first example, the teacher developed a thorough understanding of the concept of *symmetry* in a sixth-grade math class. She modeled symmetry, she had pairs of students use their bodies to form symmetrical and nonsymmetrical images, and students cut folded paper to create examples of symmetry. Their examples were used to discuss types of symmetry and nonsymmetrical contrasts. When it was time to use the textbook to do the math exercises, they had a well-developed concept of the word.

In the second example, another teacher helped students create a whole-class semantic map of terms related to *racism*. As they talked about these concepts and suggested ways they could be visually represented, ideas were recorded on chart paper. From this discussion, students created individual posters using pictures from magazines to represent the concept of racism. As they chose each picture, they were evaluating its depiction of the vocabulary terms introduced during the lesson.

Both of these teachers followed guidelines from research regarding appropriate direct and explicit vocabulary development (Blachowicz & Fisher, 2000). Specifically, teachers (1) helped students establish multidimensional knowledge about the words they were teaching; (2) encouraged students to connect what they knew and experienced with specific concepts; and (3) provided multiple opportunities to help students develop subtle distinctions between related words that occurred in the same semantic field.

CONCLUSION

In this chapter, we have discussed word consciousness as part of the vocabulary curriculum, that is, in terms of how it contributes to vocabulary growth. However, we want to be clear that we do not consider word consciousness simply as a motivational trick to encourage students to memorize vocabulary words, an otherwise unpalatable activity. Rather, word consciousness contributes to literacy in a number of respects.

First of all, word consciousness—and especially an understanding of the power of word choice as a communicative tool—is essential for sustained vocabulary growth. Words are the currency of written language. Learning new words is an investment, and students will make the required effort to the extent that they believe that the investment is worthwhile. The world of schooling contains tens of thousands of words that most children never hear in their homes or in everyday conversations. In order to learn these words, they need to become conscious of how words work and ways they can use them as tools for communication.

Second, word consciousness is essential to effective writing. As students learn to negotiate the written world, sensitivity to word choice enhances their ability to communicate their ideas. Richard, a sixth-grade student, said:

> The most useful thing I learned as a writer this year is the Gift of Words. . . . I like how you take a sentence and transform it, like "*I'm afraid*'" to "'*heart pounding fear.*" I'm going to try to make my work better by using more Gift of Words. Sometimes I don't use them. I don't know why because I can take a sentence and BOOM, it's a lot more powerful. (in Skobel, 1998, p. 23)

Third, word consciousness also contributes to reading comprehension.

Word-level fix-up strategies (e.g., figuring out the meaning of an unfamiliar word from context) are essential items in one's comprehension strategy toolbox. Morphological and syntactic awareness are particularly valuable in this realm. In addition, developing enhanced word consciousness contributes to critical reading. Students with enhanced word consciousness become more critical consumers of literature when they pay attention to an author's use of words in the books that they read. More generally, the ability to reflect on the meanings of words is an essential part of understanding decontextualized language. The language of text uses a richer vocabulary than conversation not only because of differences in content but also because the means of effective communication in textbook language are different. Beyond just having larger vocabularies, students need to understand how and why these words are used.

Teachers play a vital role in bringing word consciousness to the fore. We believe that when teachers "up the ante" by using sophisticated vocabulary in their classrooms, teach words fully so that student internalize rich word schemas, and create learning communities in which students can explore word use with a vocabulary coach at their side, they are giving their students tools they need to become successful in the world of schooling and beyond.

REFERENCES

Anderson, R. C., & Nagy, W. (1992). The vocabulary conundrum. *American Educator, 16*(4), 14–18, 44–47.

Anglin, J. M. (1993). Vocabulary development: A morphological analysis. *Monographs of the Society for Research in Child Development, 58*(10, Serial No. 238).

Babbitt, N. (1975). *Tuck Everlasting.* New York: Farror, Strauss & Giroux.

Baktin, M. M. (1981). *The dialogic imagination: Four essays by M. M. Baktin.* (M. Holquist, Ed.; C. Emerson & M. Holquist, Trans.). Austin: University of Texas Press.

Baumann, J. F., Kame'enui, E. J., & Ash, G. (2003). Research on vocabulary instruction: Voltaire redux. In J. Flood, D. Lapp, J. R. Squire, & J. Jensen (Eds.), *Handbook of research on teaching the English language arts* (2nd ed., pp. 752–785). Mahwah, NJ: Erlbaum.

Blachowicz, C., & Fisher, P. (2000). Teaching vocabulary. In M. Kamil, P. Mosenthal, P. D. Pearson, & R. Barr (Eds.), *Handbook of reading research* (Vol. 3, pp. 503–523). Mahwah, NJ: Erlbaum.

Bruner, J. (1986). *Actual minds, possible worlds.* Cambridge, MA: Harvard University Press.

Chafe, W., & Danielewicz, J. (1987). Properties of spoken and written language. In R. Horowitz & S. J. Samuels (Eds.), *Comprehending oral and written language* (pp. 83–113). San Diego, CA: Academic Press.

Diaz, R. M., Neal, C. J., & Amaya-Williams, M. (1990). The social origins of self-regulation. In L. Moll (Ed.), *Vygotsky and education* (pp. 127–154). New York: Cambridge University Press.

Fischer, U. (1990). *How students learn words from a dictionary and in context.* Unpublished doctoral dissertation, Princeton University.

Fischer, U. (1994). Learning words from context and dictionaries: An experimental comparison. *Applied Psycholinguistics, 15*(4), 551–574.

Fleischman, P. (1980). *The Half-A-Moon-Inn.* New York: HarperCollins Trophy.

French, F. (1986). *Snow White in New York.* Oxford, UK: Oxford University Press.

Graves, M. (1987). The roles of instruction in fostering vocabulary development. In M. McKeown & M. Curtis (Eds.), *The nature of vocabulary acquisition* (pp. 165–184). Hillsdale, NJ: Erlbaum.

Graves, M. (2000). A vocabulary program to complement and bolster a middle-grade comprehension program. In B. Taylor, M. Graves, & P. van den Broek (Eds.), *Reading for meaning: Fostering comprehension in the middle grades* (pp. 116–135). Newark, DE: International Reading Association.

Graves, M. F., & Watts-Taffe, S. (2002). The place of word consciousness in a research-based vocabulary program. In A. Farstrup & S. J. Samuels (Eds.), *What research has to say about reading instruction* (3rd ed., pp. 140–165). Newark, DE: International Reading Association.

Hayes, D. P., & Ahrens, M. (1988). Speaking and writing: Distinct patterns of word choice. *Journal of Memory and Language, 27,* 572–585.

Henry, S., Scott, J, Wells, J., Skobel, B., Jones, A., Cross, S., Blackstone,T. (1999). Linking university and teacher communities: A "think tank" model of professional development. *Teacher Education and Special Education, 22*(4). 251–267.

McKeown, M. (1985). The acquisition of word meaning from context by children of high and low ability. *Reading Research Quarterly, 20,* 482–496.

Miller, G., & Gildea, P. (1987). How children learn words. *Scientific American, 257*(3), 94–99.

Minick, N. (1987). Implications of Vygotsky's theories for dynamic assessment. In C. S. Lidz (Ed.), *Dynamic assessment* (pp. 116–140). New York: Guilford Press.

Moll, L. C., & Whitmore, K. F. (1993). Vygotsky in classroom practice: Moving from individual transmission to social transaction. In E. Forman, N. Minick, & C. Addison Stone (Eds.), *Contexts for learning: Sociocultural dynamics in children's development* (pp. 19–42). New York: Oxford University Press.

Nagy, W., & Scott, J. (2000). Vocabulary processing. In M. Kamil, P. Mosenthal, P. D. Pearson & R. Barr, (Eds.) *Handbook of reading research* (Vol. 3, pp. 269–284). Mahwah, NJ: Erlbaum.

National Institute of Child Health and Human Development. (2000). *Report of the National Reading Panel: Teaching Children to Read.* (NIH Publication No. 00–4754). Washington, DC: U.S. Government Printing Office.

Paterson, K. (1977). *Bridge to Terabithia.* New York: Harper Trophy.

RAND Reading Study Group. (2002). *Reading for understanding: Toward a research and development program in reading comprehension.* Prepared for the Office of Educational Research and Improvement (OERI), U.S. Department of Education. Santa Monica, CA: RAND Education.

Roberts, B. (1992). The evolution of the young child's concept of word as a unit of spoken and written language. *Reading Research Quarterly, 27,* 124–138.

Rosenblatt, L. (1978). *The reader, the text, the poem: The transactional theory of the literary work.* Carbondale, IL: Southern Illinois University Press.

Schwartz, R., & Raphael, T. (1985). Concept of definition: A key to improving students' vocabulary. *Reading Teacher, 39*(2), 198–205.

Scott, J., Asselin, M., Henry, S., & Butler, C. (1997, June). *Making rich language visible: Reports from a multi-dimensional study on word learning.* Paper presented at the annual meeting of the Canadian Society for the Study of Education, Newfoundland.

Scott, J., Blackstone, T., Cross, S., Jones, A., Skobel, B., Wells, J., & Jensen, Y. (1996, May). *The power of language: Creating contexts which enrich children's understanding and use of words.* A micro-workshop presented at the 41st annual convention of the International Reading Association. New Orleans: LA.

Scott, J., Butler, C., & Asselin, M. (1996, December) *The effect of mediated assistance in word learning.* Paper presented at the 46th annual meeting of the National Reading Conference, Charleston, SC.

Scott, J., Jamieson-Noel, D., & Asselin, M. (2003). Vocabulary Instruction throughout the school day in 23 Canadian Upper-Elementary Classrooms. *The Elementary School Journal, 103*(3), 269–286.

Scott, J. A., & Nagy, W. (1997). Understanding the definitions of unfamiliar verbs. *Reading Research Quarterly. 32*(2), 184–200.

Scott, J. A., & Wells, J. (1998). Readers take responsibility: Literature circles and the growth of critical thinking. In K. Beers & B. Samuels (Eds.), *Into focus: Understanding and supporting middle school readers.* Norwood, MA: Christopher-Gordon.

Skobel, B. (1998). *The gift of words: Helping students discover the magic of language.* Unpublished MEd thesis, Simon Fraser University, Burnaby, BC.

Snow, C. (1994). What is so hard about learning to read? A pragmatic analysis. In J. Duchan, L. Hewitt, & R. Sonnenmeier (Eds.), *Pragmatics: From theory to practice* (pp. 164–184). Englewood Cliffs, NJ: Prentice-Hall.

Vygotsky, L. S. (1978). *Mind in society.* Cambridge, MA: Harvard University Press.

Watson, R., & Olson, D. (1987). From meaning to definition: A literate bias on the structure of word meaning. In R. Horowitz & S. J. Samuels (Eds.), *Comprehending oral and written language* (pp. 329–353). San Diego, CA: Academic Press.

Werner, H., & Kaplan, E. (1952). The acquisition of word meanings: A developmental study. *Monographs of the Society for Research in Child Development, 15*(1, Serial No. 51).

Wertsch, J. V., Tulviste, P., & Hagstrom, F. (1993). A sociocultural approach to agency. In E.Forman, N. Minick, & C. A. Stone (Eds.), *Contexts for learning: Sociocultural dynamics in children's development* (pp. 336–356). New York: Oxford University Press.

Willingham, D. T. (2002) Allocating student study time: "Massed" versus "distributed" practice. *American Educator, 26*(2), 37–39, 47.

13

Keep the "Fun"
in Fundamental

*Encouraging Word Awareness and Incidental
Word Learning in the Classroom
through Word Play*

CAMILLE L. Z. BLACHOWICZ
PETER FISHER

This chapter sketches out a research base for word play in the classroom based on four principles: (1) Word play is motivating and an important component of the word-rich classroom; (2) word play calls on students to reflect metacognitively on words, word parts, and context; (3) word play requires students to be active learners and capitalizes on possibilities for social construction of meaning; and (4) word play develops domains of word meaning and relatedness as it engages students in practice and rehearsal of words. Each principle is examined in turn, and then exemplars of word play and supporting scaffolding are presented. The chapter concludes with options for web-based word play as well as other resources.

The title of this chapter comes from a teacher participating in staff development on word play who noted, "Well, this puts some of the 'fun' back in fundamental. Vocabulary instruction can be pretty grim sometimes." This comment dovetailed with our own experiences in working with reluctant readers in clinics and classrooms where word play proved to be a powerful learning and motivation tool, particularly for children whose home experiences do not involve linguistic play. These two observations helped us set the first goal of this chapter—to link word play and the development of word awareness in students with the research on metacognition and vocabulary instruction. In this age of evidence-based practice, such a link is needed for teachers to ground the inclusion of word play in the curriculum. Our stimulus came from reviews of vocabulary instruction and development that emphasized the importance of vocabulary (Baumann, Kame'enui, & Ash, 2003), suggested that researchers address the application of vocabulary research to teachers' practical problems (Blachowicz & Fisher, 2001), and that vocabulary learning should be emphasized as a metacognitive activity (Nagy & Scott, 2001). From the work we review, we propose research-based principles for using word play in the classroom. Our second goal is to share some examples of instruction consistent with these principles and discuss the ways in which they develop effective strategies, good habits, and the love of words in learners.

THE RESEARCH BASE FOR WORD PLAY IN THE CLASSROOM

We believe the evidence base supports using word play in the classroom. Our belief relates to these four research-grounded statements about word play:

- Word play is motivating and an important component of the word-rich classroom.
- Word play calls on students to reflect metacognitively on words, word parts, and context.
- Word play requires students to be active learners and capitalizes on possibilities for the social construction of meaning.
- Word play develops domains of word meaning and relatedness as it engages students in practice and rehearsal of words.

Word Play, Motivation, and the Word-Rich Classroom

All teachers know the motivational value of play. Things we enjoy and view as sources of pleasure stay with us throughout our lives. The motivated learner is the engaged learner who has a personal sense of self-confidence in participating in learning activities (Au, 1997), participates in a knowledgeable and strategic fashion, and is socially interactive (Guthrie & Wigfield, 1997). This engagement and enjoyment is highly correlated with achievement in all areas of literacy (Campbell, Voelkl, & Donahue, 1997) including vocabulary learning. In one highly controlled study of vocabulary learning in the middle grades (Beck, Perfetti, & McKeown, 1982), a curious phenomenon surfaced. Out of all the classrooms involved in the research project, students in one classroom learned more incidental vocabulary—words no one was attempting to teach. When trying to locate the source of this learning, the researchers were unable to come up with any instruction or materials that could account for the difference. Then one researcher noted a poster of interesting words in the classroom. When the teacher was asked about it, she noted that it was the "word wall"—a place where students could write new words they encountered in reading, in conversation, on TV, or in their daily experiences. If they could write the word, talk about where they heard or saw it, and use it, they received points in a class contest. Very little expense, instructional time, or effort was involved, but the students became "tuned in" to learning new words in a way that positively affected their learning. They actively watched and listened for new words and shared them with their peers. They were motivated word learners.

Self-direction is an important component of motivation. With students who are English language learners, some degree of choice about word learning is important. Jiminez (1997) found that middle school readers were more motivated and learned more vocabulary when they could have a say in selecting some of the words they were to learn. Using the Vocabulary Self-Collection Strategy (Haggard, 1982), a strategy that helps students develop selection and learning strategies, motivated students to say, "I used to only think about vocabulary in school. The whole world is vocabulary" and "I hear words everywhere that would be good to use" (Ruddell & Shearer, 2002, p. 352). Self-selection does not water down vocabulary learning in the classroom. Fourth-grade students allowed to choose words to learn from a novel study unit chose words of greater difficulty than graded word lists would have provided them, and then they learned the words they selected (Fisher, Blachowicz, & Smith, 1991). Personal interest and choice are powerful aides to vocabulary learning.

Word play is also one element of the word-rich classroom so critical to the development of word awareness and word consciousness in students: the same consciousness that leads to greater incidental word learning. There is significant research base for having a word-rich environment in the classroom and for the development of word-aware learners. The need to increase student exposure to vocabulary is well established. Students from families entering preschool who have many opportunities for oral interactions have larger vocabularies than children who have limited interactions (Hart & Risley, 1995). The latter often lag behind in reading so that by third grade their exposure to new vocabulary through reading has been impoverished as well (Cunningham & Stanovich, 1998). All these result in learners who, by fourth grade, have much smaller vocabularies than their peers (Becker, 1977).

All students need to be surrounded by words and motivated to learn them. Reading to students is a must to expose them to vocabulary they would not encounter on their own. Just as teachers have begun to use the term "flood of books" to talk about situations where students have many and varied opportunities to read (Anderson, Wilson, & Fielding, 1988), so, too, "flood of words" is an important issue for general vocabulary development.

Wide reading is another hallmark of word learning, with many studies suggesting that word learning occurs normally and incidentally during normal reading (Nagy, Herman, & Anderson, 1985). Reading to children has been shown to have an effect not only on their recognition knowledge of new words but also on their ability to use these words in their own retellings (Dickinson & Smith, 1995); so a wide variety of materials used for reading to children and for their own reading is necessary to develop the word-rich classroom. Word play can round out the word-rich classroom by providing another way to encounter, practice, and become interested in these building blocks of literacy.

Metacognition and Word Play

Question: What vehicle do you use to take a pig to the hospital?
Answer: A hambulance, of course.

Corny? Yes. Metacognitive? Definitely. Anyone who understands the pun has performed a metacognitive act. First there must be the association of *ham* with *pig*, the segmenting of the first syllable of ambulance and replacing it with the syllable *ham*, and then using the meaning of *ambulance* as a vehicle for hospital transport. The groan or laugh that results is our metacognitive check. We get the joke and we exhibit cognitive flexibility, the ability to look at the same thing in different ways. Many children, however, don't get it. Watch a child react to a book like *The King Who Rained* (Gwynne, 1970), which focuses on humorous interpretations of various expressions. Some students interpret the expressions literally. They don't have the knowledge to draw on for word meaning, nor do they have the flexibility to think about words and word parts in more than one way. So a joke about having a "frog in my throat" is horrifying rather than funny. Creating and sharing jokes, riddles, and puns can help develop this flexibility.

Traditionally, vocabulary instruction has focused on learning meanings of words (Watts, 1995). Words are considered individually, not in a domain or context, and the learning is typically receptive, not constructive. Students are either given a definition or asked to look one up, often resulting in hilarious mistakes, as the young girl who described an *acute angle* as "a very good looking angle." An alternative approach is to consider vocabulary instruction as metalinguistic development (Nagy & Scott, 2001). The ability to reflect on, manipulate, combine, and recombine the components of words is an important part of vocabulary learning (Tunmer, Herriman, & Nesdale, 1988). Phonological awareness (being able to segment speech sounds, such as removing *am* from *ambulance*), morphological awareness (the awareness of word-part meanings), and syntactic awareness (how a word functions in language) all play important parts in word learning (Carlisle, 1995). There is also evidence that this type of learning is developmental over the school years (Anglin, 1993; Roth, Speece, Cooper, & De la Paz, 1996).

Using morphology along with context is the most effective way to unravel the meanings of new words. Syntax is needed to determine if the letters *T-E-A-R* mean a *tear* in the eye or a *tear* in fabric. You can't phonologically recode those letters without a context. Then context enables you to check your understanding by reading further to see if your choice makes sense (Tunmer, 1990). Indeed, the learning of definitions is often hampered by the lack of use of a word's part of speech to help understand what a word really means and how it is used (Fischer, 1990; Scott, 1991). It has been proposed that the greater metacognitive ability of children functioning in two languages is the result of their operating on words as objects and examining words and word parts in an analytical way (Taeschner, 1983). Word play, punning, joking, and other forms of word manipulation can make this happen. So, developing an environment in which word play and word awareness are integral is an appropriate goal for the classroom. Later in this chapter, we share ideas for word play in order to develop flexible ways of thinking about words.

Word Play and Active Social Construction of Meaning

Besides immersion in words, talk is critical to word play and word learning. Discussion in the classroom (Stahl & Vancil, 1986) and around the dinner table (Snow, 1991) is another correlate of incidental word learning. While this type of learning through exposure cannot guarantee the learning of specific words, it does develop a wide, flexible, and usable general vocabulary as well as the opportunity to learn from others. "Two heads are better than one" is especially true in vocabulary learning. There is rarely any word presented in a classroom context that does not elicit some meaning, association, or idea from some member of the class.

As in all learning situations, having the learners actively attempt to construct their own meanings is a hallmark of good instruction. Learning new words as we have new experiences is one of the most durable and long-lasting ways to develop a rich vocabulary. Words like *thread, needle, selvage, pattern, and dart* are naturally learned in the context of learning to sew, just as *hit, run, base,* and *fly* take on special meanings for the baseball player. Answering and asking questions that invite students to evaluate different features of word meaning or different issues of a text is another way to become actively involved in discovering meaning (McKeown, Beck, & Worthy, 1993). For example, answering and explaining one's answer to the question "Would a recluse enjoy parties?" helps students focus on the important features of the word *recluse*. This discussion makes the process of figuring out meanings visible to learners.

Teachers can also make word meanings and relationships visible for students by having them actively construct word meaning. Chart games, collections, pen-and-paper games, manipulative category games, and art and drama not only physically display attributes of meanings but also provide memory organizers for later word use. For example, in coining the word *inoculatte*—the first shot of coffee that gets you through the day—the student who drew the picture (see Figure 13.1) provided a pun with the attendant actual word meanings for memory.

Word Play, Semantic Relatedness, Practice, and Rehearsal

Many studies have shown the efficacy of putting word meaning into graphic form such as a map or web, a semantic feature chart, or advanced organizer (Johnson, Toms-Bronowski, & Pittelman, 1982). It is critical to

FIGURE 13.1. Inoculatte.

note, however, that mere construction of such graphics without discussion is not effective (Stahl & Vancil, 1986). Other approaches that stress actively relating words to one another are clustering strategies that call for students to group words into related sets. These include brainstorming, grouping, and labeling (Marzano & Marzano, 1988), designing concept hierarchies, constructing definition maps related to concept hierarchies (Bannon, Fisher, Pozzi, & Wessell, 1990; Schwartz & Raphael, 1985), and mapping words according to their relation to story structure categories (Blachowicz, 1986). All these approaches involve student construction of maps, graphs, charts, webs, or clusters that represent the semantic relatedness of words under study to other words and concepts.

In word play, category games, such as Scattergories, are the "play" versions of these techniques. Word picture games such as Pictionary that use art to display meaning, acting-out games such as Charades, and synonym games such as Password and Taboo all emphasize semantic categories and relatedness and provide for practice and rehearsal. Besides the obvious active learning involved, word play also provides a vehicle for use and rehearsal, the creation of a personal record including visualization in graphics and drawing (Pressley & Woloshyn, 1995), and kinesthetic representations in drama (Duffelmeyer, 1980). Discussion, sharing, and use of the words are necessary components of active involvement, as is feedback and scaffolding on the part of the teacher.

In summary, we ground word play in the classroom in the research base that suggests it develops word awareness by engaging learners in learning and wanting to learn new words and developing their metacognitive ability. The evidence base suggests that, for effective word play in the classroom, teachers should (1) create a word-rich environment; (2) call on students to reflect metacognitively on words, word parts, and context; (3) encourage active engagement with discussion; and (4) emphasize relatedness in rehearsal and practice. We now present examples of word play that achieve these objectives.

PRACTICE: MAKING IT HAPPEN

Creating a Word-Rich Environment

Materials

A classroom full of materials is essential for growing good readers and for exposing them to a wide selection of vocabulary (Cunningham & Stanovich, 1998). Variety in levels of materials and topics is a *must*. Literacy materials should be chosen for motivational as well as instructional value. Besides

books, newspapers, magazines, reference materials, and technological references such as CD ROMs are necessary to meet the needs of all readers. A variety of excellent magazines are available for young children (e.g., *Lady Bug*,
Ranger Rick, *National Geographic for Kids*) and upper elementary or adolescent students (e.g., *BMX*, *Skateboarder*, *Guitar*). Subscriptions to daily newspapers and weekly newsmagazines provide ongoing connections to current
events and an introduction to adult reading. Magazines in content areas such
as science (*Contact*) or history (*Cobblestone*) or regional magazines such as
Illinois History or *Merlin's Pen* provide current and motivating material related to the curriculum. Internet news groups and topical forums also require
reading and give a "hot-off-the-press" feel to the reading curriculum. Classrooms should also have small-group and large-group sets of books, novels,
anthologies, short stories, and magazines. Teachers often like to create sets of
related books centering around one topic. For example, for a unit on the sea, a
third-grade teacher collected books on several different levels. As part of the
unit, she included a book about whale rescue, one about the life cycle of
whales, and a third about whale habitats. The first book is about at grade
level, the second a bit easier, and the third a bit more difficult. She used these
as core books for the unit and then allowed students to seek out related materials. As the students engaged in small- and large-group discussions, the
teacher listed thematic vocabulary that crossed all the books (e.g., *baleen,
blowhole, spout, sound*).

Students with easy access to books read more and encounter more vocabulary than students who have to go down the hall at fixed periods to a
school library or fetch books from high shelves. A comfortable place to
read, a collection of good books, magazines, and newspapers; and the ability to develop a personal collection through book orders all increase the
number of new words students encounter and practice on a daily basis.

Games

Games are useful for vocabulary practice and rehearsal. We suggest a variety of card, board, and other games to promote vocabulary development.

Card Games

Cards emphasize semantic relationships by working on the pairing principle. A pair is made when you match a word with a synonym, a definition,
an antonym, a cloze sentence in which it makes sense, a picture symbolizing
its meaning, or an English translation. Have students prepare a deck of at
least 40 word-card pairs from words across their curriculum. For example,
you may emphasize synonyms such as:

| altitude | | height |

Cards are shuffled, and seven are dealt to each player. Each player can choose a card and discard one card in turn. Pairs may be placed on the table. The first player to pair all cards wins.

The same decks of word cards can be used to play more traditional games. For "Go-Fish," all the cards are dealt, and players pick one card from the player on their left in turn. Pairs may be placed on the table. The first player to pair all cards wins. For "Old Teacher," a variation of Old Maid, an extra card is prepared with a drawing of the teacher—or some generic teacher. This is played like fish. The person who is left with this card is the "Old Teacher."

In all card games, students must read their pairs and can be challenged by another student if the group does not agree with the pair. The dictionary settles disputes. If the challenger is correct, she or he may take an extra turn. If the challenger is incorrect, the player gets an extra turn.

Race-and-Chase Board Games. Race-and-chase games require a poster board game board and moving pieces. Many teachers like to construct generic race-and-chase boards that can be used with many sets of cards. A 2″ × 3″ index card cut in half or thirds is an excellent size for word cards. Moving pieces can be commercially purchased at teacher stores or taken from garage sale games. In addition, dice or spinners are useful.

One of the easiest race-and-chase formats is "Synonym Match." The stack of word cards is placed in the center of the board, and the synonym cards are arranged face up. Each student rolls a die and picks up a word card. If the student can correctly locate the synonym match, he or she can move the number of spaces on the die. The group and the dictionary again serve as the check. A harder version requires the students to use words in original sentences.

Memory Games. Like commercial memory games, word memory, or "Concentration," involves finding matches and remembering cards. Play this game with about 25 cards—12 word cards, 12 match cards, and 1 wild card. All the cards are shuffled and placed face down. In each turn, a student turns up and reads two cards. If the cards are a match, the student takes the cards. If they are not a match, they are turned over and left in the same place. Students may use the wild card only if they can supply a suitable match orally. This can be checked at the end of the game by looking at the remaining card. The student with the most cards wins.

Bingo. This popular game can be played by any size group. Students each have sets of word cards from which they construct a 5 × 5 (25-space) bingo card. They lay out their cards in any manner they choose, placing a "free" card in the space of their choice. The caller chooses definitions from the definition pile and reads them out. Students can place markers on the words that match. The first student to mark an entire row, column, or diagonal wins. Students check by reading the words and definitions. The cards are reshuffled, each student's cards are rearranged, and the winner becomes the caller for the next game.

Adapting Commercial Games. Besides teacher-made games, many commercial games can be adapted for class use. For general word learning, *Scrabble, Probe, Pictionary, Pictionary Junior,* and *Boggle* are excellent. Teachers can add dictionary use as a component of play. *Facts in Five* and *Scattergories* are variations of the category game and can build general word learning. *Outburst* and *Outburst Junior* help develop networks by association. All are worthwhile for general vocabulary development.

Crosswords and Other Puzzles. Browsing any newsstand or bookstore will emphasize the popularity of word puzzles. Involvement in creating and doing puzzles can build a lifelong interest in words for students. Crossword puzzles are probably the most popular type of word puzzle. They are so familiar that we won't go into detail about them here. One thing for teachers to note is that, although crosswords are familiar to most adults, the process is not familiar to most children. Take the time to work through a puzzle with your students until they get the general idea of how they are completed. Keeping blank grids in your classroom for creating puzzles is also a wonderful way to stimulate thinking about words and definitions.

Codes. Students love secret codes. Decoding a word, phrase, or sentence demands a substantial use of context and inference. Many books of coded and encrypted messages can be purchased at bookstores, supermarkets, and newsstands.

Jumbles. Jumbles, or anagrams, call for readers to unscramble words and letters to match a clue, sometimes in cartoon form. Most newspapers run a daily jumble that can provide good classroom material—as well as an incentive to browse the paper each day. This can be a good starter in middle school or high school homeroom periods.

Computer Play and Exploration. Many commercial programs are available for word play. For example, some create crosswords, semantic maps, or word clusters, and there are electronic dictionaries and thesauruses. Students can also use the computer to create text or HyperCard personal word banks that can be easily alphabetized, coded, and clustered.

Internet Resources

There are a number of vocabulary websites that teachers and students can consult.

> *www.vocabulary.com.* This website can be used by both teachers and students in middle school or above.
>
> *www.wordsmith.org/awad.* A.Word.A.Day (AWAD) has a theme of the week, such as words of German origin or words related to Halloween.
>
> *www.randomhouse.com/features/rhwebsters/game.html.* The game on this website is called "Beat the Dictionary," and it is basically a version of online "Hangman."
>
> *http://rhyme.lycos.com.* This website contains a rhyming dictionary and thesaurus program.
>
> *www.wordexplorations.com.* This site describes itself as an advanced English vocabulary site that will expand visitors' vocabulary by focusing on Latin and Greek elements used in English.

Word Play Emphasizing Metacognitive Manipulation of Words and Word Parts

Students become interested in riddles and jokes in the early grades, and "pun-o-mania" hits in the middle grades. Riddle and joke books abound and quickly circulate in most classrooms. Creating riddles, jokes, and puns is one way to stimulate exploration of words and to build interest and flexibility in word learning.

Word Riddles

Mike Thaler (1988), a prolific author and conference speaker, has collected many ideas for riddle and joke making. One way to make word riddles that are questions with pun-like responses is to choose a subject and generate a list of related terms. For example, if your subject is *pig*, your list might contain *ham*, *pork*, *pen*, *grunt*, *hog*, and *oink*. You take the first letters off one of the words and make a list of words that begin with that letter pattern. For example, if you chose *ham*, you would make a list that began with *am* such as *ambulance*, *amnesia*, *amphibian*, and *America*. Then you put back the missing letter and get *hambulance, hamnesia, hamphibian,* and *hamerica.* Then you would make up riddles for the words.

Riddle: How do you take a pig to a hospital?
Answer: In a hambulance!
Riddle: What do you call it when a pig loses its memory?
Answer: Hamnesia!

Taking students through five steps ensures that the process is transparent to the students: (1) shared experience, (2) think-aloud through the riddle, (3) group creation, (4) independent scaffolded creation, and (5) independent practice. Students can be further supported by having many books of jokes, riddles, and puns that give pleasurable practice as they become "riddlers."

Name Riddles

Thaler (1988) also suggests Name Riddles. Look for names with the related word part. For example, remaining in the "pig mode,"

Riddle: What pig discovered the theory of relativity?
Answer: Albert Swinestein!

Hink Pink

Hink Pink asks students to come up with a pair of rhyming words to match a defining phrase. Each word in the pair is the same number of syllables. The person who creates the phrase clues the guesser with the term Hink Pink (two 1-syllable words), Hinky Pinky (two 2-syllable words), Hinkety Pinkety (two 3-syllable words), and so forth.
For example,

Clue: Hink Pink—an angry father. (Answer: mad dad)
Clue: Hinkety Pinkety—an evil clergyman. (Answer: sinister minister)

Hink pinks are fun, and often students can come up with more than one answer for a clue. Any meaningful answer is acceptable. The trick to understanding hink pinks is to learn to write them. Start with the answer, which is usually an adjective paired with a noun. These words must share the same number of syllables and rhyme, for example, *mad dad* from above. To write the question, brainstorm synonyms for each word (e.g., synonyms for *mad = angry, irritated, upset*; synonyms for *dad = father, pop, pater*). Pick one from each set to make the riddle (e.g., What's an angry father, an irritated pater, or an upset pop?).

Encourage Active Engagement with Discussion

Many activities we have described call upon students to speak with others to clarify thinking. There are other playful ways in which talk can be encouraged in word play, such as playing guessing games and engaging in drama and drawing games.

20 Questions

This game can be adapted to help students think about words they are learning. The student who is "it" selects a word card from a prepared stack. Other students ask up to 20 yes/no questions. A turn ends with a "no." If one correctly guesses the word, that player becomes "it" for the next round. If students do not guess the word, "it" gets another turn.

Categories

One of the most popular pencil-and-paper games is Categories. Draw a suitable size grid (e.g., 2 × 2 for young students; 5 × 5 for older students), and label each row with a category. Then choose a word whose number of letters matches the number of columns. For example, students in a ninth-grade study hall working on the Civil War constructed the grid shown in Figure 13.2. Players are given a designated time limit to fill in as many squares as they can, after which points are totaled. Taking each student's card individually, players get 5 points for every category square they fill in which no other player has filled; 2 points for every category square filled in

	A	R	M	I	E	S
Specific Confederacy Words		Rebel				
Specific Union Words						Sherman
Military Words		Rifle		Infantry		Sniper
Battles and Places	Atlanta					

FIGURE 13.2. Categories grid for the Civil War.

that others have filled in, but with other words; and 1 point for every category square filled in where someone else has the same term. Inappropriate entries may be challenged and carry no point totals if they are not suitable.

Word Challenge

Word Challenge is another category game in which the categories are established to focus on particular word characteristics. For example, categories might include synonyms, antonyms, or related words (see Figure 13.3). The rules for Word Challenge are the same as for categories.

Word Fluency

Word Fluency is a technique that encourages students to use categorization to learn vocabulary (Readence & Searfoss, 1980). It is especially useful in a one-to-one or small-group situation. The task is to name as many words as possible in 1 minute. The teacher or student chosen to be monitor tallies the words as the student says them. If the student hesitates for 10 seconds or more, the tutor suggests looking around the room or to think about an activity they recently completed. After the student's initial effort, the tutor models naming words in *categories,* which is much easier and faster than choosing random words. The rules for scoring are (1) no repetitions, no number words, no sentences; (2) one point for each word; and (3) one point for each category of four words or more.

Students see this as a challenge and enjoy it. They want to try to beat their own score. Once a student is familiar with the activity, the tutor can provide categories from topics that have been studied recently: animals, science, or families, for example. The student must only name words that could be in these categories. Recently a tutor in our Reading Center wrote

Word	Autonym
hard	*soft*
sensible	*silly*
healthy	*sick*
neat	*sloppy*
praise	*scold*
friendly	*spiteful*

FIGURE 13.3. Word Challenge grid—alphabet antonyms (students have to choose antonyms that all begin with the same letter).

in her log about using Word Fluency with her student, Serge: "The word fluency was so much fun. Serge left it until last, but he had so much fun with it, I think he will choose it much earlier tomorrow." She felt that this activity provided a good review of the vocabulary for Serge and, more importantly, demonstrated to him that he knew "lots of words."

Drama

Drama can be used in three ways to promote word play: Synonym String, Situations, and Charades. First, use drama to build a set of related words, the Synonym String. Form the class into two teams and present each team with a starter word, such as *walk*. The group needs to come up with as many synonyms as they can and illustrate each dramatically. For example, they might *stroll, saunter, sashay, amble*, and so forth. A thesaurus can be helpful, or the teacher can present a list of words. Synonym Strings can lead to a discussion of denotative and shades of word meanings.

Second, students can use dramatization of words to create meaningful Situations that clarify word meaning (Duffelmeyer, 1980). Prepare a set of word cards, each containing a word, its meaning, an example of a situation, and a question. For example, the word might be *irate*; the situation might be to act out the situation of an irate father talking with a son who came in late for curfew; and the question might be, "When have you been irate?" Form groups of students and give one card to each group. The actors have time to discuss the word and plan a skit (limit to 5 minutes). They can use the situation on the card or plan their own. When presenting their skit, one member of the group writes the word on the board and pronounces it. The skit is acted out, and a cast member asks the audience the question and meaning of the word. At this point, the teacher can provide feedback, and all class members enter the word in a vocabulary file along with the meaning and some personal context.

Third, Charades can be played with phrases or single words. Words or phrases are written on word cards and placed in a stack. Students are divided into teams. One member of a team draws a card and attempts to act out each word or syllables of the word using a series of signals. A timekeeper from the other team keeps track of the time, and the team with the lowest time score after a full round wins. The related game Guesstures is a playful form of acting out words that older students love.

Art

Students love to play with words using art and drawing to create visual riddles. Not only does art provide a multisensory way to provide keys to word learning, but it also can provide a playful way for students with nonverbal talents to relate to word learning. For example, for high school students studying word parts, a drawing activity was a natural way to show learning. If students are studying Latin forms (e.g., *tri* = three, *ped* = feet, *bi* = two, *corn* = horned, *optis* = eye), they can create and label their own original animals. For example, a bicornoptistriped (two-horned, three-footed animal with an eye) was drawn, as shown in Figure 13.4.

Emphasize Relatedness in Rehearsal and Practice

Most school curricula deal with common word categories, such as synonyms, antonyms, similes, and metaphors. But what about acronyms, portmanteau words, imported words, slang, collective words, and other creative categories of words?

Consider portmanteau words. When you pack a suitcase, or portmanteau, sometimes you scrunch things together to make room. For example, you might put your socks in your shoes. *Portmanteau* words are packed words formed by merging portions of one word with another. For example, *smog* is a common portmanteau word based on a combination of *smoke* and *fog*. English has a rich history of creating new words in this way, a tendency readily picked up by Madison Avenue, journalists, and comic book writers. Advertising has given us the *motel* (*motor* + *hotel*), cartoons *zap* (*zip* + *slap*), science the *beefalo* (*beef* + *buffalo*), and political journalism *insinuendo* (*insinuation* + *innuendo*) (McKenna, 1978). Include these in your investigation of words to help build broad categories of vocabulary. Teachers often have students build bulletin board lists or word walls of these fascinating types of words, such as the following categories:

FIGURE 13.4. A bicornoptistriped triped.

- Acronym: a word formed from the initial letters of other words (e.g., *scuba* = self-contained underwater breathing apparatus).
- Anagram: a word or phrase formed by scrambling the letters of a word (e.g., *lake/kale*).
- Borrowed words: words used in English from other countries (e.g., *cafe, lariat, pretzel*).
- Collective words: words that label a group, typically of animals (e.g., a gaggle of geese, a pride of lions).
- Malapropism: use of an incorrect word for a similar sounding one (e.g., My Gramma has very close veins).
- Onomatopoeia: a word whose sound relates to its meaning (e.g., *buzz, gulp*).
- Oxymoron: a phrase composed of words that seem contradictory (e.g., plastic silverware).
- Palindrome: words or phrases that read the same forward or backward (e.g., *mom, dad, Able was I ere I saw Elba*).
- Spoonerism: an unintentional transposition of sounds (e.g., Please pass the salt and shecker papers).

Students also like to make collections of personal interest words, such as "All the Words About . . . " books. In these books, students collect words related to a topic, a hobby, a person of interest, and so forth, and soon the class library has such collections as "All the Words About Baseball," "All the Words About Ferrets," and "All the Words About Wesley Snipes." Students are fascinated by other students' collections, and these books, many illustrated or collaged, circulate widely.

A FINAL WORD

In this chapter, we have presented a research base for word play in the classroom. This grounding supports four goals for classroom word play: (1) create a word-rich environment; (2) call on students to reflect metacognitively on words, word parts, and context; (3) encourage active engagement with discussion; and (4) emphasize relatedness in rehearsal and practice. There is convincing evidence that classroom practice reflecting these principles will encourage incidental word learning as well as developing word awareness and interest in students. In addition, our own experience working with struggling readers is that, almost universally, they have not participated in word games either at home or at school. When we invited them to do so, they often become animated and motivated. They look forward to those parts of our sessions together and frequently take games home to play with parents and siblings. We have found that parents who are anxious to improve their child's literacy rarely think of word games as something that can be done at home. However, when they try them and see the joy that they can bring to a previously reluctant learner, they ask for more. Consequently, we view games and word play as valuable commodities in the curriculum and a way to encourage links between home and school. They are vehicles for putting the "fun" back in one of the most fundamental aspects of learning during the school years—vocabulary development.

REFERENCES

Anderson, R. C., Wilson, P., & Fielding, L. (1988). Growth in reading and how children spend their time outside of school. *Reading Research Quarterly, 23,* 285–303.

Anglin, J. (1993). Vocabulary development: A morphological analysis. *Monographs of the Society for Research in Child Development, 58*(10, Serial No. 238).

Au, K. H. (1997). Ownership, literacy achievement and students of diverse cultural backgrounds. In J. T. Guthrie & A. Wigfield (Eds.), *Reading engagement: Motivating readers through integrated instruction* (pp. 168–182). Newark, DE: International Reading Association.

Bannon, E., Fisher, P. J. L., Pozzi, L., & Wessel, D. (1990). Effective definitions for word learning. *Journal of reading, 34,* 301–302.

Baumann, J. F., Kame'enui, E. J., & Ash, G. E. (2003). Research on vocabulary instruction: Voltaire redux. In J. Flood, D. Lapp, J. R. Squire, J. M. Jensen (Eds.), *Handbook of research on teaching the English language arts* (2nd ed.). Mahwah, NJ: Erlbaum.

Beck, I. L., Perfetti, C. A., & McKeown, M. G. (1982). The effects of long-term vocabulary instruction on lexical access and reading comprehension. *Journal of Educational Psychology, 74,* 506–521.

Becker, W. C. (1977). Teaching reading and language to the disadvantaged—what we have learned from field research. *Harvard Educational Review, 47,* 518–543.

Blachowicz, C. L. Z. (1986). Making connections: Alternatives to the vocabulary notebook. *Journal of Reading, 29,* 643–649.

Blachowicz, C. L. Z., & Fisher, P. J. L. (2000). Vocabulary instruction. In M. L. Kamil, P. B. Rosenthal, P. D. Pearson, & R. Barr. (Eds.), *Handbook of reading research* (Vol. 3, pp. 503–523). New York: Longman.

Campbell, J. R., Voelkl, K., & Donahue, P. L. (1997). *NAEP 1996 trends in academic progress.* (NCES Publication No. 97–985). Washington, DC: U.S. Department of Education.

Carlisle, J. (1995). Morphological awareness and early reading achievement. In L. Feldman (Ed.), *Morphological aspects of language processing* (pp. 189–209). Hillsdale, NJ: Erlbaum.

Cunningham, A. E., & Stanovich, K. E. (1998). What reading does for the mind. *American Educator, 22,* 8–15.

Dickinson, D. K., & Smith, M. W. (1994). Long-term effects of preschool teachers' book readings on low-income children's vocabulary and story comprehension. *Reading Research Quarterly, 29,* 104–122.

Duffelmeyer, F. A. (1980). The influence of experience-based vocabulary instruction on learning word meanings. *Journal of Reading, 24,* 35–40.

Fischer, U. (1990). *How students learn words from a dictionary and in context.* Unpublished doctoral dissertation. Princeton University.

Fisher, P. J. L., Blachowicz, C. L. Z., & Smith, J. C. (1991). Vocabulary learning in literature discussion groups. In J. Zutell & S. McCormick (Eds.), *Learner factors/teacher factors: Issues in literacy research and instruction* (pp. 201–209). Fortieth yearbook of the National Reading Conference. Chicago: National Reading Conference.

Guthrie, J. T., & Wigfield, A. (Eds.). (1997). *Reading engagement: Motivating readers through integrated instruction.* Newark, DE: International Reading Association.

Gwynne, F. (1970). *The king who rained.* New York: Simon & Schuster.

Haggard, M. R. (1982). The vocabulary self-collection strategy: An active approach to word learning. *Journal of Reading, 26,* 203–207.

Hart, B., & Risley, T. R. (1995). *Meaningful differences in the everyday experience of young American children.* Baltimore: Brookes.

Jiminez, R. J. (1997). The strategic reading abilities and potential of five low-literacy Latina/o readers in middle school. *Reading Research Quarterly, 32,* 224–243.

Johnson, D. D., Toms-Bronowski, S., & Pittelman, S. D. (1982). *An investigation of the effectiveness of semantic mapping and semantic feature analysis with intermediate grade level students* (Program Rep. No. 83–3). Madison, WI: Wisconsin Center for Education Research, University of Wisconsin.

Marzano, R. J., & Marzano, J. S. (1988). *A cluster approach to elementary vocabulary instruction.* Newark, DE: International Reading Association.

McKenna, M. (1978). Portmanteau words in reading instruction. *Language Arts, 55,* 315–317.

McKeown, M. G., Beck, I. L., & Worthy, M. J. (1993). Grappling with text ideas: Questioning the author. *The Reading Teacher, 46,* 560–566.

Nagy, W. E., Herman, P. A., & Anderson, R. C. (1985). Learning words from context. *Reading Research Quarterly, 20,* 233–253.

Nagy, W., & Scott, J. (2001). Vocabulary processes. In M. L. Kamil, P. B. Mosenthal, P. D. Pearson, & R. Barr (Eds.), *Handbook of reading research* (Vol. 3, pp. 269–283). New York: Longman.

Pressley, M., & Woloshyn, V. (1995). *Cognitive strategies: Instruction that really improves children's academic performance* (2nd ed.). Cambridge, MA: Brookline Books.

Readence, J. E., & Searfoss, L. W. (1980). Teaching strategies for vocabulary development. *English Journal, 69,* 43–46

Roth, F., Speece, D., Cooper, D., & De la Paz, S. (1996). Unresolved mysteries: How do metalinguistic and narrative skills connect with early reading? *Journal of Special Education, 30,* 257–277.

Ruddell, M. R., & Shearer, B. A. (2002). "Extraordinary," "Tremendous," "Exhilarating," "Magnificent": Middle school at-risk students become avid word learners with the Vocabulary Self-Collection Strategy (VSS). *Journal of Adolescent and Adult Literacy, 45,* 352–363.

Schwartz, R., & Raphael, T. (1985). Concept of definition: A key to improving students' vocabulary. *The Reading Teacher, 30,* 198–205.

Scott, J. (1991). *Using definitions to understand new words.* Unpublished doctoral dissertation. University of Illinois at Urbana–Champaign.

Snow, C. E. (1991). *Unfulfilled expectations: Home and school influences on literacy.* Cambridge, MA: Harvard University Press.
Stahl, S., & Vancil, S. (1986). Discussion is what makes semantic maps work in vocabulary instruction. *The Reading Teacher, 40,* 62–69.
Taeschner, T. (1983). *The sun is feminine: A study of language acquisition in bilingual children.* Berlin, Germany: Springer-Verlag.
Thaler, M. (1988). Reading, writing and riddling. *Learning, 17,* 58–59.
Tunmer, W. E., (1990). The role of language prediction skills in beginning reading. *New Zealand Journal of Educational Studies, 25,* 95–114.
Tunmer, W. E., Herriman, M. L., & Nesdale, A. R. (1988). Metalinguistic abilities and beginning reading. *Reading Research Quarterly, 23,* 134–158.
Watts, S. M. (1995). Vocabulary instruction during reading lessons in six classrooms. *Journal of reading behavior, 27,* 399–424.

Index

Academic vocabulary, 69
Acronyms, 181, 234
Active engagement, encouraging, 230–233
Affictionaries, 165
Affixes, 160, 163–164, 181. *See also* Prefixes;
    Suffixes
Age, vocabulary acquisition and, 29
Alphabet, knowledge of, 146–147
Ambiguities, 181
Anagrams (jumbles), 181, 227, 234
Anansi and the Moss-Covered Rock, 58t
Anemonyms, 190–191
Antonyms, 167, 181, 203
Aptronyms, 180, 187
Art, 232–233
Assessment, of vocabulary, 30, 33, 35–36
Association level, of word knowledge, 106

Beginning literacy stage, 148–152
Bingo, 226–227
"Birdwalking," 70
Books. *See* Literature, children's
Borrowed words, 234
Brainstorming, 73–74

Call It Courage, 18
Caps for Sale, 58t
Card games, 225–226
"The Case of the Blueberry Pies," 23–24
Catchphrases, 180, 196
Category games, 224, 230–231, 230f
A Chair for my Mother, 58t
Charades, 232
Classification, 59–60, 72–75
Classroom discussions
    direct vocabulary instruction in, 21–22
    emergent stage, 145–146
    encouragement of, 230–233
    on language use by good authors, 209

Clifford at the Circus (Bridwell), 36
Cloze procedure, 168
Codes, 227
Collective words, 234
Collocations, 181
Commercial games, adapting, 227
Comprehension. *See also* Reading,
    comprehension
    influencing factors, 15–16
    level of word knowledge and, 106
Comprehension strategy instruction, 89
Computer programs, 227–228
Concept development, in-depth, 213–214
Concept sorts, 146, 154
Concepts, 103
Concrete prompts, 89
Consonant alteration, 127
Content area dictations, 154–155
Context clues, 162
    effectiveness of, 14–15, 22, 23
    expectations from, 22–24
    general, 167
    metacognitive instruction on, 169
    types of, 166–167
    for vocabulary acquisition, 14–16, 110
Contextual analysis, 161
    elements of (*See* Context clues)
    guidelines for teaching, 167–169
    instruction, rationale for, 161
    integration with morphemic analysis, 169–171
    pitfalls, 169
    teaching, 161–163, 166–169
Contextual redefinition, 168–169
Coordinates, 181
C(2)Q, 168
Cross-curricular instruction, 128
Crosswords, 227
Curious George Feeds the Animals, 58t
Curious George Gets a Job, 67

Definitions, as context clues, 167
Demonyms, 180, 187–188
Derivational morphological patterns, 125–127
Dialogic reading, storybook reading
     intervention and, 44
Dictionaries, 153
Direct vocabulary instruction, 108, 113
     counterarguments, 14–15
     in early childhood classes, 69–72
     effective strategies for, 15, 17–21
     in grade 3 and above, 46
     importance of, 13–14
     multiple exposures to words and, 111–112
     ongoing, 25–26
     overheard conversations activity, 18–19
     richness of, 17–18, 20–21
     spelling–meaning connection and, 130–134
     strategies for, 46
     subject matter terms for, 111–112
     successful, 25–26
     timing/opportunities for, 21–22
     vs. indirect vocabulary instruction, 110–
        111
     with wide reading, 110, 112
     word line activity, 19–20
     word selection for, 16–17
Directive contexts, 22
Drama, 232
Dual coding theory (DCT), 105–106

Early elementary classrooms, teaching word
     meanings in, 75–76
Early intervention, 42–43
Emergent stage, 144–148
English, written vs. spoken, 204–206
English language learners
     beginning literacy activities, 151–152
     emergent stage, 147–148
     transitional literacy activities, 154–155
Eponyms, 180, 186–187
Ethnicity, word knowledge gaps, 61
Euphemisms, 181, 198
Example–nonexample activity, 19, 20f
Examples, as context clues, 167
Experiences, literacy, 140
     early, differences in, 41–42
     gaps in, 62
     language exposure and, 142–144, 143f
Explicit instruction, 46–48, 88–89
Expressions, 193–197. See also specific types
     of expressions
Expressive Vocabulary Test, 30
External derivational morphology, 125–126

Figurative language, 182–183, 203
Figures of speech, 181, 197–198
Fog Magic, 17
Free Voluntary Reading (FVR), 109

Frequency of exposure, 156
Full conceptual knowledge, 107

Games, 73, 181, 225–227. See also specific
     types of games
General contexts, 22
General term, 103
Generation level, of word knowledge, 106–
     107
The Gift of Words project, 206–214
"Goldilocks" words, 64–65
Group interaction, 112

The Half-A-Moon-Inn, 210
Harry the Dirty Dog, 58t
Hink Pink, 229–230
Homographs, 153, 181
Homophone Rummy game, 153
Homophones, 153, 181
Hot Hippo, 58t
Hush! A Thai Lullaby, 58t
Hyperbole, 181

I Lost My Bear, 58t
Idioms, 180, 183, 193–194
Imagens, 105
Indirect vocabulary instruction, vs. direct
     vocabulary instruction, 111
Initialisms, 181
Instruction, 101–102. See also Direct
     vocabulary instruction
     comprehensive, components of, 159–160,
        202
     content-specific terms in, 113–114
     dual coding theory and, 106
     early, linking to practice, 48–50
     explicit, 46–48, 88–89
     indirect approaches, 108–109
     levels of word knowledge and, 106–108,
        107–108
     literature, research principles, 49, 49t
     modes of representation and, 104–106
     outline for, 112–114
     reference and, 102–104
     target lexicon for, 104
     timing of, 156
Integration
     of morphemic and contextual analysis,
        169–171
     of spelling and vocabulary (See Spelling–
        meaning connection)
Intermediate grades, spelling–meaning
     connection, 6, 123, 124f–125t, 125
Internal derivational morphology, 126–127
Internet resources, 228

Jamberry (Degen), 146
Jumbles (anagrams), 181, 227, 234

The King Who Rained (Gwynne), 221
Knowledge
    generative, of words, 207–212, 208*f*, 212*t*
    of word learning, 203–204
    of written language (*See* Orthographic
        knowledge)

Language. *See also* Oral language; Written
        language
    exposure to, 156
    experience and, 142–144, 143*f*
        quality of, 155–156
    of novels, 210
    of school, 68–69
Language and Reading Success (Biemiller), 31,
        35
Learning
    from context, 14–16, 63
    ecological models of, 142–144, 143*f*
    fun aspects in, 181–182
    outside classroom, 25
Letter knowledge, 42, 146–147
Lexical knowledge, assessment of, 122–123
Lexical representations, 121
Linguistic structures, 105
Listening to storybooks, vocabulary
        acquisition and, 43–46
Literacy development
    context of, 140–141
    layers of orthography and, 141, 142*f*
    student-related problems, 139–140
    vocabulary development and, 140
Literature, children's. *See also* Reading;
        specific children's books
    choosing, for read-alouds, 34–35
    to create word-rich environment, 224–225
    for The Gift of Words project, 208–209
    reading several times, 32–33
    as source for vocabulary words, 17
    storybook reading activities, shared, 69
    target vocabulary and definitions, 58*t*
    in vocabulary instruction, 37–38
    vocabulary knowledge from, 67–68
Living Word Vocabulary (LWV), 31–32, 35
Logogens, 105
Logology, 183. *See also* Word play
Long-term transfer, from prefix instruction,
        97
Low-income children, 60, 62, 63, 69, 82

Magazines, 225
Malapropism, 234
Materials, classroom, 38, 224–225
Math, word selections for, 128–129
Maze cloze, 168
McDuff Moves In, 58*t*
Memory games, 226
Metacognition, word play and, 221–222

Metalinguistic awareness, word consciousness
        as, 201, 202–203
Metaphors, 181, 203
Metasemantic awareness, 203
Misdirective contexts, 23
Monkey and Crocodile, 58*t*
Morphemes, 120
Morphemic analysis
    definition of, 160
    guidelines for teaching, 164–166, 172
    independent use of, 165
    instruction, rationale for, 161
    instructional elements of, 163
    integration with contextual analysis, 169–
        171
    pitfalls in learning, 166
    research on teaching, 161–163
    teaching affixes and roots, 163–164
Morphological awareness, 203
Morphology, 118–119
    English spelling system and, 120–121
    instruction in, 121–122
    orthographic representation of (*See*
        Spelling–meaning connection)
"Motherese," 64, 65
Motivation, for learning/using words, 206–
        208, 219–221

Names
    business/store, 180, 193
    first/personal, 185–186
    nicknames, 180, 191–192
    pen names, 192–193
    power in labeling, 59–60
    proper, 103, 180
    riddles, 229
    town/city, 188, 189*t*, 190
National Research Council, 97–98
National vocabulary, 104
Neologisms, 181
Nondirective contexts, 22–23
Nonimmediate talk, 65

Odonyms, 190
Onomastics. *See also specific types of
        onomastics*
    definition of, 184
    psychological aspects of, 184–185
    types of, 180
Onomatopoeia, 234
Oral language
    derivational morphological processes in,
        127
    experiences, shared storybook reading
        activities, 43–46
    resources, 140
    vocabulary, 29, 140
    vs. written language, 204–206

Orthographic invariants, 142
Orthographic knowledge, 119. *See also*
        Written language
    assessment of, 122–123
    development of, 143
    reading/spelling and, 121–125
    synchrony of literacy learning and, 141,
        142*f*
Overhead transparencies, in prefix teaching,
        89, 90, 91–92
Overheard conversations activity, 18–19, 19*f*
Oxymorons, 181, 234

Palindromes, 181, 234
Partial conceptual knowledge, 107
Personal word journals, 25
Pete's a Pizza, 58*t*
Phonemic awareness, developing in English,
        147
Phonological awareness, 42, 145
Phonology, derivational morphological
        patterns, 125–127
Phrases, descriptive, 209, 210–211
Picture books, wordless, 212
Picture walks, 71–72
Portmanteau words, 181, 233, 233*f*
Positive Outcomes While Enjoying Reading
        (POWER), 109
Practice (rehearsal), 223–224, 233–234, 233*f*
Prefix removal and replacement strategy, 94–
        95
Prefixes, 160–161
    absorbed, 135
    as context clue, 170–171
    definition of, 83–84, 163
    frequency list, 87, 88*t*, 96
    research on teaching, 84–86
    teaching, 81–82, 163–164
        clarification in, 89–90
        example of, 91, 92*f*, 93*f*, 94
        explicit instruction for, 164–165
        frequency of, 87–88
        general approach to, 88–89
        introduction of concept, 89
        limitations of, 96–98
        motivation in, 90
        order of, 87
        overview of, 89–90
        preliminary considerations, 87–88
        research on, 84–86
        reviewing/prompting, 92, 92*f*, 93*f*, 94,
            95–96
        value of, 83–84
Preschool, teaching word meanings in, 75–76
Primary grades
    assessing word knowledge in, 30, 35–36
    vocabulary levels in, 28–29
    vocabulary promotion in, 32–38

Prompting, in prefix instruction, 95–96
Pronunciation, 127, 155
Prosody, 205
Proverbs, 180, 194–195
Pseudonyms, 180
Puzzles, 227

Race-and-chase board games, 226
Read-alouds
    book selection for, 34–35
    checking comprehension of, 145–146
    scheduling, 38–39
    Text Talk strategy for, 70–71
    vocabulary acquisition from, 34
    word explanations and, 36
Reading. *See also* Wide reading
    accuracy, 140
    automatic, 140
    during beginning literacy stage, 149
    to children (*See* Read-alouds)
    comprehension
        vocabulary instruction and, 100–101
        vocabulary knowledge and, 82
        vocabulary levels and, 28
        word consciousness and, 214–215
    difficulties, 15, 44–46, 122
    orthographic knowledge and, 122–125
    in semantic map creation, 74
    storybook activities, shared, 69
        in preschool to grade 2, 43–46
        target vocabulary words in, 45
        teacher-directed vocabulary instruction
            and, 45
    student exposure to, 140
    with word explanations, 36
Reading vocabulary, size of, 82
Rebuses, 181
Reference, 102–104
Referential representation, 102
Registers, of language, 204
Rehearsal, 223–224, 233–234, 233*f*
Review process, in prefix teaching, 92–96, 92*f*
Rhymes, 146
Rich instruction, 17–18, 20–21
Riddles, 228–229
Root word, 128, 160–161
    as context clue, 170–171
    definition of, 163
    explicit instruction for, 164–165
    meanings, acquisition of, 47
    teaching, 163–164

Scaffolding opportunities, 209–212, 212*t*
Science, word selections for, 129
Self-direction, motivation and, 220
Self-selection, of words, 112
Semantic context clues, 166–167
Semantic maps, 73–75, 74*f*, 75*f*

Semantic relationships, 223–226
Settings, for student's stories, 210–211
Shared storybook reading literature, research
    principles, 48–49
Sight words, 149, 150f
Similes, 181, 197
Singular term, 103
Situational model, 102
Situations, 232
Slang, 180, 183, 195
Slogans, 180, 196–197
Snow White in New York (French), 211–212,
    212t
The Snowy Day (Keats), 50–54
Social studies, 129, 162–163
Socioeconomic status, 61, 68
Sorting games, 73
Sound–symbol relationships, 148
Sources, for vocabulary words, 17
Specific word instruction, word consciousness
    and, 213–214
Spelling
    morphology and, 120–121
    orthographic knowledge and, 121–125
    of prefixes, 83
Spelling–meaning connection, 119–120
    definition of, 119, 120
    direct vocabulary instruction, 130–134
    instruction, 129–135
    intermediate grades and beyond, 123,
        124t–125t, 125
    selection of words/patterns and, 127–129
    student exploration, 134–135
Spoken language. See Oral language
Spoonerism, 234
Storybook intervention, 54–55
    description of, 50–51
    reading activities, 51–53
    vocabulary activities, 53–54
Storybook reading. See Reading, storybook
    activities, shared
Structural analysis. See Morphemic analysis
Student exploration, of spelling–meaning
    connection, 134–135
Subject matter terms, 111
Suffixes, 160–161
    as context clue, 170–171
    derivational, 163, 164
    inflectional, 163
Superordinates–subordinates, 181
Surnames, 185–186
Sustained Silent Reading (SSR), 109
Synonym cloze, 168
Synonym String, 232
Synonyms, 167, 181, 203
Syntactic awareness, 203
Syntactic context clues, 166
Syntax, 222

Target words, direct instruction of, 46–47
Teacher, 208, 208f. *See also* Classroom
    discussions
Television commercials, as source for
    vocabulary words, 17
Text, 68–69
Text Talk, 70–71
Toponyms, 180, 188
Transitional literacy stage, 152–155
Twenty questions, 230

Uninterrupted Sustained Silent Reading
    (USSR), 109
Utterance, 68

Venn diagrams, 73
Ventriloquism, 210
Verbal association knowledge, 107
The Very Hungry Caterpillar, mother–child
    discussion on, 65–67
Vocabulary
    crucial facts about, 82–83
    differences, of children, 42, 47
    gaps in knowledge of, 60–61
    generative knowledge of, 201–202
    information organization of, 119
    instruction (*See* Instruction)
    levels, in primary grades, 28–30
    promotion, 32–36
    size, 82, 101
Vocabulary acquisition
    early, student-related problems, 139–140
    by listening to storybooks, 43–46
    rates of, 36–37, 38, 61
    from reading aloud to children, 34
    sequence, 30–32
    sources of, 67
    talking with children and, 64–67
Vocabulary lists, 110–111
Vocabulary Rule, 170–171
Vocabulary Self-Collection Strategy (VSS),
    112, 220
Vocabulary–spelling connection. *See* Spelling–
    meaning connection
Vowel alteration, 126
Vowel reduction, 126–127

Wide reading, 108–109, 113, 160
    with direct vocabulary instruction, 110,
        112
    in The Gift of Words project, 208
    new word exposure and, 110
    word learning and, 221
"Word a day" strategy, 37
Word associations, 181
Word awareness, word play and, 220
Word Challenge grid, 231, 231t
Word combinations, 104

Word consciousness, 160, 214–215
    classroom promotion of, 206–214
    definition of, 201, 202
    as metalinguistic awareness, 201, 202–203
    motivation and, 206
    specific word instruction and, 213–214
    spoken *vs.* written English and, 204–206
    word learning knowledge/beliefs and, 203–204
    word play and, 220
Word ending sounds, 148–149
Word explanations, reading with, 36
Word families, 149, 150f, 165
Word Fluency technique, 231–232
Word formations, types of, 181
Word Frequency Book, 83, 87
Word games, 181
Word identification, 29
Word knowledge, 122–123
    definition of, 104–105
    development of, 62–64
    levels of, 106–108
    reference and, 102–104
Word learning
    knowledge/beliefs on, 203–204
    model for, 62–64
    sequence, 30–32
    wide reading and, 221
Word line activity, 19–20, 20f
Word manipulations, types of, 181
Word meanings
    active social construction of, 222–223, 223f
    deriving from context, 23–24
    teaching in preschool and early elementary
        classrooms, 75–76
Word play, 183–184, 234–235
    active social construction of meaning and,
        222–223, 223f
    categories of, 180–182 (*See also specific
        word play categories*)
    definition of, 179–180
    emphasizing metacognitive manipulation,
        228–230
    emphasizing relatedness in rehearsal/
        practice, 233–234, 233f
    encouraging active engagement/discussion,
        230–233
    fun from, 218–219
    function of, 181
    metacognition and, 221–222
    motivational value of, 219–221
    research review, 182–184
    semantic relatedness and, 223–224

Word riddles, 228–229
Word sort activities, 134–135, 153
Word study activities, 155–156
    for beginning literacy stage, 148–152
    for emergent stage, 144–148
    selection of, 139
    transitional literacy stage, 153–155
Word study notebooks, 135
Word walls, 220, 233–234
Word Wizard activity, 25, 72–75
Word-learning strategies, 160
Word-of-the-Week sheet, 72
Word-rich classrooms, 219–221
Word-rich environment, creation of, 224–
    228
Words
    defining characteristics of, 101
    description of, 102
    as generalizations, 103
    high-frequency lists, 110–111
    individual instruction for, 160
    introduced, listing of, 36–37
    metalinguistic awareness of, 203
    morphologically related, 126
    multiperspective examination of, 129–
        130
    number of, for vocabulary instruction, 14,
        111
    overgeneralization of, 63
    phonological representation of, 62–63
    rare, 64, 67
    selection of, 16–17, 35
    self-selection of, 112
    talking around, 65–67
    Tier 1, 2 and 3, 35, 65
    usage frequency, 14
Writing, word consciousness for, 214
Written language
    derivational morphological patterns, 125–
        127
    development, 141
    knowledge of (*See* Orthographic
        knowledge)
    layers of, 141, 142f
    resources, 140
    student exposure to, 140
    vocabulary, 140
    vs. spoken, 204–206

Yoko, 58t

Zip cloze procedure, 168